"Live from Bedford Stuyvesant the livest one representing BK to the fullest"

—The Notorious B.I.G.,
"Unbelievable," 1994

UNBE

LIEVABLE

The Life, Death, and Afterlife of The Notorious B.I.G.

A VIBE book by Cheo Hodari Coker

A
VIBE
BOOK

A
VIBe
BOOK

WHERE
HIP HOP
LITERATURE
BEGINS

Published by VIBE Books, New York, New York.
an Imprint of Augustus Publishing
www.augustuspublishing.com

Printed in United States of America

Editorial Director: Rob Kenner

Cover Design: Jason Claiborne

Inside Design by Mark Shaw

Library of Congress Cataloging-in-Publication Data

Coker, Cheo Hodari.

Unbelievable: the life, death, and afterlife of the Notorious B.I.G.
/ by Cheo Hodari Coker.—1st ed.

PRINT ISBN: 978-19358836-1-6
EBOOK ISBN: 978-19358836-0-9

10 9 8 7 6 5 4 3 2 1

First Edition

Dedicated to my unbelievable grandfather,
the notorious Lt. Col. Bertram W. Wilson, a Tuskegee airman
who flew with the 100th Fighter Squadron during World War II.
The finest man I have ever known.
I miss you, Granddaddy. Every day.

CONTENTS

FOREWORD	THE THRILL IS GONE by Bönz Malone	IX
INTRODUCTION	ALL ABOUT THE BENJAMINS?	1
CHAPTER 1	DOLLY MY BABY	12
CHAPTER 2	THINGS DONE CHANGED	26
CHAPTER 3	IT WAS ALL A DREAM	46
CHAPTER 4	GIMME THE LOOT (I'M A BAD BOY)	72
CHAPTER 5	WHAT'S BEEF?	118
CHAPTER 6	MO MONEY, MO PROBLEMS	140
CHAPTER 7	ONE MORE CHANCE (THE REMIX)	188
CHAPTER 8	YOU'RE NOBODY TILL SOMEBODY KILLS YOU	208
CHAPTER 9	THE LONG KISS GOODNIGHT	234
CHAPTER 10	WHO SHOT YA?	254
EPILOGUE	SKY'S THE LIMIT	274
AUTHOR'S NOTE, ENDNOTES		278
ACKNOWLEDGMENTS		286

THE THRILL
IS GONE

FOREWORD

by Bönz Malone

66 Everyone has a talent. What is rare
is the courage to follow that talent to
the dark place where it leads. 99

—Erica Jong

When Christopher "Biggie Smalls" Wallace was searching for a record deal in 1992, he came up to see me at Island Records, where I was working in A&R at the time. He rolled through with my man Matt-Life and offered me a brash challenge—from one Brooklynite to another. We would play cee-lo, the classic curbside hustler's convention dice game. And if he won? Well, I guess I would owe the brother a record deal.

Maaan, it was on! We rolled them bones from 5 P.M. till after 8. I was snappin' my fingers so hard they started bleeding. All of a sudden, the Notorious one started playin' hot. On the last roll, he threw a pound and told me I better "Go get a pen" so he could sign that contract.

Five years later—and forty-eight hours after the murder of my friend Christopher—I sat in my lonely studio apartment, thinking of how close we became, the meals we had together, and about how different both of our lives might have been if I hadn't rolled that game-winning head crack. One toss of the dice, in effect, delivered the Notorious B.I.G. straight to Bad Boy Entertainment.

Biggie was damn crafty; I'd never known any aspiring artist to get down for his crown with an A&R guy like that before. I'd never seen an MC standing in front of his building wearing a Bermuda shirt and shorts, draped with a .357 Magnum, either. When I asked him why he had the strap, he said, "Somebody called my crib and said they were comin' to get me... so I'm waiting for 'em."

Ultimately, this was a B.I.G. brother who believed that *real* people do *real* things. A grown-ass man who knew the difference between gun powder and divine power and trusted only the will of God, the luck of the draw, and the loyalty and respect of his fam—plus the whole Hip Hop Nation.

Biggie's voice is still on the air and his name is still in the air seven years after his family laid him to rest. Some people swear he's the greatest MC of all time.

Others have portrayed him as a thug, a sex symbol, or a crime lord. Personally, I could live with the death of Biggie Smalls the image. But now, I'm forced to live without Christopher Wallace the person. And that's a difficult reality to face.

I have yet to read this book, although I've been asked to write the foreword. Without knowing what secrets and revelations unfold herein—and just to prove that what's true in one place is universally true in all places—I will share with you the same counsel I once gave the king:

"There are two sides to every one-way street and there's only one question that puts you on that yellow line in its center: Will you be an artist or a gangster? Both create images of hero worship. Both have plenty of underlings present to watch you destroy yourself at the height of your career. All young men are faced with this question once they get introduced to the street life. Although hip hop was created to defuse gang violence, it doesn't have the power to exempt you from making a choice. It can only help absolve you to yourself, in one way or another."

The title of this book may be *Unbelievable,* but for an only child raised by his mom, the story certainly is not. Christopher Wallace made his choice to be the Bad Boy of the block so that his moms could walk the streets with juice. So that his kids and his crew could live off the lyrics he wrote for them and own property from their publishing. Because he believed it was all going to pay off for him one day, not pay him off some day. If Satan stepped to Christ himself and offered Him all the kingdoms of the earth, then jumping out on St. James Place with 24-inch dubz ain't nothing for the devil to do! It can happen to you too. And if you're like me, it already has.

Christopher Wallace and I were friends and I respected him, but so did those that hated him—because he had become both the artist and the gangster. Biggie absolved the two personas to himself with such command of presence that it became impossible to differentiate between them. Like many of our associates in the rap industry, he knew that the pen is mightier than the sword. He also knew that a pen *and* a sword make a king. The "nonchalance" of his delivery was labeled legendary from the moment he picked up the habit. It will live in infamy until the industry he conquered one day implodes. May the story of his life show both the blessing and the malediction of someone who did more for others than for himself, and who had the courage to make the wrong choice for the right reason.

The only way to serve God is to be a gangster of His will, in one way or another. Believe that.

ALL ABOUT THE BENJAMINS?

66 Stereotypes of a
black male misunderstood
And it's still all good... **99**

"Just relax, man. Kick back. It's all good."

The Notorious B.I.G. sat in the cabana area near the pool at the Four Seasons Hotel in Beverly Hills wearing his trademark Versace sunglasses, sipping from a glass of lemonade and puffing on a potent marijuana-filled cigar in clear defiance of a posted NO SMOKING sign. It was a sunny afternoon on February 14, 1997, and Christopher Wallace was very much in character as B.I.G., the hustler god he personified on his hit records. But the cane resting near his deck chair was not just a player accessory—he truly had trouble getting around since the car crash that fractured his right leg five months earlier. He was taking his time, slowly re-learning how to walk on his own.

Old friends like D-Roc and Lil' Cease kept popping in to see if he needed anything. His pager buzzed incessantly with women sending Valentine's Day wishes. He ignored most of them because he'd already spoken with the first and most important love of his life, his mother Voletta Wallace. Valentine's Day was also her birthday. He told her he was sorry he couldn't help her celebrate in person, but that he was happy to be right where he was. New York was cold, and B.I.G. was way out west to make a music video, drop some rhymes , smoke some sticky green bud, and play in the sun.

I thought of the kid I met three years earlier, standing in unlaced Timberland boots on his block in Brooklyn. He'd recently returned from the Hamptons, a plush Long Island suburb where he and Sean "Puffy" Combs had filmed the video for B.I.G.'s first hit single, the rags-to-riches tale "Juicy." Combs would eventually buy a $2.5 million house in the exclusive area. But Wallace remembered being unnerved by the quiet, wondering aloud how someone could make real rap records if they "woke up in the morning hearing birds and crickets."

"This is a long way from Brooklyn," I said to B.I.G., taking his "kick back" advice and loosening my Gap tie, but refusing a hit from the blunt.

"I know, right?" B.I.G. said with a laugh. "A few million miles."

I was fresh from my cubicle at the *Los Angeles Times* where I worked as a staff writer. So far I'd been frustrated in my efforts to publish a Sunday Calendar cover story on B.I.G. even though his next album, the follow-up to the double-platinum debut *Ready to Die*, was sure to be the biggest release of the spring. If you listened to any urban radio station for half an hour, B.I.G.'s deep voice and fearsome flow were inescapable. On music television it was the same thing.

Even those who were unaware of what made Wallace so "B.I.G." were quite familiar with his "Notorious" side—chronicled all too eagerly by the same mainstream press that ignored the artistry of his meticulously crafted records. Most infamous was Wallace's tragic falling out with Tupac Shakur, a close friend who became a bitter rival. After months of very public disputes with Wallace and Combs, Shakur was fatally shot on September 7, 1996, while sitting in the front seat of a car driven by Marion "Suge" Knight, CEO of Death Row Records. Even before Pac died—six days later, on Friday the 13th—there was widespread speculation about Wallace's supposed connection to the crime. He always avoided dissing his old friend on wax or in print, often sounding genuinely hurt and confused by the rift. Seven years later, the crime remains unsolved.

As he sat in the shade of his cabana that afternoon, Wallace seemed completely relaxed. But despite his laid-back demeanor, it's safe to say that there was a lot on his mind—and not just because he was in California so soon after Shakur's murder. B.I.G was always the type to keep things running through his head. Unlike most other rappers, he never carried lyric notebooks into the studio. He would construct those intricately rhyming narratives inside his formidable brain, then step to the microphone and record them "off the dome."

B.I.G. sat watching kids splash around in the pool without a care in the world. "This shit is beautiful," he said, taking a sip of lemonade. "You got palm trees and all type of stuff right here. I wouldn't want to lose it for nothing in the world."

Two young white kids, looking like they just stepped out of a Polo ad, approached the 6'3" 300-pound rapper to get an autograph. Kenneth Story, a tall bald security guard posted just outside the cabana tried to stop them. But B.I.G. nodded, allowing them past, requesting a pen.

"What's your name?" he asked, smiling.

Once feared, now revered, the Notorious B.I.G. was a real star; no doubt about it.

B.I.G. believed that his forthcoming double album, *Life After Death... Till Death Do Us Part* was going to take his career to the stratosphere. With the perfect mix of R&B grooves and hardcore hip hop, this was the record that could silence his critics, unite the coasts, and win over anybody still caught up in the overblown East Coast versus West Coast rap war. He would be the one to erase three years of heated tension, if not for love, then for money.

B.I.G. had not yet recorded his verse for "It's All About The Benjamins," Puffy's ode to hundred-dollar bills that would become one of the hottest jams of the coming summer. But when talking bout the current state of rap music, the conversation invariably came back to economic empowerment, a.k.a. cash money.

"I've noticed that change from when I first came out in '92 to now," B.I.G. said. "Everybody's trying to get paid." And getting paid seemed as good a reason to make peace as any other. "Why would you want to limit your money? Why would you want to be a rapper that could only get money on the East Coast, and have other rappers only get money on the West Coast? Why not blend all this shit together?"

The plan was simple: Spend some time out west, stop by the radio stations, let California know he not only had love for the West Coast but that he'd loved Pac as well. Earlier that week, Puffy Combs had appeared with Death Row artist Snoop Dogg on *The Steve Harvey Show* as a show of unity, to prove that successful black men could come together regardless of any geographic locations, affiliations, or bad blood between them.

"I thought it was something that had to be done," Wallace said. "It was a conversation that was held by Snoop, myself, and Puffy so long ago. I'm glad it took place, too. 'Cause that's all it would take is for Snoop to say, 'It ain't no beef,' for me to say, 'It ain't no beef,' Puff to say, 'It ain't no beef.' Then the fans would be like, 'It ain't no beef.' It's time for it to be over, man. Let's just get money man."

But when I asked him "Is money really power?" he paused before answering.

"*You* answer that question," B.I.G. replied, a tinge of sarcasm in his deep voice. "Do you think money is power?"

"Yes," I said, keenly aware of how money had changed his life, for one.

"I think so," he said, nodding. "Money can't get you love, but it can get you respect."

There was no disputing the fact that people's attitudes toward him changed dramatically once he stopped hustling on street corners and started his music career. No longer was he "Considered a fool cause I dropped out of high school," as he rapped in "Juicy." But now he was besieged by people he called "playa haters." His fame had begun to alienate some of his hardcore fan base. Grimy rap heads wondered aloud why Biggie traded in his Timberland boots for alligator loafers. Instead of being happy for his success, many people simply resented it.

"I'm not that nigga on the streets no more," B.I.G. said, sounding a bit frustrated. "I can't be acting like it's something that I'm still going through. That would be unbelievable. No, B.I.G. is not selling no drugs, so why would you want to hear a song about that? I got other problems. These goddamn haters, man. They just can't say 'Damn, this nigga was from Brooklyn, he took a talent he had and just built that shit into something so strong. I'm proud of him.' " B.I.G. shook his head in disgust. "They can't even say that shit."

"Everyone knows you're big," I said. "But are you still hungry?"

"Starving," he replied. "I got a point to prove. That sophomore jinx... so many new artists who came up, their second album was trash. I know everybody want to know, 'Can he do it again?' I want everybody to know that I can. I want to *exceed* their expectations. Go to an even further length. I went all out on this one, man."

That was Biggie for you. But when I asked about Tupac, the Notorious B.I.G. didn't answer my questions. Christopher Wallace did.

"Tupac, at one point, was my dawg," he said with a smile, his voice softening. "Funny muthafucka, too." You could hear affection and regret in his words: two emotions very much at odds with Biggie's public persona.

"There's a lot things people didn't know about him," Wallace continued. "That nigga could make a nigga laugh, man. And he liked to laugh... He liked to hang out and get drunk. He had such a serious outlook. In his interviews and everything, he just seemed so angry, but at the same time, so charming. It would fuck people's heads up. He liked that title as a troubled muthafucka. You know what I'm saying? He liked that type of shit. He kept everybody on their toes."

Wallace's voice trailed off and he sat silently for a moment before continuing.

"I'm realizing that nothing protects you from the inevitable. If something is gonna happen, it's gonna happen, no matter what you do. Even if you clean your life up. What goes around comes around, because karma is a muthafucka.."

More contemplative silence.

"When he died, that shit fucked me up," Wallace said, voice low. "I know so many niggas like him, too. So many rough, tough muthafuckas. When I heard he got shot, I was like, 'He'll be out in the morning, smoking some weed, drinking Hennessy or whatever.' You ain't thinking *him*. You ain't thinking he going to die."

B.I.G. sat up in his lounge chair, shifting his weight.

"You just keep thinking, a nigga making so much money, their lifestyle should be more protected. You know what I'm saying? Their lives should be more protected where things like a drive-by shooting ain't supposed to happen. That shouldn't have happened, man. He's supposed to have lots of security. He ain't even supposed to be sitting by no window."

We sat and talked until the sun went down. Then it was time for him to go get a tattoo on Sunset Boulevard with some of his crew.

Playing back the interview tape during my long drive home, I heard Wallace say something that haunted me then, and still haunts me to this day.

"It's crazy for me to even think about saying this," he said, his voice reverberating through my Honda Civic hatchback. "Thinking that a rapper can't get killed, because he raps. That shit can happen, and I'm stupid to even think that it couldn't."

Twenty-five days later, shortly after midnight on Sunday, March 9, 1997, Christopher Wallace was the victim of a drive-by shooting, almost six months to the day after Shakur was shot. He too was sitting by a window.

And now there he was, flat on his back. Naked. Tubes hanging out of his mouth, his right hand resting on his chest, near the twin heart-monitor leads stuck to his pectorals. The photo caption in Randall Sullivan's book *LAByrinth* said it all: "Notorious B.I.G. dead on a gurney at Cedar's Sinai Medical Center in Los Angeles. His killer has never been caught."

I nearly dropped the book. I was outraged. I went to my bookshelf and picked up Cathy Scott's *The Killing of Tupac Shakur*, flipped to the center, and found an equally gruesome photograph of Shakur on a coroner's table. How could they publish these tasteless pictures? The only factor in Scott's defense was the rumor about Pac faking his own death, a flimsy journalistic argument at best. But the casket at Christopher Wallace's funeral was open. There's never been any doubt about his death. The only conceivable reason for Sullivan to run such a lurid picture would be to compete with Scott's book, which Sullivan characterized as being "finished fast and dirty"—a criticism that could well be leveled at his own work. After complaints from Wallace's family, Sullivan's publisher removed the autopsy photo from the book's paperback edition.

About the only time you see death photos are in books about mobsters. You see a picture of, say, the Sparks steakhouse hit in John H. Davis's *Mafia Dynasty*, and the subliminal message is, Crime doesn't pay—and here's the proof! Scott and Sullivan depicted Shakur and Wallace like dead gangstas or dead niggas or both—as if they had it coming. While these books do offer some insights into various details of the still-unsolved murders, they offer very little insight into who Wallace or his friend Shakur really were, as people or as artists. Though their faces adorn the covers of these books, they are only incidental characters caught up in webs of police corruption and showbiz intrigue.

And no wonder. The authors of these books were mostly interested in their murders. To find out who these rappers were, they could only rely on second-hand accounts, press clippings from magazines like VIBE, music videos, and CDs. No wonder they fell for the hard poses the artists portrayed in their music. They had no way of knowing what a natural comedian Wallace could be. Yet as soon as someone pulled out a camera, his smile would disappear, his eyes would go dead, and *boom*—there was the photo he knew you wanted, the hard-ass thug, chin raised like, "What?!"

I placed both books side by side on my desk, opened to the autopsy photos. Here were two men who had so much love for each other, turned against each other by forces beyond their control. And now pictures of their dead bodies were available at bookstores everywhere. Whose corpse would fetch the highest price? They deserved better than to be pitted against each other this way. Their families deserved better. But the people responsible for those books never spent any time around these men, never looked into their eyes. They didn't understand their music, much less their lives. Wallace and Shakur weren't people to them— just two more black corpses.

If you've picked up a copy of Unbelievable just to find out who killed Biggie, then you've come to the wrong place. Go get one of the aforementioned books. Enjoy.

On the other hand, if you want to find out who Christopher Wallace really was, how a sheltered Catholic school honors student was transformed into a drug dealer and then into the world's greatest rapper and unlikeliest playboy, then read on. If you want to know what brought Wallace and Shakur together and not just what divided them, read on. If you wonder why B.I.G.'s legend seems to loom ever larger with each passing year, what he represents in the evolution of the hip hop MC's art, or in the rise of rap as a billion-dollar indus-try, read on. If you want to understand how a man can survive the drug game only to get killed in the rap game, you've come to the right place.

While this book does deal with the facts of Wallace's death, and examines the various theories about this unsolved case, that's not really what the book is about. That is—or should be—a job for the police. This is a book about the man in full.

"It's like his life was art played out for everyone," observed Hubert Sams, one of Wallace's closest friends since childhood. "You might have heard the record where he says he was hustling to feed his daughter. But the struggle before, nobody really saw that. Nobody knew about the girls calling him 'Blackie.' Us dark brothers go through it." Though young Wallace was sensitive about his weight, his dark complexion, and his lazy eye, he was always ready with a witty comeback. "He didn't fold," Sams said. "He didn't just curl up at 226 St. James. He came out there, exposed himself to the 'hood. And further than that, he took himself to millions through the vehicle of music. But people don't realize there was a lot of pain behind him."

"You never want anybody to know everything about you," Wallace once told me. Yet that's exactly what this book will attempt to do, to tell you just as much about Christopher Wallace as it does about the Notorious B.I.G. and the world that shaped them both. If I've done my job, then after reading this book, May 21st should be just as important in your mind as March 9th, 1997.

Wallace's astrological sign was Gemini, symbolized by the Janus twins. (Tupac, born June 16, 1971, was one, too.) Geminis are creative types, known for their mercurial nature: cool, calm, and reflective one moment, fiery and warlike the next. Extremely sensitive even when appearing tough.

"Is it better to be loved or to be feared," I once asked him.

"I would say feared," he replied. "Because once you give off a perception of just being a nice guy, a lot of people tend to take your sweetness for weakness. They're like 'Oh, B.I.G., he's cool. He's a great guy.' You know? Instead of somebody being like, '*Biggie's coming*!' " he said, widening his eyes in mock terror. "'How's he gonna act? We can't get over on him.' The fear keeps everybody on their toes."

So who was he? And how do you represent such a character with so many personalities and a name for every one? There was Chrissy-Pooh, the apple of his mother's eye. There was Cwest (pronounced Quest), the closet MC messing around with his grade-school friends on boom-box mix tapes. There was Big Chris, the cat with the black hooded sweatshirt hustling with his boys on the corner of Fulton and Washington near the check cashing spot. There was Biggie Smalls, the freestyle legend and Cee-Lo champion, unofficial mayor of St. James Place. And there was the Notorious B.I.G, the dapper don portrayed in videos, riding around in yachts and helicopters with Versace shades and Coogi sweaters. *Unbelievable* attempts to capture them all, along with many other people and circumstances that made Wallace's life and work so phenomenal.

The cornerstone of this book is the six hours of interviews I did with Wallace over the course of his life, from the first time, on his block in Brooklyn on September 27th, 1994, to the final time, in his hotel room at the Westwood Marquis on March 7th, 1996—just 36 hours before he was murdered. I've done many hours of additional reporting since then —talking with numerous friends, family members, artists, producers, and others who knew him. Some interviews come from my tape archives, which go back as far as 1992.

In trying to do justice to Wallace's story, I've also drawn on numerous pieces written by fellow hip-hop journalists and others who helped me with the enormous task of researching this book. Nobody can take on a task of this magnitude entirely on their own. But I'm sick of reading other books that steal other people's hard work without giving them proper credit and respect. I list every source in the endnotes at the back of the book. The only people not listed are those who spoke with me "not for attribution" or on "deep background."

Interviewing Wallace was always a joy because he never said "no comment." He was easy to find, not pretentious in the least, and funny as hell. He told the stories of his own life in vivid detail, much like his raps. The tales were often darkly comedic, in the same way that Quentin Tarantino's *Pulp Fiction* is essentially a comedy, despite its brutal violence. Whether talking about his childhood, his experiences as a drug dealer, or the challenges of his newfound fame, Wallace always had something interesting to say. This book attempts to tell Wallace's story in the same uncut manner that he related his story to me.

The rules of storytelling dictate that every hero needs a villain to define him. The Notorious B.I.G may be the hero of this book, but that does *not* make Tupac Shakur the villain. This book explores how two friends with so much in common could become alienated by circumstances and people around them. It's a tragic tale, not unlike the split in the Black Panther Party between Minister of Defense Huey P. Newton and Information Minister Eldridge Cleaver. By telling it fully and truthfully, perhaps similar tragedies can be avoided in the future.

Once he had achieved all his goals—conquering the rap game, launching his own businesses, creating jobs for all his friends —what Christopher Wallace *really* dreamed about was a quiet family life. He said as much on *Born Again*, the posthumous tribute album released two years after his death: "Ten years from now where do I *wanna* be? I wanna be... just living man. Just living comfortably with my niggas, man. A pool and shit, smokin' plenty Indo. You know what I'm sayin'? I got my wife, just loungin' with my wife. I got my [kids]. You know, just laid back, just chilling. Living. All my niggas is living."

Then he shifted from the hypothetical to the real. "Where I *think* I'll be? In ten years? I don't think I'm gonna see it, dog," he said, laughing. "For real, man. That shit ain't promised, man. And I don't think my luck's that good. I hope it is, but if it ain't... So be it. I'm ready."

Was Christopher Wallace really ready to die? Think of all the things he had to miss. He was a successful young black man who wanted raise his family and live his life. To give his daughter T'Yanna away at her wedding and spoil her rotten. To teach his son Christopher things about being a man that his own absent father never taught him.

One day, when T'Yanna and Christopher Jordan Wallace are a little older, maybe they'll read this book. Like their father's music, this story is filled with candid moments, some of them funny, some bawdy, some violent, others down-right vulgar, and a few that are just plain sad. But it's also balanced with Wallace's humor, sensitivity, and deep insights about himself and the world around him. Like Biggie's music, this book is not for kids—or even immature adults. But despite the fact that Ms. Wallace personally endorsed my writing this book, I couldn't sanitize it because her son wouldn't have wanted it that way. "Why you taking that out?" I'd imagine him saying over my shoulder as I was editing the manuscript, debating a detail. "Yo, keep that in. Keep it real." So I did.

I just want T'Yanna and Christopher Jr. to know this: If you ever have any questions about whether your father loved you, know that, in his last hours—even before he knew they were his last hours—he was thinking only of you two. The Notorious B.I.G.'s music was filled with death, but Christopher George Letore Wallace wanted to be around to see both of you grow up. If you ever want to hear him say so in his own voice, I gave the tapes to your grandmother.

Christopher Wallace lives within you. And within all of us who loved him and his music. What else can I say about the guy? He was unbelievable.

CHEO HODARI COKER
Los Angeles; June 12th, 2003

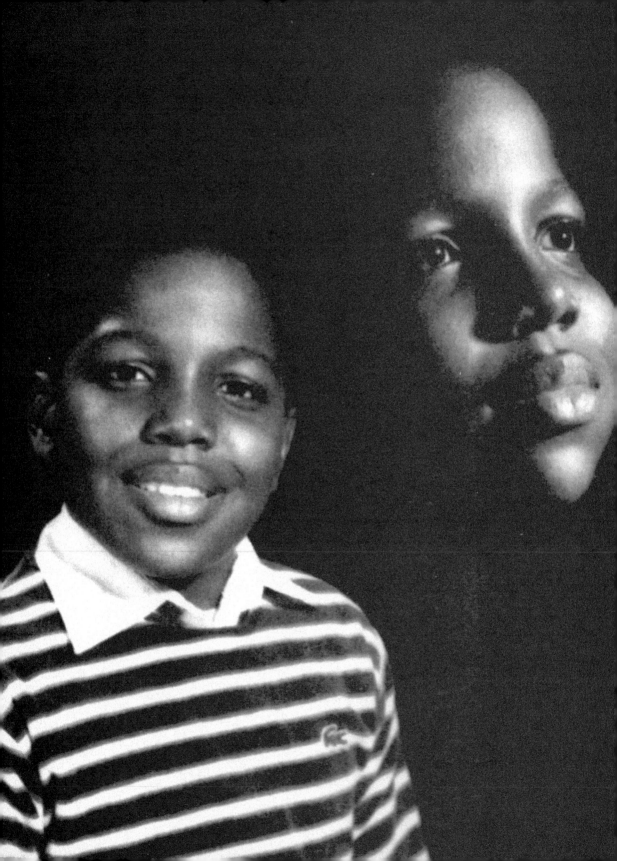

DOLLY
MY BABY

CHAPTER 1

" You I love and not another
You may change but I will never... **"**

The first time she saw the Manhattan skyline in all its splendor, Voletta Wallace gasped in awe. Miracles of glass and steel, the buildings reached upward to heights that seemed to taunt God. Nothing in Jamaica, not even the pictures she'd seen in magazines before she emigrated could have prepared her for the sheer enormity of New York City.

"There must be a lot of religious people around here," Wallace remarked to a Caribbean friend, looking out on the Bronx from a subway car soon after her arrival. "Why do you say that?" he replied. The only brick buildings she remembered in the bucolic coastal town where she grew up were places of worship, so naturally she assumed that these towers must be chapels. Her recently Americanized friend laughed.

"Those aren't chapels," he told her. "Those are apartment buildings. People live in them."

The year was 1966. Wallace's island home of Jamaica had achieved independence from British rule four years earlier, and the economy was already dangerously anemic. There was a widening disparity between rich and poor, increasing strife between political parties, and problems with everything from road maintenance to the educational system. Many Jamaicans were leaving the island for better opportunities elsewhere. Thousands went to England and Canada. But a small minority moved to another land that had once suffered under Britain's heavy-handed absentee rule: America.

Her Majesty's dreary cobblestone streets never held much appeal for Voletta Wallace. "I never saw a happy England," she explained. Her cousin Ethel had left for London years before, and had always wanted her to come visit. But Voletta never had any desire to go. America was different. She'd seen photographs of its beautiful mountain vistas and wide-open prairies. She'd heard about the abundant opportunities, the rags-to-riches success stories, the political freedom, and the fine universities. All the little bits of legend that made up the American dream appealed to her imagination. The U.S.A. sounded like the Promised Land.

The fourth of nine children, Voletta Wallace was born into a solid landowning family in the rural parish of Trelawny on Jamaica's north coast. Her mother ran the household while her father worked as a butcher. Unlike so many others on the island, she never lacked for food, clothes, or shelter. Comfortable but by no means rich, the Wallace family taught Voletta that hard work, thrift, and religious piety were the cornerstones of a happy life. She attended church every Sunday, and spent most of her free time reading books and fashion magazines, never visiting the rowdy dancehalls where other girls her age were dancing to ska, drinking, and getting pregnant.

While she was never one to rebel, Wallace realized that the last thing she wanted was to be married off as a teenager, exchanging her father's firm hand for that of a husband. She longed to see the world, to further her education, and to determine her own course in life.

At 17, she left Trelawny for Kingston, finding a job in Jamaica's bustling capitol as a switchboard operator. But she still felt unfulfilled. The city was so crowded, and oftimes dangerous, she couldn't see much of a future for herself there. By the time she was 19, Voletta Wallace decided it was time to make moves.

A postcard arrived in the mail one day from the Jules Jorgenson House of Fashion that sealed her fate. Her name was on the list because she had once purchased a watch through their mail order catalog. A friend saw the card and said it looked so official that she could probably convince the people at the American embassy she was a model traveling to New York for a fashion show. With her looks, why not? She was a beautiful young woman: 5-foot-3 and 98 pounds with long flowing hair and a slim, shapely figure. She put on her best American-made dress and went to the U.S. embassy in Kingston.

She told them she was a designer, and she needed a visa to go check out the fall collections in person.

"Most of my clothes come from the United States," Wallace told the interviewer, clipping her words with just the right amount of fashionista attitude. "I usually send for my clothes through a friend who goes to New York, but they always come back damaged, so I would like to go there and select my clothes myself."

"You want to make your complaints?" he asked.

"I made my complaints already," Wallace said curtly, cutting him short. "I just want to go up there to select my clothes."

He looked at her, then looked at the card. "The Jules Jorgenson House of

Fashion cordially invites you..." The bluff worked. Voletta Wallace was granted a 14-day visa to do her shopping. She flew up to New York, applied for an extension, and never looked back.

And so began her adventure in New York, like countless other Caribbean people before her. She started out in the Bronx, and eventually settled in the New Lots section of Brooklyn. She worked day and night, using whatever spare time she had to pursue her high school equivalency. "In Jamaica, you don't have the money to send your child for higher education," she said. "I put a great value on education when I came here." The first time she took the test she failed by one point, which only made her more determined. "What am I gonna do?" she asked herself. "Cry?" Instead, the future educator resolved to "just read, read, read." The second time around, she passed the test.

Despite her triumph, life in New York was losing its luster. Wallace took a job answering phones in a psychiatrist's office, and the surroundings were making her crazy. Though the city was pretty by night, the morning light revealed a harsh reality. One day she looked out her window and said to herself "Is *this* the beauty I wanted to come here for?" Wallace hadn't fully appreciated the misty mountains and lush tropical climate of her birthplace until her first experience with soot-colored snow. "New York was filthy," she sad. "The houses were ugly. And the people were rude." It was the general lack of respect that bothered her more than anything else. "My first shock was hearing a man use profanity toward a police officer," she recalled. "In Jamaica, that man would have been arrested and shot. But this man here was cursing out a police officer, and the officer just stepped back. I said, '*Huh*?'"

Voletta Wallace was distraught. Disappointed. "I felt like I was a swan amongst featherless fowls," she said.

She decided to try and make the best of her situation. She wasn't going to sit and sulk at home just because she didn't like her initial impression of the city. "I prayed and prayed and prayed for New York to grow on me," she said. She was determined to better herself, to achieve her dreams of self-reliance. She enrolled at Queens College where she studied nursing and worked as a home health aid. But she quickly realized that nursing wasn't for her. "I couldn't stand the sight of blood," she said. "I couldn't stand the pressure and the sickness and all that." She transferred to Brooklyn College and began taking courses in early childhood education, moving closer to what would become her true calling.

And then in 1970, four years after arriving in the States, she met another expatriate "swan" who helped make her adjustment a little bit easier.

Tall, broad-shouldered, with kind eyes and an easy smile, George Letore had

George Letore and Voletta Wallace with their son Christopher on the day of his baptism in Brooklyn, 1972.

natural charisma. A welder by trade, he was also Jamaican, having emigrated to London years before relocating to New York. It didn't matter to Voletta Wallace that he was more than two decades her senior. She thought she was in love. She delighted in the man with the quick sense of humor who was twice her size and treated her like a little girl. "To be very honest, I can't say, 'Oh, my very first impression was love at first sight,' " Wallace said. "I like older men. For some reason, all my life, I have always dated older men."

She soon became pregnant. It should have been joyous news, but there was only one problem—Letore had neglected to mention that he had a wife and family waiting for him back in London. Although she knew there was a good chance he wouldn't be around, Wallace made up her mind to be empowered instead of feeling abandoned. She had feelings for Letore, but they didn't compare to the love she felt for the new life that was kicking inside her belly. On May 21, 1972, at Saint Mary's Hospital in Brooklyn, New York, Christopher George Letore Wallace was born.

He was a big healthy baby—eight pounds—and labor was difficult for the petite mom-to-be. The child had to be delivered by cesarean section. The last thing she remembered before the anesthesia was a nurse saying, "Doctor, it's 10:21.' " Next thing she knew it was 5 A.M. and another nurse was telling her, "Mother, you have a baby boy.' "

Of course it was love at first sight. "After my son was born I found out that what I felt for George was not love, because I loved my son," she said. "*This* was love," she added, folding her arms as if she were holding the boy with the soft tuft of hair on top of his head again for the first time. "You know, this little thing right here, in my hands, that's love. Out there"—she said, dismissively waving her hand—"I don't love you. I was too focused on this little innocent right here in my hands. So I gave this person all my love, and I guess his father realized, like, 'Damn, can I get just a little bit of that?' But I couldn't give him any," Wallace said. "It was like, 'You go your way, and I'll stay with this little critter here.' And we just made life on our own." Eleven days after his birth, Ms. Wallace took her son to the place that he would call home for the next 20 years, apartment 3L in 226 St. James Place, between Fulton and Washington. Theirs was a spacious apartment, with a large living room, a dining area, a study, and three bedrooms. The one opposite the kitchen on the far end of the hall was Christopher's.

Wallace spent hours looking down at her son, just watching him sleep. She delighted in every coo, every sigh. He was so playful, and he looked up at her with such devotion. Each moment with him felt too short. She hated to leave him and go to work in the morning. "When I did," she said, "I was miserable."

"From his birth until he was two years old, I made a secret prayer in my heart," Wallace recalled. "God, I wish he could stay like this forever. I never want him to grow up. Never never never never."

If he could just stay little, and under her protection, then he would never have to venture outside their apartment, and nothing bad could ever happen to him. She knew the world outside their door could be a very dangerous place.

Just the two of us: Voletta Wallace and one-year-old "Chrissy Pooh."

Just south of the Wallace apartment lay Fulton Street, an east-west throughway that connected both sides of young Christopher's reality. At the western end was yuppified Clinton Hill, and to the east was rough and tumble Bedford-Stuyvesant. The border separating the two areas, Classon Avenue, was only five blocks to the east, but the perception gap between the two neighborhoods was canyon like. "If someone from the area did something good, the papers would describe him as hailing from Clinton Hill," one resident explained. "If they shot or robbed somebody, the papers said they were from Bed-Stuy."

In their late 19th-century heydays, both neighborhoods were among the wealthiest in New York City. The prominent people who built mansions along Clinton and Washington Avenues included pharmaceutical millionaires such as the Pfizers and the Bristols of Bristol-Myers as well as Charles Pratt, the oil executive who founded the prestigious art and design school, The Pratt Institute, at the north end of St. James Place. Those who couldn't afford mansions moved into beautiful brownstones. Victorian row houses and huge apartment buildings lined Gates, DeKalb, and Willoughby Avenues. Architects spared no detail, with sculpted gargoyles, roaring lions, wrought-iron gates, and Romanesque pillars on the exteriors, and high ceilings and intricate woodwork inside.

Emancipation, and the oppressive nature of life in the Jim Crow South, pushed many African-Americans north and west by the turn of the century. They came by train, bus, and foot, seeking a better way of life. The "Great

Migration" saw huge numbers of African Americans settle in industrial centers like Chicago, Detroit, and the mecca of the so-called "Promised Land": New York City.

As Bedford-Stuyvesant's population became blacker over the decades, white citizens' groups like the Gates Avenue Association urged their membership in 1922 to limit "the widening spread of the black belt all over Brooklyn." But it was too late. The first West Indians had begun arriving. Cubans and Puerto Ricans and Dominicans were moving north to escape the sugar cane fields. And the year 1936 marked the expansion of the Independent Fulton Street subway line which stretched all the way to Harlem. Many Harlemites seeking to escape increasingly overcrowded tenements and rising rents uptown took the A-Train to Bedford-Stuyvesant, which became one of the largest concentrations of black people in America, second only to Chicago's South Side.

When the Japanese bombed Pearl Harbor on Dec 7th, 1941, the U.S. Navy lost many of its mightiest warships, including the Brooklyn-built *U.S.S. Arizona*. The Navy needed new ships quick. Thousands of workers answered the call, including people who were previously locked out of the Brooklyn Navy Yard: African-Americans and women. The Yard became the area's largest employer.

When the war ended, many black people lost their jobs to returning soldiers. Having risked everything to move, they weren't about to go back down south. So they stayed put. And just like in Harlem, which was once a Dutch and Jewish neighborhood, Bedford-Stuyvesant experienced a major bout of white flight. The white folks took much of their money with them, but kept the apartments, slashing rents, and turning some of them into flophouses. Formerly proud buildings suffered the neglect of basic repairs and upkeep.

After the neighborhood had been abandoned by both the white and black middle class, Bedford-Stuyvesant became the very picture of Langston Hughes's "Dream Deferred." In 1966, the same year Voletta Wallace came to New York, the Brooklyn Navy Yard closed. Unemployment was on the rise. The prominent buildings in Clinton Hill and Beford-Stuyvesant still stood, but the paint had faded. Politician's promises of more jobs, better schools, and clean, safe streets didn't materialize. Bedford-Stuyvesant increasingly led the city in violent crime, infant mortality, and unemployment. The Pfizers of Clinton Hill gave way to street pharmacists selling heroin and cocaine on the corner.

Strictly speaking, 226 St. James was in Clinton Hill, but in 1971, when Voletta Wallace moved in, it was far from cushy. "Two blocks over there was a methadone center," she observed. "There were a lot of addicts that would congregate around that block." And then at nighttime she would hear the sounds of the city. "Those weren't fireclappers out there," she recalled. "It was gunshots. All those police sirens couldn't have been false alarms. I was scared to death."

But she stayed. She had a beautiful apartment that she could afford, and she was close to where she worked and went to school. And on the bright side, Clinton Hill was a community filled with many young, working class West Indians like herself, proud and frugal, who kept to themselves and closed ranks, keeping their old traditions alive. And then there was everyone else.

As long as Christopher stayed inside, came home on time, and minded his business, he'd be just fine.

"I was a sweet little boy," Christopher Wallace once said, looking back on his childhood. Then he laughed, rolling his eyes.

"I was a sneaky nigga, man," he admitted. "I was *real* bad, you know? And you know what made shit worse? Muthafuckas would tell Moms that I did something, but she just wouldn't believe them. She'd be like, 'Not *my* Christopher.'"

And why would she believe them? Polite, attentive, articulate, Christopher was considered a darling by family and friends alike. He never gave his mother any reason to suspect otherwise.

"He was adorable," said his mother, her eyes lighting up. "Just cuddly and kissable." He loved watching *Sesame Street* and reading Winnie the Pooh stories, thus earning the nickname "Chrissy Pooh."

After completing her studies at Brooklyn College, Voletta Wallace became a teacher of young children, and she'd often practice lesson plans on her son. He began nursery school at two years and five months, was writing his name in legible cursive at three, and displayed a vocabulary well beyond his age.

By the time he turned five, Wallace was bigger than many of the kids in his preschool class at Quincy-Lexington Open Door Day Care Center, but he never used his size advantage to push anyone around. If he wanted extra cookies, he'd find a student who would give him some. If he wanted to play with a certain toy, there was always someone willing to let him go first.

"He knew how to use his brain," said Melvin Blackman, his first teacher in preschool. "He had this charismatic quality. People wanted to go his way."

Among the first to go his way were Michael Bynum and Hubert Sams, his best friends at St. Peter Claver Elementary, a Catholic school located within walking distance from Wallace's apartment. Sams remembered Wallace as a student on the rise. "He had a knack for everything," Sams said. "He was on top of the class from day one. He had his ABCs down before everybody, and he was always on point, from reading to math." You name it, Chris had a gold star for it. "I don't think there's anything I could remember that he wasn't so good at," said Sams, "except for the streets." Chris, Mike, and Hubert endured their share of bumps and bruises, Sams recalled. "We weren't exposed to the raw deal until way late."

In their mothers' eyes, the St. Peter Claver uniform—yellow shirts and plaid ties—made Christopher, Michael, and Hubert look like well-groomed, successful young men on their way to learning important lessons. They learned important lessons, all right. Mike and Chris were only children, and Hubert had a little sister—none had an older brother to show them how to negotiate the rules as they moved among West Indian households, Catholic school, and the street. One thing they knew for sure: their uniforms painted targets on their backs.

"We really stood out," Sams said. "The first thing you did when you left school was you snatched your tie off, right away."

From the second they hit the block, there was tension with the public-school kids. The trio could feel the eyes watching their every move, the unspoken challenge: *They think they better than us?* Going to play video games at the arcade on Fulton Street became a rite of passage. "We didn't have anybody to tell us, 'When you go to the arcade, don't jingle your quarters, because the big kids will take them away from you,'" said Sams. "Back in that era, it was, Yo, if his sneakers are right, we can jump him. It was really, really raw."

Even something as simple as a bus pass could be a test of will. One had to adapt and overcome or perish. "After a while, you either got used to somebody

Graduation day from St. Peter Claver Elementary, 1982. That's Captain Chris holding a paper in hand; best friends Heartbreakin' Hubert and Master Mike are at right.

taking your bus pass, or you fought for it," said Sams. "We chose the latter."

At that time, Wallace was the smallest of the trio, but had the most forceful personality. It was his idea to form The Hawks, a little protection crew that was, in effect, the original junior mafia. The three friends all bought hats with hawk insignias at a store around the corner. Wallace gave them nicknames and he even made up a theme song, which they all had to memorize. "Everybody's talking about the Hawks because we nice," went the rap. "Heartbreaking Hubert, Captain Chris, and Master Mike... If you mess with the Hawks you're forecasting your luck. Why's everybody always picking on us?"

Acting on his mother's advice, Chris preferred to use words to fight his battles. The Hawks could resort to other means if they had to, sometimes going as far as carrying around box cutters. But they were smart enough never to use them.

Doing well in school wasn't good enough for Christopher, because he found that easy. What he wanted was the neighborhood respect that was so elusive. It wasn't just about trying to make friends with the American kids. It was about becoming part of the *fabric* of the 'hood, to be out there wearing the right clothes, the right sneakers, doing exactly what they were doing.

Not that Christopher Wallace felt alienated from his Jamaican heritage—quite the contrary. His mother never wanted him to forget where he came from. "Christopher grew up in Jamaica," she says. Every summer until he was sixteen years old, they would go back down to Trelawny for a couple of months. Christopher loved island life, riding around on a donkey, soaking up the sunshine and fresh air. He loved the jerked pork, curried goat, roasted fish, and red-pea soup. He loved being around his Jamaican relatives, especially his grandparents and his uncle who worked as a disc jockey at local reggae clubs.

Voletta Wallace wanted her to remember that he came from a family that owned land, that he was somebody special. But when he got home, that knowledge didn't change his day-to-day reality. Christopher Wallace just wanted to be like the other kids he saw playing downstairs on St. James. His mother would barely allow him to wander past the front stoop of their building. Even when he did, she'd watch him from the window above like the eye in the sky at a casino.

"Put a label on me," Ms. Wallace said. "Overprotective? I don't care."

She tried to make up for not letting him out by giving him stuff that would keep him inside. The boom box he wanted ("Either the Sharp or the Sony," he specified), tapes by the Fat Boys and Run-D.M.C., and best of all, a slew of video games. Most kids at the time wanted either Atari, Intellivision, or Colecovision. Wallace had all three. Although it went against Ms. Wallace's old-school West-Indian upbringing—the "spare the rod and spoil the child" approach—she thought it was a small price to pay to keep her deeply intelligent child off the streets.

When he played with his neighbors Mike and Arty Bynum, whose West Indian mother shared Voletta Wallace's views on most of the kids in the neighborhood, it was all video games, blanket tents, and kung-fu movies on channel 5. "A typical Saturday for us would be hanging in the house all day," Arty recalled. "We'd get little bowls, and put in chips, Skittles, and cut-up fruits, like mangos, tangerines, cherries. We'd have a little picnic thing going on there... eating our snacks and talking about how we wanted to have all the things that Ricky Schroeder had in *Silver Spoons*." It was as if Christopher was kept in a protected bubble, an oasis where, if Mom had it her way, he could stay forever.

But the longer the two of them stayed in Bedford-Stuyvesant, the more Ms. Wallace became aware that her son was at risk. She'd see the teenage boys hanging out on the corner every day while she waited to catch the bus. So angry. So sullen. So rude. So devoid of the sort of cultivation she'd grown up to expect and respect, men like her father and brothers. She'd seen the faces of mothers who had to bury their own children. She was determined to see that her son would never become another casualty.

Later on Christopher started inviting other kids from the neighborhood up to play his video games, charging them each a quarter. She didn't complain, as long as he stayed home. Her greatest fear was that her son would end up like the other kids she saw all over the neighborhood. The ones that ran the streets all hours of the day and night, stealing candy from the bodega, opening fire hydrants on scorching summer days, and in some cases, getting mixed up in violence. Christopher wanted to get out there too, but his mother wasn't having it.

"I don't want you out there because I see those other kids," she would tell her son. "First of all, they look dirty. And what mother would want their kids to be out there playing from morning until night without supervision?"

Everything that scared Voletta Wallace about living in Brooklyn enticed her son. It was all so close, and yet tantalizingly out of reach. And then one afternoon, when he was hanging out on the stoop, someone who was a part of that neighborhood fabric, spotted him and walked over. His name was Chico Delvec.

"Why you never come off the stoop?" Chico asked.

"Cause my mom won't let me do the things you do," Wallace replied.

Their friendship was sealed over videogames upstairs in the apartment. Wallace started making friends with other kids in the neighborhood by charging them a quarter for each turn, just like at the arcade down the street. Each had something the other didn't have and the other wanted. For Chico, Wallace had video games, a full fridge, and just about every gadget you could imagine. And Chico had something Wallace valued above all else—freedom.

His mom didn't mind him inviting friends over. Going out was the problem.

And so his double life began. As long as he kept his grades up and kept up a respectful attitude at home, his mother would never suspect that he had a completely different personality when he was on Fulton Avenue.

"When she would go to work or to school, I'd be all over the place, you know what I'm saying," he recalled with a chuckle. "I'd be outside with niggas, smoking cigarettes and drinking Calvin Coolers. Just doing shit that I knew I wasn't supposed to do."

On weekends, however, when Ms. Wallace was home, it was a different story.

"Ma," he'd ask. "Can I go outside?"

"No," she'd say.

"Come on, let me go outside."

"I don't want you out there."

I'm out there all the time, he thought to himself. *You just don't know about it.*

"She just made me want to keep doing it," Wallace said years later. "Why does she not want me to play skellie, or 'run, catch and kiss,' and do shit that little boys are supposed to do? Keeping me in the crib—that shit ain't doing nothing but stifling me, man. Let me loose a little, give me some air. I ain't got no brothers and sisters or nothing. You gone all the time. What? You just want me to be a lonely bastard?"

Wallace was known to exaggerate from time to time. His early years weren't nearly as impoverished as he'd later portray them in songs like "Juicy." Living in a "one-room shack" with "no heat" where "Christmas missed us" might have been a reality for other kids in the neighborhood, but not in the Wallace household.

The funny thing about the "keep it real" ethos of rap is that it compelled artists to make their music as bleak as the streets—even if their real lives didn't match up. O'Shea Jackson, for example, grew up in a sheltered middle-class household in South Central Los Angeles. He was never arrested and never gang-banged a day in his life. But as Ice Cube, Jackson's rap persona in the group N.W.A, he was one of the fiercest gangsters ever to walk the earth, his rhymes dripping with an authenticity that enthralled listeners would had sworn was 100 percent "real."

It was a similar situation when Christopher Wallace grew up to become Biggie Smalls—art did not exactly imitate life. Just for the record, his mother said he never had to eat sardines for dinner, and Christmas never missed them, despite the fact that Ms. Wallace, as a Jehovah's Witness, didn't believe in the holiday.

When she did let her son outside, he had to be back in as soon as the street-lights came on, or as soon as he heard her yelling from down the block. It could be humiliating sometimes.

There was only so much that Voletta Wallace could do. A father might have been able to better understand the needs of a rambunctious boy, to provide the proper balance of freedom and swift discipline. But Christopher didn't have a father to turn to for a second opinion. He said he liked it that way.

"Don't know him and I don't want to know him," was Wallace's response when asked about his father. "I don't even remember that cat. For real. I've seen pictures. He looks like a lame. I don't need that cocksucker for nothing." He claimed he wasn't even envious of his friends who had fathers.

"I guess I knew he was a piece of shit for leaving my mom," Wallace said. "It just seemed natural for it to be just me and my mom."

The last time George Letore ever saw his son was in 1978, when Christopher was six years old. Voletta Wallace wasn't so much angry as she was confused about Letore's unexpected appearance. His son hardly knew him. The family reunion, such as it was, lasted for only a day.

After the energetic boy had gone to sleep, Letore and Wallace sat down to talk.

"I have something to give to you," Letore said

"What happened to you after all these years?" she asked. He didn't have a ready answer, and the look on her face let him know that the few hundred dollars in his hand could not begin to make up for his absence. Letore looked embarrassed. Wallace tried to explain that money was not the issue.

"Look," she said, "if you brought twenty dollars here for me to give your son, I would not turn it away. But he needs to see his father around," she said. "The least you could do is just come."

But he never came again. And as Chris grew taller, and every day a little more beyond Voletta's control, he would find other figures on the street who would fill the void that George had left.

Some nights, when his mother was home and there was no way he could sneak out, Christopher would just watch the block from his living room window. He could see the older hustlers hanging out on the corner of St. James and Fulton, drinking malt liquor and shooting dice, heads turning with every passing car, looking for the next challenge, victim, or enemy. He dreamed of the day when he'd be old enough to take his own place out there with them, doing his own thing, beyond anyone's control but his own.

It wouldn't be long now, he thought. Not too long at all.

THINGS DONE
CHANGED

CHAPTER 2

" If I wasn't in the rap game
I'd probably have a key knee deep in the crack game
Because the streets is a short stop
Either you slanging crack rock
or you got a wicked jump shot **"**

"You know what to get me Mommy? Buy me the Timberlands."

Voletta Wallace looked at the price tag on the boots her son wanted. They were well over $150—enough to buy two or three pairs of normal shoes.

"What am I, crazy?" she said.

"Ma, if you buy me this one pair, then you won't have to buy me no more shoes for the rest of the year," Christopher pleaded. At last, she agreed. But it didn't matter how many trips she made to Mano a Mano, it was never enough.

"When I bought him the Timberlands, he'd go, "Ma, get me a Tommy Hilfiger,'" she recalled with exasperation. "He didn't like it if his friends weren't wearing it," she said. No matter if they were the nicest quality, his clothes had to have the right label. She once made the mistake of buying him some Polo shirts before kids his age knew about Polo; the shirts went unworn at the bottom of his dresser.

Ms. Wallace could never could fully understand why her son was so hard to satisfy. Growing up in Jamaica, nothing was taken for granted. She was grateful to have food on the table, a clean place to sleep, and a good education. She liked fashionable clothes too, but she didn't expect to dress like that all the time.

As the family's only breadwinner, Voletta Wallace sometimes worked two jobs in addition to studying for her bachelor's degree at night. She made sure she maintained a perfect credit rating and tried save some money so her son could go to the best schools. Education had been her passport to self-reliance, and she was convinced it would be the key to her son's future as well. He was growing into a sensitive, intelligent, extremely curious little boy with an artist's eye. He could look at a picture in a magazine and draw an exact replica freehand, without tracing. The streets weren't going to claim her son. Not her Christopher.

"I made sure my son had an education, a good mattress, clean sheets, good quality clothes, and I gave him quality time," she said. "My son wasn't the pauperized kid he made himself out to be."

But Christopher was a boy growing up in America. And in America, just getting by meant you were poor. Having more than you needed was considered just breaking even. No matter how much you had, the important thing was to make it look like more than it was. Fresh wasn't just the cornerstone of an emerging hip-hop culture. It was also a way of life.

"At an early age, you learn that everything gotta be fresh," Wallace's friend Hubert Sams explained. "You can't have scuffed up Adidas. You gotta get your toothbrush, keep them fresh. That's the thing, fresh. Personality is secondary. It's about what you have on. You walk around Brooklyn in certain circles, even to this day, people look at your feet first."

No longer the runt of the Hawks crew, Wallace had bulked up considerably since the 5th grade. He'd always been a somewhat husky kid, but at age ten he fell off a city bus and broke his right leg in three places. His mother was advised to sue the City of New York, which settled the matter for a five-figure sum. After paying legal fees, she put a nice little chunk in the bank to save for his college education. His leg was in a cast for six months. Laid up in the house with nothing better to do, he ate, putting on pounds that stuck around long after his leg healed.

By the time he turned 13, he was nearly six feet tall. Though he still had a baby face, with the extra weight he was beginning to look like a man. But Wallace didn't feel all that manly. A man wouldn't have to negotiate with his moms to stay fresh. A man went out and handled his biz. He was sick of being under his mother's thumb. He wanted to get out there and test the waters beyond the stoop.

Wallace fell off a city bus at age ten and broke his leg. He had to wear a cast for six months, during which time he did a lot of eating, watching TV, and getting bigger.

Wallace had bagged groceries at Met Foods around the corner, but from his view, that was a dead end. Earning minimum wage, he'd have to save all his checks for a month or more to get the clothes he needed. And there was no point getting a $200 Adidas sweat suit without the proper shoes—if people saw you with the same kicks and gear all the time, they'd know you were broke. Forget about respect from the fellas—the girls really weren't gonna give a broke-ass nigga the time of day.

Wallace's childhood was behind him. He was about to start high school, and his mother kept reminding him how the next four years would affect the rest of his life.

His first act of rebellion was to tell her that he no longer wanted to go to Queen of All Saints school. No more uniforms, no special treatment—he just wanted to be a regular kid. When he transferred to Westinghouse High School he found the public school environment quite different from Catholic school. There was, essentially, no discipline. The student body—which included Trevor "Busta Rhymes" Smith and Shawn "Jay-Z" Carter—seemed to have the upper hand, while the teachers' chief goal was simply to maintain some semblance of order. For a kid as clever as Wallace, the curriculum just wasn't stimulating. Whenever he felt that one of the teachers had insulted his intelligence, he didn't hesitate to speak his mind.

"He did very well in school, it's just that he talked back a lot," his mother says. "He was a smart-ass." But when dressed for a junior high school dance, Wallace looked like the perfect gentleman.

"Christopher did very well in high school; it's just that he talked back a lot," his mother said. "He was a smart-ass."

"One day," she recalled, "he comes home and asks me, 'Mom, how much does a garbage collector make?' "

She just happened to know; she'd seen a magazine article that compared teachers' salaries with other professions.

The next day, Christopher went to school with the article in hand. After class, Ms. Wallace got a call from Christopher's guidance counselor.

"The guidance counselor told me how Christopher walked into class and said, 'Do you know how much a garbage collector makes, sir?' "

"No," the teacher replied.

"A teacher makes a starting salary of $22,500," Wallace informed him. "A garbage collector starts at $29,000."

"Do you have a point, Mr. Wallace?"

"Yes, sir. You said some of us inside here are gonna be garbage collectors. But we're gonna be making more money than you, so that's cool."

The longer Christopher attended Westinghouse, the more restless he became. At over 200 pounds, he had the build for football, but he didn't want to play. Career day came and went at school. Nothing really appealed to him.

Growing up in this section of Brooklyn, Wallace saw both sides of life, the legal and the illegal. Every day the men and women would walk to the C-train on the corner of Fulton in search of their daily wage. And then there were the teenagers who stood outside the train station, shooting dice, holding 40-ounce bottles in brown bags, and turning their heads back and forth so they could check out the occupants of every passing car.

"Don't be a bum," his mother warned him, her regal Jamaican accent giving the words extra impact. "You're nothing if you don't have an education."

Yet it seemed to Wallace that the corner kids, the ones who had no place to be, had every advantage over those "respectable" people who looked so tired when they got on the train in the morning, and even more worn down when they emerged from the subway station at night. The guys on the corner did what they wanted. And they stayed forever fresh.

It didn't matter how much his mother browbeat him, there was no way for him not notice those kids. They were always out there, rain or shine, 24-7-365, selling a product that sold itself, a lethal substance that would transform the neighborhood, changing his life and that of everyone else it touched: crack.

Named for its rocklike texture, this smokable form of cocaine was cooked up on countless kitchen stoves with a little water and baking soda. The tiny gray chips could deliver a rush unlike anything anybody had ever experienced. The high was immediate, potent, and kept users coming back for more. It was the worst thing to happen to the black community since the first slave vessel pulled into Jamestown in 1619.

Cocaine had been around for centuries. The Incas were cultivating coca leaves for their magical properties as early as the 1400s. By the dawn of the 20th century, everyone from Sigmund Freud to Coca-Cola was singing its praises. The all-American soda contained traces of the drug until the recreational use of cocaine was outlawed in the U.S. by the Harrison Act of 1914. That law was championed by southern sheriffs who complained that cocaine-crazy black men were raping white women in droves.

Nonetheless, cocaine became a fashionable drug among rich and famous people, many of whom believed it to be harmless. Until the early '70s, it was hard for most people to get cocaine if they weren't hanging out with rock stars or Hollywood actors. Movies like Gordon Park Jr.'s *Superfly* glamorized it. Woody Allen made fun of it. In the most memorable scene of *Annie Hall*, Allen sneezes, sending thousands of dollars' worth of blow flying around the room. Sniffing cocaine said something about you—like having Cuban cigars, the smallest cell phones, black American Express cards, and Bentleys—only "true players" had access.

Cinematic depictions of coke reached a new level in 1983 when Brian DePalma's *Scarface* drove inner-city kids crazy for the story of Tony Montana, a penniless Cuban immigrant who became a drug baron. The movie was meant to be a warning about the dangers of cocaine, but it had the opposite effect for many viewers. One montage alone—in which money-counting machines click as Tony's henchmen jump out of vans with sacks of cash while the big man relaxes with his pet tiger in an opulent mansion—fueled the dreams of countless aspiring dealers.

Richard Pryor put "freebase" on the map back in 1980 by setting himself on fire following a 72-hour smoking binge. But the high cost of making base kept that form of cocaine from becoming popular. Blow was for rich folks until the supply problem was solved by Colombia's Medellin cartel, led by a smart but ruthless man from Bogota named Pablo Escobar. Their product reached the public courtesy of street entrepreneurs like "Freeway" Ricky Ross in South Central Los Angeles. The former high school tennis star didn't invent crack, but he was among the first to offer his clients "ready rock" in 1982.

Like McDonald's founder Ray Kroc before him, Ross set up franchises and became a wholesaler—selling prepackaged rock to lower-level dealers who established their own crack houses. He even attracted the attention of a major Colombian dealer by the name of Danilo Blandon—who was later suspected of being a CIA employee who funneled drug profits to Ronald Reagan's Contras in Nicaragua.

From the dealer's perspective, crack was a wonder drug. It was easy to make, and the drug's smokable form drove customers nuts, hitting the brain's dopamine and endorphin centers instantly. Best of all, a crack high lasted less than half an hour. Users kept coming back again and again until their money was gone. Two thousand dollars' worth of powder could make you as much as $20,000 worth of crack. If you were ruthless and ambitious, it could be a gold mine.

The rock epidemic that was taking over Los Angeles was largely ignored on the East Coast. But after Len Bias, the Maryland Terrapins basketball star and Boston Celtics number-one draft pick died of a crack-induced heart attack, the drug officially entered the national consciousness. *Time* and *Newsweek* ran cover stories. President Bush held up a bag of crack during a televised address in which he announced a new war on drugs. Dan Rather did a two-hour program called *48 Hours on Crack Street* that was watched by 15 million people. The show was broadcast on September 2, 1986. Christopher Wallace was 13 years old.

"I heard about crack on the news and I was like, "That's what niggas must be doing," Wallace recalled. I knew they were fly as hell—they had $150 Ballys and bubblegoose jackets and sheepskins. I was like, 'Oh Shit. These niggas are doing it.'"

Wallace didn't know any of the specifics, but he knew he wanted in.

Chico Delvec was the bridge. It was one thing seeing kids he didn't know blow up. But seeing Chico succeed convinced him to stop sitting on the fence.

"This nigga's coming through with the butter Fila velour shit, the big cables, four finger rings," Wallace recalled. "I'm like, 'Yo, we the same age. I'm sitting here fucked up, asking my moms to throw me down money for some ice cream. And this nigga is getting cash!'"

"Come on the Ave with me," Chico told him one day, in one of those simple conversations that can change one's life forever. "Just come see what it's like and meet some of my old-timers."

Wallace's heart was racing as he walked around the corner to Fulton Street. He met some of the hustlers like Cheese, Tony Rome, and D-Roc—but the scene was too fast for him. Cars were zooming by, and you had to look in every one to make sure it wasn't a rival dealer or a cop. Wallace had the added worry that his mother might find out what he was up to.

"I ain't with that man," he told Chico, all stressed out. "The police. My moms..."

"Just chill, Chris," Chico said. "You ain't got to do nothing. Just chill."

As Wallace settled down, learned the game, and realized how much money he could make, that fear quickly turned into boldness.

"I feel like I was the bad influence," Chico said. "Because when I introduced him to the game, he just like got addicted to it"

He started off small, "hauling work" for others.

"They'd give me a little bit of paper," Wallace said. "The next thing I know, they was trying to make big moves. And they wanted me to be down. And I had my little cousin with me, my cousin Gutter. And we just got into it."

If taking drugs felt as good as selling them, he understood why the customers kept coming back for more. It was the speed that appealed to Wallace. The returns were quick, and the only limit seemed to be his own ambition.

"Within no time—*boom*!" Wallace recalled. "That's what made the shit so fascinating. It wasn't a situation where a nigga was struggling for four or five months like, 'Damn, when we gonna come up?' Within three weeks niggas was having six or seven hundred in they pocket. Niggas giving other niggas a hundred dollars to go get sneakers for them—'And get a pair for yourself.' Sweet shit like that."

Why even aspire to college? If the point was to get a job, he didn't need a degree for that. When he was a boy at St. Peter Claver, they would advise students to build on their talents and think about what they could do with it in the future. Wallace was a talented artist. There were times when he thought about becoming a commercial artist. The Pratt Institute was within walking distance of his apartment, and there were artists that lived in Clinton Hill. But a few afternoons standing on Fulton Street changed all that.

"After I got introduced to crack—commercial art? Nigga please." Wallace explained with a chuckle. "I can go out here for twenty minutes and get some real paper. There's your art, man. I didn't want no job. I couldn't see myself getting on no train for shit. I didn't want to work in no barber shop, I didn't want to do no restaurant. I wanted to sell drugs! I wanted to chop up keys, bag up work, and get paid. That's the only thing I thought I was ever gonna do."

He was seduced by the money, but Wallace was also addicted to the gamesmanship of it all, the thrill of doing something illicit in plain sight. Like so many kids at that moment in history, Wallace had "triple beam dreams," fantasies of weighing out large amounts of cocaine on precision scales, then enjoying the rewards—cars, women, and street juice. He wouldn't be the last kid with such notorious aspirations—and he was hardly the first.

The drug game, like the NBA, used to be a league for grown folks.

Street legends like Leroy "Nicky" Barnes and Frank Lucas spent years building their multi-million dollar heroin organizations from the bottom up—and were well in their thirties before they began reaping their ill-gotten gains. The Federal Government estimated that in the late '60s and early '70s, over 50% of America's heroin users lived in New York, and 75% of those junkies lived in the Harlem neighborhoods where Lucas and Barnes sold their wares.

A disciple of Ellsworth "Bumpy" Johnson, Lucas ruled West 116th Street with an iron fist. His Blue Magic "package" outsold all other brands of heroin.

"My buyers, you could set a watch by them," Lucas said. "By four o'clock we had enough niggas in the street to make a Tarzan movie. By nine o'clock, I ain't got a fuckin' gram. Everything is gone, sold. And I got myself a million dollars."

Barnes and Lucas were Harlem royalty. They had flashy cars, chinchilla furs, tailored suits, Gucci frames, women and houses all over the country. They could

be found uptown at the Lenox Lounge or Small's Paradise—the same club where a Detroit Red-era Malcolm X used to ball out with West Indian Archie and Sammy The Pimp.

Emboldened by beating so many cases, Barnes posed for a photo on the cover of the *New York Times* Sunday magazine calling himself "Mr. Untouchable." The article got the attention of President Carter, and by the late '70s Lucas and Barnes were both in prison.

But during the years when they were running the street, the most a young teenager could do was aspire to be a driver or a lookout and, over years, work their ways up the ranks. They didn't have Barnes and Lucas's overseas connections to import the stuff. You needed a Ph.D. in street sciences to make those kinds of moves.

When he started hustling, Wallace became a fixture in the neighborhood. Everybody knew the big kid on the corner. His wit and winning personality made him much more than a dealer. He was the "Mayor of St. James."

Crack made it a G.E.D. game.

As the popularity of ready rock spread, the age of the dealers got younger and younger. Teenagers were fronting in Porsches and Benzes, wearing thousands of dollars' worth of jewelry, making names for themselves. With so much money, and the exuberance of youth, the competition got nasty. Young men who once had trouble affording a Saturday Night Special now had access to Uzis and AK-47s. Jamaican posses like the Spanglers and the Showers competed fiercely for U.S. drug profits. Crips and Bloods used crack it to escalate their long term vendettas against each other, each side taking up ever deadlier arms.

Some kids didn't even care about the gang shit. They just loved the last 15 minutes of *Scarface*, and felt that killing their rivals bolstered their reputations. It was good for business. They didn't care who got hit. Drive-by shootings became routine. Innocent kids dying right next to the street soldiers.

The game was changing, and so was Voletta Wallace's boy. But she was the last to know.

"Prior to 13 years of age," she said years later, "he was just a son. A son any mother would like. At 13 he became notorious."

Ms. Wallace worked hard during the day and then took classes at night. By the time she came home, her son was usually sitting in front of the television, having left the block hours before.

The clues were subtle at first: a photo of Christopher with his friends from St. James, wearing jewelry or gold fronts on his teeth—but she never saw that stuff in person. He hid his secret identity in plain sight. Like Superman had his Clark Kent glasses and suit, Captain Chris had the benefit of his mother's doubt.

The only things he did bother to conceal from her were the fly clothes that influenced him to become a dealer in the first place.

"I used to hide all my shit on the roof," Christopher confessed. "I'd leave the house with all the busted shit my moms was giving me, act like I'm going to school, and change my whole outfit up on the roof, come down on the street, and then go to school. Every morning this was the task, I mean *every* morning."

When he got tired of the rooftop routine, he started telling his mother that he bought the stuff on the street for a discount.

"I used to hide all my shit on the roof, and leave the house with all the busted shit my moms was giving me, act like I'm going to school, and change my whole outfit up on the roof, come down on the street, and then go to school," Wallace explained. "Every morning this was the task, I mean every morning."

If she got suspicious, he had an excuse ready. "I'd tell my mom some boosters were reselling it, and I bought it off the street for like forty dollars," he recalled. "She from Jamaica; she don't know how much that Tommy Hilfiger cost."

"I remember once I saw him with a jacket," Ms Wallace said "And I said, 'Where did you get that jacket?' He said, 'Oh, it's not mine. I borrowed it.' And I said, 'You're wearing other people's clothes? That's disgusting.' And then one day, someone asked to borrow one of his shirts. And I go, "is this what teenagers do?"'

"Everyone was scared of his mother," recalled Wallace's friend Damion "D-Roc" Butler. "Mrs. Wallace don't *play*. When I used to stay at Big's house, if we came in at, like, three in the morning, trying to tiptoe in the crib, she would be right there. She'd direct you into the living room and sit you down on the couch. And she wouldn't just be talking to Big. She'd treat everybody like her son. She'd say, 'Don't come in here this late. Y'all gotta be careful. You smell like reefer.' She'd just always be on us, but not in a bad way. I mean, you can't be mad at somebody who cares, you know?"

While Wallace maintained a positive front at home, he didn't bother to keep up the same level of deception at school. The former honor-roll student started missing classes days and weeks at a time. By the end of his sophomore year, the truancy letters began to pile up, and he was running out of excuses.

"I have a warrant for your arrest," his mother told him one day, waving the paper in his face. "You don't go to school, and the cops are out there looking for you. When they find you, they're going to arrest you and put you in a home."

That got to him. "He was so scared," she said.

For a minute, anyway. But the money made things easier.

"We were making $1200, $1300 a day," Wallace remembered. He felt his mother's frustration, but at the same time, he couldn't see any reason for continuing with school. A high school degree seemed irrelevant; college was not even an issue.

"My mother was going to school for a long time," Wallace said. "It was hard. And I used to see her. School was hard. I was like, man, this ain't the shit for me. And I just started saying, Fuck it. I'm not doing this shit."

It broke his mother's heart. Even with him missing as many classes as he did, she felt that he still could have graduated with minimum effort.

But Christopher was adamant. He wasn't going back for his last year of high school, no matter how much she pleaded.

"How are you gonna live?" she would ask him, over and over. "I'm thinking about your future. What are you going to do out there? Walk about and be a bum? Have your mommy feed you and clothe you?"

The thought wasn't keeping Wallace up at night.

"All of us dropped out of school," he said. "We were sitting on six and seven grand a week, just living, y'know what I'm sayin'? And we had all the chicken-head bitches on our dicks and shit. We were just doing our thing."

Christopher Wallace was sixteen years old, and he thought he had life all figured out. Of course, he didn't. The game was unpredictable, stressful, and sometimes scary. Life in the fast lane wasn't all it was "cracked up" to be.

When West Coast and Southern hustlers referred to crack dealing as "grinding" they weren't just talking about the texture of the product. They were also describing the lifestyle—the same thing brothers in Brooklyn meant when they spoke of "the struggle." Selling drugs was life on the swivel. Constantly looking over your shoulder. Always wondering if this was the day you were going to get busted.

Sometimes Wallace felt that he was working so many hours, he might as well get a real job. What looked like easy money turned out to be hard work

"I'd wake up around nine o' clock to catch the check cashing place at nine fifteen," Christopher Wallace recalled. "The crack heads got checks from Social Security, and on Saturday they all get their welfare checks. And when they cash those in, they usually want to buy drugs. So we'd be up early—as soon as they got their money, we're gonna be the first person they see."

"Every day between 4:30 and 7:00 we'd come hustle right on the corner," Wallace said. "The train station would be flooded with business people from all over the area. And they'd see us every day. Every day they'd come out of the train and get hit with a cloud of marijuana smoke." Their radio was blasting rap music, their dice game was taking up the whole block. "They'd look at us like we the scum of the Earth," Wallace said.

But you had to be out there, because that area of Fulton Street was an open market, and competition was cutthroat. You got lazy, you lost your customers. It was as simple as that. As on Wall Street, time was money.

"Everybody popped up with their own package," said one former dealer familiar with the Fulton Street drug scene. "You be at one bodega, and you looking across the street and somebody else there, and you're both hollering for the same customer. Whoever treated the customer better might have a chance."

The dealer's relationship with his client was close by necessity. From the crack-fiend's perspective, the quality of each "jack," or vial of crack, depended on the dealer, the quantity and texture—rocky or crumbly—how much they cut it, and what they cut it with. If a certain dealer sold a certain quality product, and you felt like you could trust him, that's who you dealt with.

From the dealer's perspective it was different. You had to know your clientele to avoid going to jail. Selling just one vial of crack to an undercover cop could land you behind bars for a year. A pocketful of jacks could send you upstate for the rest of your natural life. And with the advent of TNT—the NYPD's Tactical Narcotics Task Force, street dealers knew they were public enemy number one.

"TNT sends you somebody new every day" said the former dealer. "They'd send you a decoy with marked money, and the van would come right after. You had to be selective. Had to do your homework. Some people didn't sell to anybody they didn't know—straight up. Or you had to come up with a good customer and stand there and vouch for them like, 'I know this guy, hook him up.' Sometimes you'd be paranoid, you'd get a twenty, and then run into the Arab store and break it real quick."

If it wasn't the cops busting the block, it was the crack heads short-changing you. If you were charging ten bucks, they would try to give you eight. After a while it added up. If they kept shortchanging you, you had two choices—refusing to serve them, or beating their ass the next time they came up short.

"The drug game is so up and down," Wallace observed. "There's so much shit that can happen." When business was bad, it was very bad. During a drought or a police crackdown, it wasn't unusual to make $300 in a week. Or nothing at all.

And even when the money was good, he never saved it. Seven thousand a week might get split six or seven ways. He could easily blow his $1500 on clothes, shoes, and weed. Next thing he knew, he'd be headed uptown to spend the last of his funds buying more weight so he could cook it up and start all over.

When he was on the block, "Big Chris" had no conscience—it was all about the dough. If someone wanted some shit, you sold it to them—no matter who that person was. You might have started out with scruples, but the longer one remained in the game, the looser those principles became.

"Once he got to the point where Fulton street became his real stomping grounds, he wasn't even Chris no more," said Hubert Sams.

Sams was a student at Thomas Jefferson High School, where he played full-back on the football team. When he wasn't at practice, he'd sometimes visit his old friend Captain Chris, who was spending most of his time with his cousin Gutter and a new friend everyone called O.

"You playing football?" Wallace asked, sounding impressed. Then the old humor came back. "Man, you gonna break something."

"I'm all right, yo," Sams said with a smile. "I'm all right."

"You getting' big though," Wallace said.

"This nigga ain't big," Gutter said, wrestling Hubert to the ground and laughing.

The Christopher Wallace Sams knew at sixteen was very different than the kid he knew at six. He was still funny. He still had people following his lead. But the whole context had changed. Wallace's "dibbling and dabbling" days—when he'd buy just a little and sell when he got the chance—were over. "When I went to see him, we weren't chilling at his house anymore," Sams recalled. "He was on the block."

That's when the changes began to sink in. "Being sixteen, you think about hanging out with your friends as play time. But I realized Big wasn't out there playing. Yeah, there were some jokes being cracked, but it wasn't a game out there. I think that mighta helped me not fiend to get in the game. Cause I saw what it was really about. And the motivation was money, man. The motivation was money."

"We used to have this rule that was, 'We ain't serving to no pregnant ladies," Wallace said. "And there was a pregnant lady who used to come see us every day from Jersey that used to want, like, 90 capsules. I'm like, Fuck it. I mean if I don't give it to her someone else will."

"It ain't like she gonna go home and be like 'Well, Biggie didn't give it to me, I'm going to sleep.' She's gonna get high. So I'm going to handle my business. And niggas was like 'Yo, you foul.' "

But Wallace remained unapologetic. "I didn't get in this game to feel sympathy for nobody. I got in this game because I can't do nothing else. This is what's going to help me eat. So I can't pass up no muthafucka. That's bread and butter, y'knowhatumsayin'? If I don't do that, I don't eat."

So he stayed out there, chasing the dollar and trying not to get caught.

Sams recalled visiting Wallace on Fulton late one evening when the police almost got his friend. They had gone into a bodega to get the hustler's staple—a turkey hero with cheese.

"We weren't on the Ave, so we didn't see them roll up," Sams said—"they" meaning the cops, of course. "Chris is a well known figure. So when they hit the block, they know they're looking for the big guy. Usually he stashed his stuff. He didn't have it on him. And they'd talk to him like, 'You know you got it.'"

This time was different. "They walked in the store right behind us, and we at the counter," Sams recalled. "He had a few jacks in his hand. As soon as they came in, he threw them in his mouth. I saw him. They might have seen him. But it was kinda smooth. He was on point. You had to be."

The police officers patted both young men down.

"Open your mouth," one of the cops said to Wallace.

"What?" Wallace said, eyes wide.

That's when the cops grabbed him—and Wallace switched to plan B.

"*Aggh! Aggh!*"

"He just fell down and started screaming," Sams remembered. "So now they trying to wrestle with him." People in the store began crowding around to see the cause of the commotion, and the cops got distracted.

"They're looking up and away—one's got his knee in his back," Sams said. "So he looks up at me and he's whispering 'Take the jacks! take the jacks!' Like he wants me to bend down and take them out of his mouth. But the cops is standing right there."

The look on Sams' face told Wallace that idea wasn't going to work. "So he just keeps screaming," Sams said. "Yo, he could have won an Oscar. He was acting like they were killing him. And then he started crying."

At this point, the cops stood him up.

"Get out of here, man," they said. Frustrated, they turned and left.

"After they left and started getting in the car, he just turned around and started screamin'!" Sams said, laughing almost as loud as Wallace did.

"When he started laughing at 'em, I was like 'Yo, I wouldn't have did that.' Cause I wouldn't have wanted them to come back with a hard on for me. But that was his attitude man. He felt like he was almost untouchable. Almost."

Despite the money he was making on the street, Wallace was still camped out at 226 St. James in his sweaty-ass room in the back, with sneakers and fast-food containers stacked sky high. Despite all his talk of being a man, he wasn't ready to leave home. And though he knew he was doing wrong, he liked the idea that his mother thought he was a good guy. In some ways, both of their psyches depended on it.

"Shit, sneakiness was winning," Wallace recalled with a grin.

How deep was his mother's denial?

"I thought crack bottles were perfume bottles," Ms. Wallace said.

It's hard to believe that anyone could be so naïve—on the level of Lois Lane never suspecting that Clark Kent was Superman when his only disguise was a pair of wire rimmed glasses and a tie.

Never underestimate the power of denial, particularly when it comes to single black mothers and their only sons.

There was the time that Wallace and his friend O left a batch of cocaine that they'd just cooked into a gooey white paste on a plate in Wallace's room. They had plenty of time to kill before they could crack it up and put it into vials, so they put the plate of wet paste under a fan and went downstairs to hang out.

"We go outside and get something to eat, and just happened to be in there with some broads, spending too long in there" Wallace recalled.

By the time they returned, they discovered that his mother had decided to come home early that day. When they went in his room, the plate was gone.

"Ma, you go up in my room?"

"Yeah"

"Did you see a plate on my bed?"

"The plate with the mashed potatoes?" she replied, sounding mildly annoyed. "They were so hard on the plate I had to flush 'em."

"WHAT?!"

"I threw some in the garbage.

"WHAT?!"

"I'm like taking crack out the garbage," he said, savoring the comedy of his story. "She got barbecue turkey wings all on the shit, and niggas are looking at me like 'You fucked up.'"

Eventually he did.

Standing out on the corner in early 1990, Wallace and some of his friends got arrested. Wallace had a loaded, unregistered gun on him—but no drugs. Because it was his first offense, and because he was only seventeen, the judge was lenient, and he was given five years' probation.

After the gun charge, it became impossible to hide what he was doing from his mother. It didn't help when the police came by the apartment to tell Ms. Wallace that her son was out on the corner selling drugs. They said one day they'd catch him with a few vials on his person and that would be all they needed to lock him up for a very long time.

"I think you have the wrong boy," she told them, even then. "Not my Christopher."

Her own son was the one who had to break it to her. "I really had to sit down and tell her that what they were saying was true."

Even if she suspected something was going on, it was hard to confront the truth. Her son had strayed from the path. He was no longer someone to be proud of.

"My moms was looking at me like I was crazy," Wallace recalled, his voice softening. Other than the death of his friend "O"—who got shot around the same time—disappointing his mother was one of the few memories from Wallace's street life that caused him visible remorse.

"My moms was just flipping out," he says. "She'd be watching the news, seeing stuff about how crack is plaguing the city. She'd just lose her mind and go in my room and throw all my shit away. She'd be like, 'I don't want this shit in my house! If you're gonna do this shit under my roof you gotta leave.' You know me, Mister Bold and Beautiful. I'm like, 'Alright. I'll go.'"

He came back within two weeks. Relieved but also reluctant, Ms. Wallace let him back in. He assured her that he had learned his lesson and was out of the game. Every morning she'd catch the bus to work, and every morning he'd be back on the corner near the check-cashing place. It was a separate but equal existence, neither one trying to tread on the other's space.

His mother sealed their new arrangement by taking out a life insurance policy on her son. After he signed it, she looked him in the eye and said, "Do you know what you just signed? You signed away your *life*."

But it was the life he had chosen for himself.

"I'd never say she accepted it," Wallace said about his mother's attitude about his dealing. "But I was basically uncontrollable. I wouldn't stop no matter what."

And so he was out there every day, gathering a crew around him that was down for whatever. Chico and Gutter were the guys that held him down. Older cats like Cheese and Tony Rome looked on like overseers. To the untrained observer, they just looked like neighborhood kids who kept moving around. The crew was always changing positions to avoid being too conspicuous. But no matter where he went, you could always saw the big guy.

James Lloyd a.k.a. Lil' Cease was a thirteen-year-old who saw him all the time.

"I used to come back and forth from school, doing my thing, and Big, he right there on that corner, hustling with the rest of the dudes. He'd be out there, shooting dice, breaking fools off while waiting for customers."

Trife and Larceny were some of the other youngsters who hung around. Also in the mix was Kimberly Jones, a friend of Lil' Cease's sister who was known as

Lil' Kim to distinguish her from another girl named Kim. Money L lived nearby. D-Roc (short for Rockefeller) lived over on Bedford Ave, but Wallace would often visit him for a piece of his grandmother's pineapple upside-down cake. Butler remembered being impressed by Wallace's intellect. "He was so smart," said D-Roc, "you could ask him questions like, How many miles is Pluto from Earth? And he could break it down."

Wallace became a fixture on that corner .Everyone knew him, from little kids to old men, beat cops to bodega owners. Mothers on their way home from work. Often he'd be out there telling jokes, smoking trees, just holding court on the "Ave" like he was a politician meeting with his constituents. One of his friends said he was "like the mayor or some shit." The moniker stuck: Big was now The Mayor of St. James. He was in the bodegas so much that he even learned a little Arabic so he could joke around with the shopkeepers.

"He was a clown," remembered Jan Jackson, a sweet, heavyset girl who lived right around the corner from St. James. "That's the only way I can put it, a clown, but a charismatic clown. He would be standing out there all the time. He approached me one day when I was on the pay phone. And he just came up to me and started a conversation. And then every day after that, when I came home from work, he would be there and we would have a conversation. And it just started from there."

Jan progressed from fixing him a plate of rice and beans to becoming Wallace's first serious girlfriend. They were so close, some people assumed they were kin.

What started as a friendship would last the rest of Christopher's life. They got along because, on the surface, both were the kind of people that white (and some black) society discriminate against. They were overweight, poor, and dark-skinned. But they understood each other. Jan wasn't trying to change him. She could handle his mood swings. She could even understand the fact that he was hustling—and not be one of those people looking at him like he was a piece of shit.

"That man had so much sex appeal," she says. "It's not even funny. I couldn't think of five men that I've met since then that have the charisma of his one body. 'Cause when you'd meet him, he was just like... he was my friend," she says. "We would just talk, and laugh, and you would feel so much at ease, and you wouldn't have a care in the world. It was like nothing or no one else was there."

The time they spent together would be simple but meaningful. He told her about the things he wanted to do if he had enough money.

"The cars. Always the cars," Jan said, laughing at the memory. "Always going to buy his mother a house in Florida. 'Oh, I'm gonna get a house in Florida.

Oh, and I'm gonna have two houses, one for the boys, and one for me and you.' "

How all this was going to happen she didn't know. Nor did he. He always assumed that his future lay in the game. But fate had other plans for Wallace.

Christopher had this hobby, see—he liked to rap. When he wasn't busy on the Ave, he spent most of his time rhyming. and he knew he was getting better. And as more people heard him, they would say he was the best in the neighborhood—possibly even better than that.

IT WAS ALL A DREAM

A DREAM

CHAPTER 3

66 You never thought that hip hop would take it this far
Now I'm in the limelight cause I rhyme tight
Time to get paid, blow up like the World Trade **99**

Christopher Wallace came along at a pivotal moment in rap's evolution.

Born in 1972, he was a member of the last generation to remember what black music sounded like before hip hop was even a possibility. He was old enough to remember the soulful sounds of the Dramatics, Blue Magic, Teddy Pendergrass, Stevie Wonder, and Marvin Gaye. He was familiar with the explosive theatrics of Parliament-Funkadelic, Earth, Wind & Fire, and Kool & the Gang—and the father of funk, James Brown. He knew the isolated moments of disco genius—Chic, Diana Ross, and Donna Summer. Then there were those childhood trips to Jamaica, where jazz and mento, reggae and soul formed an ever-present sonic backdrop—sometimes seasoned with a bit of toasting, Jamaica's form of proto-rap. All of these influences, consciously or not, filtered through his ears, shaping his ideas and opinions about music.

Christopher was barely walking when some of the most groundbreaking events in the continuing evolution of black music were taking place. When DJ Kool Herc began setting up his massive sound system in the courtyards and project recreation halls of the South Bronx, it was more than an event—it was a unifying force in a community where gangs and crime ran rampant. Afrika Bambaataa and his Zulu Nation had a similar philosophy, but he played music a little differently. He could slip any record into the mix and make it funky. The *Andy Griffith Show* whistling theme. Billy Squire. Thin Lizzy. The more obscure the better. Pop music garbage became hip hop symphony. In fact, that was the unspoken motto of the art form—taking other people's trash and turning it into gold.

Grandmaster Flash provided the final piece to the puzzle. An electronics whiz from Samuel Gompers Vocational School, Flash figured out how to preview one record while playing another. This allowed him to go beyond the blends heard in disco clubs. He could isolate the break—that part of any old record that makes time stand still. Like the first few seconds of John Bonham's drums on Led Zeppelin's "When the Levee Breaks," or the Phelps "Catfish" Collins guitar solo on James Brown's "Get Up, Get Into it, Get Involved." Some dancers would wait for these special parts of the record to show off their new dance steps. They became known as break boys, or B-boys for short.

While Herc, Bam, Flash, and other pioneers manipulated the dance floor like scientists in a laboratory, they needed someone to hold sway over the crowd— a Master of Ceremonies, Microphone Controller, or simply, MC. Catchphrases that started off as spontaneous remarks became the cornerstones of style. "Throw your hands in the air, and wave 'em like you just don't care," said Cowboy. "Yes, yes y'all," said Kid Creole. Along with his younger brother Melle Mel, these three formed the nucleus of Flash's eventual Furious 5.

Slowly but surely, people began to flock to jams to hear what the MCs were saying as much as what the DJs were playing, and rappers stepped to the forefront. Just as DJs once competed to see who had the best sound and style, MCs began competing with one another.

"When you battlin' on the mike you could say some shit about a motherfucker and piss him off," said Harlem native Alonzo Brown. Along with his best friend Andre Harrell, they formed the old-school rap duo Dr. Jekyll and Mr. Hyde. "You would rhyme about a nigga's moms," said Brown. "You would rhyme about a nigga being broke. You would rhyme about taking a bitch and his bitch be right there. But because you had the mike, you had all the power."

Tapes of those park jams and battles circulated throughout the five boroughs, but nobody was in a hurry to go to the studio and make a record. When the Sugarhill Gang made a hit record in 1979 with "Rappers Delight," it pissed a lot of people off. Most hip hop fans had never heard of Big Bank Hank, Wonder Mike, or Master Gee. Most of their rhymes were familiar, though, since they were lifted from MCs like Grandmaster Caz and Raheem. But the floodgates were opened, and soon records like Afrika Bambaataa's "Planet Rock" were preserving new sounds and states of mind. Not long after that, Grandmaster Flash and the Furious Five showed that hip hop could also carry "The Message."

And then in 1983, some kids from Hollis, Queens, changed the rules of the game all over again. Run-D.M.C. stripped rap down to its elements: two MCs and one DJ, minus all the fancy clothes and gimmicky routines. Run-D.M.C. were B-boys, not in practice, but in stance. Black Lee jeans and matching jackets, unlaced Adidas sneakers, and that "I don't give a fuck" body language. When they took the stage, you got the impression that they'd just stepped off Linden Boulevard, gotten into a car, and driven to the venue. "Sucker MCs" was not trying to cross over to the R&B charts. Run-D.M.C. showed the world what rap was supposed to sound like and marked a line in the sand. Anything that came before them was old school; anything that came after was new school.

Christopher Wallace listened intently to Run-D.M.C. and all the great MCs who came after them. LL Cool J brought similes and sex appeal to the MC's arsenal. Boogie Down Productions reflected the ravages of the crack trade through songs like "9mm" and "Criminal Minded." Ultramagnetic MCs dropped "Critical Beatdown" with Kool Keith's on-beat, off-beat style of rhyming and Ced Gee's mysterious samples and effects, zooming ahead while looking in the rearview mirror. In 1987 Eric B. & Rakim dropped *Paid in Full,* perhaps the most timeless rap album ever made. Rakim's voice that made everything move in slow motion. He was the closest person to being holy in hip hop, as if what he was saying was as old as the Nile but futuristic at the same time. Slick Rick and EPMD kept the energy building, switching up styles and sounds and making some of the greatest records hip hop ever heard.

And let's not forget Biggie's predecessor for the title of Brooklyn's finest: Big Daddy Kane. This kid from Flatbush got down with Marley Marl's Queens-based Juice Crew by ghostwriting rhymes for Biz Markie. He ended up emerging as one of the fiercest battle MCs ever. His distinctive voice was so rich and smooth he almost sounded like he was crooning when he rapped. His metaphors were simple but potent: "So full of action," he said, "my name should be a verb." If Frank Sinatra was an MC with a high-top fade, he'd be Big Daddy Kane.

During those golden years between the end of 1987 and the middle of 1990, it seemed as if every single record that came out and every MC that came forward eradicated what came before it. And Christopher Wallace was there, absorbing it all. Hip hop never had a more devoted, attentive listener. The first time he heard "Rappers Delight" and "Planet Rock" he wrote every word of the lyrics down in a notebook. Wallace and Hubert Sams collected as many "Uptown tapes" as they could get their hands on. They would listen over and over to those old-school sessions recorded live at places like Harlem World and T-Connection

After school, when the three of them were able to get together, Sams and Wallace would go to Mike Bynum's house to mess around with his turntables and try to make songs in the three hours before Mike's parents came home.

Wallace came up with the MC name Cwest, and Sams and Bynum became his DJs, the Techniques. They messed around with crude boom-box tapes until Wallace met Donald Harrison, a New Orleans–born jazz saxophonist who had played with Art Blakey's Jazz Messengers. Harrison lived on St. James and he had a home studio that he let them experiment with. He also shot film footage of Wallace in the studio and at street-corner jams in the neighborhood.

"I used to fuck with Donald all the time," Wallace said. "He got my ears tuned into jazz music. He put me onto Herbie Hancock and Terence Blanchard." They joked about the fact that Wallace shared a close physical resemblance to Harrison's friend, the jazz pianist Cyrus Chestnut. "Niggas don't even know I know Cyrus," said Wallace. "I knew Cyrus way before I ever thought about this rapping."

Though they didn't rise to the level he would achieve later, those first songs of his teenage years showed elements of his distinctive rhyme style.

"He wrote really intelligent stuff using big words and rhyme schemes," Sams said. "He'd say some wild stuff. We always knew he had potential."

But as the trio grew older, their interests began to differ. Sams, whose mother died when he was 16, got busy with high school football. When he hung out with Wallace, they didn't work on music. Bynum, who went to Sarah J. Hale High School, also drifted away from music. And Wallace, who was knee deep in the street game, viewed rhyming as strictly a hobby.

Sure, he made tapes with the turntables at Chico's crib, but they were tapes for the Avenue. Mabusha "Push" Cooper used to put on little shows on the block, and Wallace would routinely massacre the competition during the open mike segment. It wasn't anything he took seriously.

"I would play around with lyrics, do some parties," Wallace said. "I wasn't looking to get discovered. I was having fun."

Rhyming was his hobby. Selling drugs was his occupation.

Now that he didn't have to worry about school, Wallace began going out of town for extended stretches of time. He caught the Greyhound bus down to Raleigh North Carolina where hooked up with an older New York hustler by the name of Robert Cagle, a.k.a. Zauqael. They both recognized that they could get seriously paid down south by bringing in powdered cocaine from New York. They would rent a hotel room, give somebody a little weight to work off, then sit back and watch the profits roll in.

"Back when Big first came down I didn't know he could rap," Zauqael recalled by phone from a state prison. "Back then it was different. The drug game was kinda big at the time. And the rap game wasn't really that promising. But he was telling me that his name was Big, and he could rap. He didn't make a big deal out of it; he just said he could rap. And I figured everybody knows how to rap, you know?"

One evening they were chilling in a room at the Day's Inn watching the Sidney Poitier and Bill Cosby movie *Let's Do It Again* on TV. "One of the characters was named Biggie Smalls," Zauqael recalls. "And I said, Listen, Ain't you say your rap name is Biggie? I said, Listen. That's a better name for you right there. Biggie

Smalls. And he said, Yeah, I like that. 'Cause it was gangster plus it was funny. But I told him, if you're gonna be named that, I hope your MC game is nice."

"Yo, I am nice," Biggie assured him. And then to remove all doubt, he started freestyling.

"I said, Son, is nice, but we drug dealers right now," Zauqael recalled with a laugh. "I was keeping it real." One night he took Biggie to a local club called the Zoo. Zauqael convinced the DJ to let him kick a few rhymes. Then he passed the cordless mike to Biggie. "When he started rhyming the place went crazy."

Between 1990 and 1992, Wallace and Zauqael were doing so well, they bought a three-bedroom house together at 2700 Alpha Drive in Raleigh. Biggie was a good roommate. He had a great sense of humor that Zauqael couldn't stay mad at him, even when he caught Wallace stealing his Häagen-Dazs and stuffing the container with bread to cover his ice-cream capers. Wallace mostly kept to himself, writing in a notebook of rhymes in his spare time. On one of their trips to the mall, Zauqael encouraged him to buy a rhyming dictionary. "I can't write like this," Wallace said. He looked up a couple of words, but preferred listening to the words in his own head.

On his trips back home to New York, Wallace watched as people he knew got played trying to get into the rap game. Nobody was going to catch *him* kissing some A&R man's ass.

"I would see niggas breaking their backs making demos," he recalled, "going to Funky Slice in Brooklyn, getting the crazy, crazy drum machine beats, bullshit breaks with the fucked-up mikes, sounding mad cheesy. I'm hustling on the block in the morning seeing niggas saying 'Yo man, I'm about to shop my demo. I got a meeting at Warner Bros. I'm like 'Word, go do your thing, baby.' I knew I was nicer than them niggas. But I hate rejection, man."

He'd never have to worry about it.

When he wasn't selling drugs on Fulton Street, Wallace hung out with D-Roc and his peoples on Bedford Ave, across the Classon Avenue border in the heart of Beford-Stuyvesant. Here he hooked up with a crew called the Old Gold Brothers and a DJ named 50 Grand, who lived closer to St. James, on Gates and Fulton. He wasn't trying to make music; it just kind of happened.

"I put all my time into hustling, 100% of my time," Wallace said. "But at the same time, we'd be on corners and niggas would go in the basement and bring 8 or 9 bags of weed with us, and just listen to music."

One day 50 invited Wallace, D-Roc, and a few other guys over to his crib. "We get to his basement, and he's got two turntables and a mixer," Wallace recalled. "I was like 'Oh word, you got equipment, kid?' He was like, 'Yeah.'"

Wallace and DJ 50 Grand linked up one afternoon in 50's basement. "I get busy, son," Big said. So they made a tape.

"Word? You got a tape deck? "

"Yeah."

"I get busy, son," Wallace said.

"Word? Get the fuck out of here."

"No, for real, I get busy," Wallace emphasized.

50 Grand stepped behind his turntables and pulled out two copies of *Ultimate Breaks and Beats, Volume 24*. He pressed the square button on both his Technics 1200 turntables and placed the needle on track four: The Emotions' "Blind Alley," widely known as the backing track for Big Daddy Kane's "Ain't No Half Steppin." The breakbeat hit the speakers, a luscious groove with a ticklish piano melody. Wallace grabbed the mike and started rhyming like a man possessed. Not a single person in the room could take their eyes off him. He flowed over the beat with such command it was shocking. This didn't sound like an amateur who rapped as a hobby—his freestyles were as good, if not better, than anything on the radio. When he finally paused, 50 Grand looked up from his turntables.

"Let's make a tape," 50 Grand suggested.

Wallace shrugged.

"Why not? Fuck it."

Hearing his voice played back on a tape, even if it was just for kicks, tickled Christopher. He might have told his friends he didn't want to be an MC. He might even have believed it sometimes. But he couldn't help himself. When he wasn't out on the corner, he'd be back in his bedroom blasting his cassette player, either stuff he taped off the radio, cassettes he bought at the Wiz, or now, his own voice. He didn't sound bad, either. Not bad at all.

DJ Mister Cee shook his head.

If only he had a nickel for every person who came up to him backstage or at the barbershop, talking about how they'd discovered the next big rap star. It was a cliché. Now here was his neighbor, DJ 50 Grand, saying the same thing.

"I'm telling you," 50 Grand said. "Biggie is nice. You need to check this kid."

"A'ight. A'ight," said Mister Cee, who was about to go on tour with Big Daddy Kane. "When we get back, I'll listen to it then," he said, blowing 50 Grand off.

The tour ended on September 23, 1991. Mister Cee was barely back in his house for an hour when he heard the knock on his door again. It was 50 Grand.

"I ain't even unpack yet!" Mister Cee protested. But 50 had the tape in his hand, and he was clearly on a mission.

"Just listen to it," said 50.

Cee popped it in the deck and turned up the volume. The beat came on. And five seconds later, Mister Cee couldn't breathe.

He wasn't even in his apartment anymore.

Just like that it was 1985 and he was a 17-year-old kid at Sarah J. Hill High School in Brooklyn, pounding his fist on a table to keep rhythm while his best friend, Antonio Hardy, captivated the crowd with his rhythmic gift of gab. Everyone knew Hardy was nice, but Cee saw something special. He saw the birth of Big Daddy Kane.

The voice coming out of his speakers was a little higher than Kane's baritone, but damned if it didn't give Cee the same chills. And it had the nerve to ride Kane's beat as well as Kane did. Cee couldn't stop playing it. He rewound it over and over, and each time it got better.

"I always felt like it was just inevitable for me to have heard that tape," Mister Cee said later. "Because of all the things that was involved in it. Bed-Stuy Brooklyn. Rhymin' over the 'Blind Alley.' It was a message from God that I had to hear that tape. I just really believe that."

When Cee looked up at 50 Grand, he was damn-near teary eyed.

"Yo, I gotta meet this dude," he said.

A few weeks later, 50 and Christopher Wallace showed up on Mister Cee's doorstep on Gates and Bedford. The future of hardcore hip hop wore a dirty white T-shirt, boots, and some grungy black jeans. Cee though he looked "grimy, hungry." He didn't waste too much time with small talk.

"I'm gonna try to get you a deal," he said. "I said I can't make any promises to you, but I'm gonna try to make some things happen for you."

Wallace looked at Mister Cee skeptically, sizing him up

"Yo, you know man, you know, don't be promising me nuttin' Duke. You can't do nuttin' for me, just tell me straight up man," he said. "Don't try to gas me."

"That was like the first thing he said to me," Mister Cee recalled. "Before even saying 'What up.' Those was his first words to me."

Unbeknownst to Mister Cee, Wallace had tried working on a demo with Daddy-O from the group Stetsasonic, who lived right around the corner. Wallace had mad respect for Daddy-O, but for whatever reason, things didn't work out. And Mister Cee was catching the brunt of it.

"Listen man, don't be promising me nothing. If you can't do it, just say you can't do it," Wallace told Mister Cee. He could take getting shot at, but not shot down. Making a tape for his friends on the Avenue was one thing. Risking rejection and ridicule was something else.

"I wanna re-create the demo," Mister Cee said. "I have some equipment here. What I wanna do is re-create the demo. I wanna redo it. Record it in my house. Make it nice and clean. And try to present it to *The Source* for their 'unsigned Hype' situation or whatever."

Wallace looked at Mister Cee and made a spot judgment. He decided that he was going to trust him. "Whatever, whatever you wanna do," Wallace said in his deep voice. "You know. Whatever." He knew there was a risk, but Cee's enthusiasm seemed genuine. And he wasn't asking him for anything.

Mister Cee sent the tape to Matteo Capoluongo, one of the editors at *The Source*. Writing under the name Matty C, he started a column called "Unsigned Hype," and he knew talent when he heard it. Artists who appeared in his column had a nasty habit of becoming superstars. An MC from Chicago by the name of Common Sense sent in his stuff and soon landed a deal with Relativity. Mobb Deep, DJ Shadow, and DMX were some of the up-and-comers whose eventual success came as no surprise to those who read Matty C's column.

As soon as he heard Biggie Smalls, he knew it was something special.

"Biggie was like Kane reincarnated to me," Matt said. "It was like the essence of the classic hip hop feeling I got when I first heard Kane."

Matty raved about the tape. He played it for anyone who came by his office. He couldn't stop talking about it.

Before he left his magazine job to become senior V.P. of A&R for Loud Records, other talent scouts would call him to see which aspiring rappers were ready for prime time. In those days, just knowing that an artist was about to be featured in "Unsigned Hype" was enough to generate a buzz that could get them signed. Some A&R reps learned the hard way that not calling Matty to hear a tape featured in his column meant missing out on a potentially career-breaking artist.

Matty had written about these two kids from Queens called Poetical Prophets, and he gave their demo to his friend Bönz Malone, a writer for *Spin* magazine who had just gotten an A&R job at Island Records. Malone loved the hardcore

duo and signed them under the name Mobb Deep. There was only one problem—this other A&R kid liked the group too. He was pissed that someone else
had gotten to them first.

The A&R kid couldn't afford to make the same mistake twice. Rap stars were
here today, gone this evening. You never knew who would be the next cat to
heat up the street. So the second he heard about the demo featuring Biggie
Smalls and his DJ 50 Grand, he picked up the phone and called *The Source*.

Reminding Matty about Mobb Deep, the A&R kid asked, "What else you
got?"

"I got some other things," Capoluongo said.

"Why don't you come up here?" said the A&R kid. "We should meet."

So Capoluongo went to this kid's office. He was sitting behind a large desk
with a television tuned to MTV. He nodded when Matty came in, but barely
looked up from his sushi. He acted as if he wasn't the one who initiated the
meeting.

After some quick but stiff pleasantries, Capoluongo played him the tape that
Mister Cee gave him. The kid listened to it, nodding his head, but not revealing
any emotion one way or the other.

Then the tape shut off. There was silence in the room for a moment. The
A&R kid smiled. Suddenly he seemed more laid-back.

"What does he look like?" was the first question out of his mouth.

"Well," Matty said after a brief pause, "he's fat. He's a big guy."

"How big?" the kid asked. "Heavy D big? Or Fat Boys big?"

"Call Mister Cee. You have to meet him."

The guy wasn't even signed yet, and already this A&R kid was thinking about
how to market what he'd heard.

That would always be Sean "Puffy" Combs's special genius.

The revolution will not be televised—it will be marketed. And people close to Combs
saw—from as far back as 1988, when he was a nineteen-year-old freshman at
Howard University—that he was the Huey P. Newton of hip hop hustle.

That famous photograph, with Newton sitting in a wicker chair wearing a
leather jacket and beret, a rifle in one hand and a spear in the other, was a more
effective recruiting tool for the Black Panther Party than any rally, speech, or
10-point platform the organization could ever put out. Combs, too, would learn
the power of using an image. His first lesson started with, of all things, a real
revolutionary situation on Howard University's campus—a student take over.

"They wanted to put David Duke on our Board Of Directors," remembered
Combs's college friend (and future employee) Deric "D Dot" Angelettie. Actually,

it was not the former Klansman, but Lee Atwater, a key Republican strategist for George Bush Senior's presidential campaign. Atwater may have had a soft spot for the blues, but as the architect of the racially divisive Willie Horton ad, he was not thought of as an ally for black folks.

Founded in 1866, Howard was the largest, most prestigious historically black university in the nation. The concept of a right-wing politico being part of such an institution didn't go over well with the student body. Students had other grievances, too: Some wanted changes to the curriculum and complained about the facilities. They didn't want to wait for a institutional response. Compromise was not an option.

"So," remembered Angelettie, "we took over the school."

Led by Ras Baraka, son of the famed black revolutionary author (and Howard alumnus) Amiri Baraka, a group of students escorted people out of the administration building, padlocked the doors, and drew up a list of demands. They had seized the nerve center where all the school's academic and financial records were kept, effectively bringing Howard to a standstill. They could hear the security guards outside, preparing to take back the building, so they seized their moment.

"A group of us went on the roof, with our hands in the air," Angelettie recalled. "We got sticks, we got bats—some of us had chains around our necks. And someone took a picture."

The whole thing was documented; there were dramatic photographs of police storming the building and hauling students out. Combs, who had not taken part in the protest, made a montage of all the images and printed up posters.

"He made hundreds of them, and sold them for ten and fifteen dollars apiece," Angelettie recalled, sucking his teeth. "That's the type of nigga I saw. All this protest shit is well and good, but who's getting paid off of it?" Angelettie laughed at the memory. "He was ready."

Combs was born ready. The sporting life was in his blood.

Few hustlers want their sons in the game. They want them to own the team one day, to have the money and the influence to trade pieces around the chessboard, like so many sacrificial pawns. Otherwise, why even play?

The goal is to have their family legacy and illicit money purified by the actions of sons with clean hands. It worked out that way for former bootlegger Joe Kennedy, as his sons John, Robert, and Edward made famous inroads in politics. Vito Corleone, Mario Puzo's fictional mobster from *The Godfather*, always wanted a purer life for his sons, especially Michael. And surely Melvin Combs wanted his son Sean Jean Combs, born November 4, 1969, to soar to heights he would never be able to achieve himself.

"Pretty Melvin" was known for his style and his laughter. He had a fur coat so long that it reached his ankles and he made sure his beautiful wife, Janice, a fashion catalog model, never lacked for stylish clothes or jewelry.

"He was a street man, a hustling man," Janice Combs said about her husband. "We met at a party in the Bronx. He used to love to dance. We used to crack up on him because he thought he was the baddest thing."

Melvin had much greater ambitions than driving his cab—some of them admittedly dangerous. But he felt the inherent risks were worth it. Harlem's favorite son was out there making moves on Lenox Avenue so that his progeny would never have to.

So when Melvin Combs was discovered murdered on January 26, 1972, in Central Park, dead from a point-blank gunshot wound, Janice Combs made a decision. After identifying the body, she made up her mind that Sean, and the daughter kicking in her belly, Keisha, would never know how their father died.

If they asked, Sean and Keisha would be told that their father was a businessman who died in a tragic car accident.

She also decided that her two kids would never want for anything. Even though she only had a high-school degree, she'd work three jobs if she had to. No welfare or public housing. Sean would go to the best schools, and he'd never, ever end up anywhere close to the elements that killed her husband.

Sean, nicknamed Puffy by childhood friends because of the way he would huff and puff when he didn't get his way, was raised a charmed child. By the time he was eight, he was a model in print ads for Baskin-Robbins, and had appeared in *Essence* magazine, which was edited by one of Janice's life-long friends from the neighborhood, Susan Taylor. He was the kind of happy kid who loved the spotlight—who danced harder than anyone else at family gatherings and house parties, who couldn't resist mugging for the camera when anyone wanted to take a picture—just like his father.

The family still lived in Harlem, but they moved in with Janice's mother to a middle-class apartment complex, Esplanade Gardens, filled with retirees and frugal professionals. Of course, the street was still out there, never far away, but Sean never saw much of it, as far as his mother knew. But Sean did hear the music coming out of clubs like the famous Harlem World near where he lived. He also heard his friends in grade school talking about what went on at the parties, relating tales told to them by their older brothers and sisters.

By the early '80s Janice had relocated the family to Mount Vernon, a Westchester County suburb about half an hour north of New York City. Congested streets, glass-littered concrete, and the sound of children splashing around in water from an open fire hydrant was replaced by wide-open vistas, manicured lawns, and the sound of children splashing around in backyard pools.

The house they moved into was nice enough, but it didn't have a pool. Sean wanted a pool more than anything in the world. The white kids across the street all had pools.

"They would never invite me over," Combs said. "I used to cry. My moms made sure that she got me a pool that was two times bigger than theirs. It took her like a year to save for it, and it was the only Christmas gift—no socks, nothing."

Soon water wasn't enough. Janice Combs always gave her son the best, but he always wanted more. He had this urge, this thirst, that he could never explain, to be in the mix, to stir things up, to earn his own money his own way.

During lunchtime at Mount St. Michael Academy in the Bronx, the Catholic school his mother sent him to, Sean made a habit of asking other students for fifty cents. By the end of the lunch period he'd have several dollars in his pocket—along with the lunch money his mother had given him. He worked in restaurants, amusement parks, anywhere to earn an extra buck. In Mount Vernon, even though he was too young to have a paper route, he figured out a way to falsify his birth date, and then he hired other kids take on other routes and collected a percentage of their earnings, managing them so to speak.

He had to mix it up.

And on those occasions when he'd go back to Harlem, to visit his grandmother and to hang out with childhood friends who would eventually become his bodyguards—guys like Anthony "Wolf" Jones and Paul "Big Paul" Offord—he'd hear stories about "Pretty Melvin."

"As I got older, I knew about street life, so I knew who was hustlers," Combs said. "I would constantly hear how good everybody was living back in those days—furs, and how we was the only people in Harlem to have a Mercedes-Benz, and all that. And I also started hearing other stuff from other people. When I started putting two and two together, I was like " 'Come on, man, my pops was hustling or something.' "

The *New York Times* laid out the details of his father's death in stark, terse terms. And Combs began asking more questions. His father, one of New York's biggest hustlers, shot in the head. Central Park West. Uptown.

"All the stories I heard about him—he was a good man and all that—he was hustling," Combs eventually realized. "He was running numbers or selling drugs or whatever. He wasn't known as a gangsta."

Combs suddenly had a newfound fascination with the street life he had always been sheltered from. It was a part of his legacy. And like a whole generations of "haves" before him, he suddenly had an interest in the "have-nots," especially now that he knew he was remotely connected to the street.

"The majority of kids in the suburbs was made, you know," Combs said. "Their parents made them a certain way. These kids from the ghetto had no choice. They didn't have shit, but they were real."

That was the thing he loved about hip hop: the realness. It was gritty, wild music, and it was getting wilder all of the time.

As Puff became a teenager, the music was beginning to come of age: Boogie Down Productions, Eric B. & Rakim, Big Daddy Kane. Street kids were becoming millionaires off crack, and uptown hustlers like Rich Porter, AZ, and Alpo ran the streets in this new crack/hip hop economy.

The music had also gone further underground. No longer was it important for artists to cross over like Run-D.M.C. and get a song played on the radio. Street and mix-tape respect meant everything. And the realest things were happening in New York City clubs like the Latin Quarter and the Red Parrot, and perhaps the most famous of all, the Rooftop in Harlem.

And Puff was right there, sneaking out of the house, getting in the mix, trying to be down. Fronting—and getting over.

"Parties at the Rooftop—that shit was one of the most incredible experiences ever," Combs recalled. "This was when crack first came out—niggas fourteen and fifteen riding around in jeeps with the tops off. If you wasn't hustling, you wasn't on the list. I wasn't hustling," he added, "but I had to make sure my gear was up to par."

Dances like the wop, that serpentine side-to-side move, originated at the Rooftop. "You'd have niggas wop like you've never seen niggas wop," Combs recalled. "We talking about some shit that looked like a fuckin' African dance."

He was beginning to realize his goal: to find the bridge between the Polo-and- Birkenstocks world of his private Catholic school and the Fila-and-Dapper-Dan realm of the Harlem streets he so much wanted to be a part of. One thing was certain—all the kids were listening to the same music. Even if they couldn't get into the same parties, their radios were tuned to DJ Red Alert, Mr. Magic's Rap Attack, and the Awesome Two.

Music was the bridge. And if people couldn't cross between the worlds on that bridge yet, Combs was going to figure out the way to entice them across.

Handsome, fresh-dressed, and armed with a bright smile, Combs became popular on campus from the moment of his arrival in the Fall of 1987. He had a certain style about himself, a way of doing things. He attracted people to him, and knew how to get them to do things for him.

"I could get anything I wanted on campus," Sean Combs said about his years at Howard. "If I needed an English paper, I knew where to go. If I needed an exam or some weed, I knew where to get it."

"Puff would have *GQ* magazines, you know?" said Ron "Amen-Ra" Lawrence, another fellow Howard student from New York who was ahead of Combs.

"Even at his early stages, you could see his fashion," said Lawrence. "Every time I saw Puff he had on something slick. If it wasn't a shirt and tie, he had on a slick suit, and then he would flip and then he'd be rocking some hip hop shit. The way he's doing it now? He was doing it that way back then."

> **"I could get anything I wanted on campus," Combs said of his years at Howard University. "If I needed an English paper, I knew where to go. If I needed some weed, I knew where to get it."**

Combs came to Howard to study business, but was quickly learning more outside the classroom than in it. He thought fast on his feet—especially on the dance floor—learning all sorts of valuable lessons in the club that he would later apply to the music business. He also began assembling the crew that would transform all of them into millionaires in a few years.

Ron Lawrence grew up with Salt-N-Pepa's producer Hurby "Luv Bug" Azor—and had his own aspirations for getting into the music business. Musically he was advanced—beyond his conservative looks.

"Ron was the bookworm producer guy, he wasn't the party-throwing guy," said Matty C, who would occasionally return from NYU to go home to Washington D.C. for Howard University parties. "He was the first guy on Howard's campus to have an SP1200 drum machine."

"It wasn't an SP1200, it was an MPC-60," Lawrence said, laughing. He taught himself what he needed to know and soon he was building beats. "It was all trial and error," he admits. "When you read those manuals, it was Chinese."

Whatever he learned, he started teaching to Angelettie, who was a DJ back in Brooklyn. Howard was in need of a hipness injection, and Angelettie wanted to be the one to administer it.

"When I got down there, it was a lot of New York people, but it wasn't a lot of hip people there. Like, you know what I mean? Like, you have people from Detroit and California and Miami and the South and they all had their cliques," Angelettie said.

"Even within the New York clique, we had the hardcore characters—the characters who smoked chronic and wanted to hang out every night. Then you had the New York clique that was, like, half and half. Some of them rolled with us, but some of them were real book smart and you had the ones that didn't fuck with us at all. We hung with different people, you know?"

Although he should have been in class, Angelettie spent most of his freshman year trying to make a scene. He'd mess with girls, wake up late, and barely make it to class. But he did have his turntables. And slowly but surely, he was getting hired to DJ for the sorority parties at Alpha Kappa Alpha and Delta Sigma Theta.

It was at one of those parties during his sophomore year, that he first met the freshman Combs. Already Puffy was his trademark flamboyant self.

"You know you always had them guys that do all the dancing?" Angelettie said. "He was one of those dudes. Puffy's in the middle of the dance floor getting all the young big-booty chicks on his dick because he's dancing and doing flips. Him and his partner, they're doing all that dancing shit."

Angelettie and Combs kept running into each other. It became clear that they had similar attitudes about music, and both were extremely popular. They decided to join forces and promote parties together. They formed "A Black Man and a Puerto Rican Productions." Combs stacked the deck by inviting some of the biggest rap celebrities of the day to his parties, people like Heavy D, Guy, Slick Rick, and Doug E. Fresh. Other New York kids at Howard came around too—future business partners like Chucky Thompson, Mark Pitts, and Don Pooh. And Puffy's syndicate was not content with just promoting parties. Angelettie and Harve Pierre used to rhyme against each other in the Blackburn Rec Center. Lawrence asked them to form a group with him called Two Kings and a Cipher.

Soon, the guys who used to run the party scene in D.C., Todd Johnson and Maynard Clark, were a thing of the past. It got to the point where if any major rap artist was coming through to Washington, Puff and his crew threw the hottest after-party. Sometimes the after-parties were liver than the concerts themselves.

"We had our own club every Friday night," Angelettie remembered. "We rented a church basement and called it The Asylum." Their breakthrough came when the students asked them to throw Howard's biggest-ever homecoming party.

"We had over 8,000 kids come to this Masonic temple with a fence around it," Angelettie recalled. "We only had one entrance in. Kids were literally climbing up the fence, crawling in through the second-floor windows trying to come downstairs into the main room." That's when the fire marshal showed up.

Angelettie and Combs tried to reason with him. "We looked outside and there's a potential for us to make another $25,000, $30,000 easy. We're charging $30 or $40 a person because it's ridiculous in there. Some kids are paying $50 or $70 just to get into the joint. We both got on our knees and begged. The fire marshal was like, 'Nah, it's over.' "

But it was just getting started.

At the parties, Combs and crew studied what kids from different parts of the country were wearing, what kind of music they responded to. He learned how to approach them, how to make them react. The parties were just as important as the classes or the morning lectures they were supposed to be attending. From these events they learned lessons about marketing and promotion that would make them richer than if they had been the doctors, lawyers, and accountants that their parents sent them to Howard to become.

Howard University became to the black music business what Harvard was to Hollywood sitcom writers. Pierre, Lawrence, Angelettie, Thompson, Myrick, and Pooh not only became some of Combs's first employees when he launched his own record label, they also became, in their own right, some of the most influential producers, A&R executives, and artist managers in black music.

"We learned that if you touch one person, this person can reach at least a thousand others," Angelettie said. "We learned how to make fliers and our fliers went from real cheap to getting sexier. We learned a lot about marketing. That's why Puffy's parties are still the shit, because we learned what attracts. What do women want to hear? You know, how do the speakers sound? Should we have balloons? Should we have candles? All that shit came from just watching people."

And Combs always thought big.

"It was something he really wanted," remembered Ron Lawrence. "He was like, 'You know, one day I'm gonna have a record company.' And at the time you'd be, like, 'Yeah right.' It was hard to see the vision because everybody was either an MC or a DJ. Nobody was thinking about being president of a record company. For him to be thinking that far ahead..." Lawrence said, sounding awestruck. "Man."

The first thing Combs had to do was to learn, up close, exactly how a record company was run. It was through a fellow Mount Vernon resident, rapper Heavy D, that Combs first met Andre Harrell, the CEO and founder of Uptown Records—a Harlem man who would teach him everything he needed to know about making hit records.

Harrell—who started out as the first half of the old-school rap duo Dr. Jekyll and Mr. Hyde—realized very early that he was never going to be a superstar. He decided that the real power was backstage. He took a job working as a $200-a-week assistant for Russell Simmons, the man who once managed him. At one point the two shared an apartment in Lefrak City Housing complex in Queens.

They had very different approaches to the music, in part because they came from different backgrounds—Harrell from the Bronxdale Projects and Simmons from a suburban home in Hollis, Queens. But their ongoing friendly argument gave each a better understanding of what motivated the other.

"My shit was the fly shit," Harrell explained. "His shit was more alternative."

When Simmons founded Def Jam Records with Rick Rubin in 1985, it became the first rap label to get national distribution from a major label. As a result, "alternative" was beginning to encroach on the mainstream—Def Jam was the first to truly break New York rap on a national level. LL Cool J, Slick Rick, the Beastie Boys, 3rd Bass, and Public Enemy were all Def Jam artists. Run of Run--D.M.C. was Russell's little brother. Eric B. & Rakim, DJ Jazzy Jeff and the Fresh Prince, and most of the other hot rappers in the business were managed by Russell and his partner Lyor Cohen. Simmons had built a one-stop shop for hip hop.

Though Harrell was a former rapper, his interests ran toward the other side of black music, R&B. The trouble was that by the mid-'80s, most kids with any taste were into rap; R&B was pretty much dead. Jimmy Jam and Terry Lewis had their Minneapolis sound but that was "adult" music for people in their mid- to-late twenties. Prince, another Minneapolis native, was considered by many young black folks to be a "rock and roll" artist because he played electric guitar and his singles didn't hit hard enough on the urban dance floor. Michael Jackson was becoming irrelevant, too. His increasingly ghoulish appearance alienated the millions of young black kids who were devoted to him during the *Off the Wall* and *Thriller* years. New York had Full Force, a family unit of artists and producers who could do both rap and R&B. They made fun, sexy hits with Lisa Lisa & Cult Jam, but they were already signed to exclusive deals elsewhere. Harrell was convinced that there had to be someone else.

That someone was Teddy Riley. A native of Harlem's St. Nicholas projects, Riley learned guitar by ear at the age of three. By ten he was holding concerts in the project courtyard with a Casio keyboard. As a teenager, he was producing records for Kool Moe Dee and Doug E. Fresh in his apartment studio. Riley's breakthrough was the invention of a sound called new jack swing: It had all the rhythmic grittiness of rap smoothed out with fat synthesized keyboards and simulated horn sounds. Like hip hop, it was electronic, futuristic, and hard-hitting, yet it was all syncopated to classic swing beats.

"I used to see artists a little differently from Russell," Harrell said. "He thought the sound that Teddy Riley was making was the commercial side of hip hop—or not authentic hip hop. I thought it was a Harlem glamorous slick side. It was hip hop that could also be R&B."

When Andre Harrell couldn't convince Russell Simmons to sign Dwight Myers a.k.a. Heavy D—a fat but charismatic MC from Mount Vernon—Harrell quit his best friend's company and funded Heavy's first release by himself

"Andre used to try to tell me he's a sex symbol," Simmons recalled. "I said, 'Nigga, there's no girl wanna give Heavy D no pussy.' "

Harrell founded Uptown Records, teamed Heavy D with Riley and suddenly "The Overweight Lover" was in the house. Heavy D was Harrell's dream artist because he was suave and well spoken, the kind of guy who would rock your block party but at the same time you could introduce to your sister. He even made it seem cool to be fat. With the Fat Boys, obesity was something to be made fun of, but Heavy D let people see that large guys had style, too.

Combs got up every Thursday by 5 A.M. to catch the morning train from Washington to New York City to be at his unpaid internship by 10 A.M. Things got so tight he'd hide in the bathroom for hours to avoid the conductor.

By the time Heavy D introduced Harrell to Puffy, Uptown was on the upswing. It was 1988, and Heavy D & The Boyz were riding high and Teddy Riley's vocal trio Guy was in the studio working on the follow-up to their multiplatinum debut. Uptown had also secured a rich manufacturing and distribution pact with MCA. Combs was eager to get in the mix any way he could.

"He called me Mr. Harrell, even though I asked him to call me Andre," said Harrell. "The first thing I asked him to do was get me a tape from the studio. He came back with it in five minutes. The studio was ten blocks away."

Combs got up every Thursday by 5 A.M. to catch the morning train from Washington to New York City to be at his unpaid internship by 10 A.M. Things got so tight that he'd even hide in the bathroom for hours at a time to avoid the conductors. No humiliation was too daunting for Combs. He'd wash cars, get sandwiches, and stand at attention in his button-up shirt and polka-dot ties.

"I didn't give a fuck," Combs said. "I was at Uptown."

At first he was Mr. Polite—the best intern Harrell had ever had. Attentive, quiet, and hardworking, Combs' "Puffy" persona had yet to raise its head in the corporate offices. He took the Michael Ovitz/David Geffen/Bernie Brillstein approach to being an intern—all of those multimillionaires had worked their way up from the William Morris Agency's mailroom to become titans in the business. They knew as did Puffy that delivering packages and other "menial" duties gave them access to everyone. They got an inside view of how companies worked—and where all the bodies were buried.

"I did everything," Combs said. "I drove Andre's car. If they needed something delivered, I would take a cab instead of a subway and pay for it out of my own pocket. I knew it was the place to be."

Sean "Puffy" Combs as an eager young intern at Uptown Records, reporting to his mentor Andre Harrell (seated) in 1992 . Even back then, Combs knew how to dress like a CEO.

Combs soon realized that sneaking on trains to get back and forth from Howard's campus to promote parties wasn't where it was at. What was the point of going back to D.C. so he could pretend to pay attention during business administration classes? It was time to step in the arena and make real moves, which was what he'd been doing from day one at college anyway.

Like a fly on the wall, Combs would just watch, absorbing everything. He made lasting friendships with music producers and fellow Mount Vernon homeboys like Eddie F, Dave Hall, and Pete Rock. He moved into a room at Andre Harrell's plush house in New Jersey, giving him the opportunity to rub shoulders celebrities and influential executives like Russell Simmons, Benny Medina, and "Fly Ty" Williams.

Privately, Combs would talk about his ability to spot hits, but in his humble position he had few opportunities to prove his ear. Only A&R people got to make those kinds of moves. So he waited—and good things came to him.

Four hungry, haggard-kids staggered into Uptown Records' office one summer morning in 1990 with three cassette tapes full of songs in their hands. Their eyes were bloodshot and they smelled—symptoms of living in their car. They were two sets of brothers, Cedric "K-Ci" and Joel "Jo-Jo" Hailey and Donald "Devante" and Mr. Dalvin DeGrate from Charlotte, North Carolina. They didn't even have an appointment, and just happened to be lucky enough to have Heavy D hear them as they stood in the lobby harmonizing, practicing for their shot. Heavy rushed to Andre's office, Harrell heard them, and signed them on the spot.

Kurt Woodley, Uptown's A&R director, wasn't as blown away by the brothers, who were known as Jodeci. The group was quickly relegated to the state of limbo from which many signed artists never emerge, called "development."

All that began to change the moment Woodley resigned from his position to take a job at a rival label, Combs asked Harrell for the departing executive's job.

"I am your demographic," Combs told him.

The pitch worked, and Puff the A&R kid was born. He wasn't even old enough to legally buy a drink, and already Combs was a mover and a shaker. His success bred jealousy among others at Uptown—and marked the beginning of the "player hating" that Diddy still deals with more than a decade later. But more than anything, Combs was thankful for the opportunity, and he worked tirelessly to prove that there was an actual fire of talent behind all the "Puffs" of smoke.

His first assignment was to shepherd Father MC's debut album through the pop music market. Father fit the Uptown mode of R&B-flavored nonconfrontational rap, but had only a fraction of Heavy D's talent. That didn't stop Combs from making decisions that led to a gold single, and opened other doors.

For Father MC's hit single "Treat 'Em Like They Want to Be Treated," Puffy brought in Jodeci to sing on the chorus. On another song, "I'll Do 4 U," he enlisted the talents of another singer who'd been signed during the Woodley administration and was now languishing in the background—Mary J. Blige. Buoyed by a slamming Cheryl Lynn sample and Blige's sultry vocals, an otherwise forgettable song became a Top 20 hit.

As Combs began to amass power and authority, "Puff Daddy" was born. Making moves inside both the recording and styling studios, Puff produced a string of successful acts and gradually transformed Uptown's somewhat uptight image into something more urgent—and urban.

With Jodeci, the challenge was to transform four bumpkins who looked as if they'd fallen off the back of a turnip truck into the hottest vocal quartet on the East Coast. Out went the Boone's Farm apple wine—in came the 40-ounce bottles of malt liquor. Since they had nowhere to stay, Puff had them put up in a Bronx Housing project so they could absorb some flavor.

In terms of image, his assistant turned stylist extraordinaire Sybil Pennix suggested that he dress the guys in back-turned baseball caps, overalls, baggy jeans, and boots. Jodeci would do for R&B what Run-D.M.C. did for rap—they dressed like their audience. It wasn't about wearing clothes that fans couldn't afford—not yet at least. To get the teenage listeners, Puff wanted Jodeci to appear as if they'd just walked in off of 125th Street. They were speaking to the crowd as a part of the crowd—not from some lofty perch above them.

With the music, the approach was equally simple—and brilliant. When the time came to remix the group's first single, "Come and Talk to Me," Combs did something that seemed radical at the time but has now become commonplace. Instead of using the original backing track, he had one of his producers sample EPMD's underground smash "You're a Customer." The group's vocals didn't change a bit—just the beat. The result was instant street cred—an R&B record that slammed so hard even the staunchest hip hop head had to respect it.

Puff Daddy was the pioneer of hip hop soul—a simple but profound innovation that matched R&B vocals with unadulterated rap beats. The concept of blending R&B and rap was nothing new on the underground—DJ Kid Capri had been doing variations of it for years on his mix tapes. But no one ever thought to record these hybrids in the studio, press them up, and turn them into hits.

Combs couldn't operate a mixing board or program a drum machine, but he spent so much time in the studio he learned exactly how to capture the exact sound he wanted.

"I'm more like an orchestrator," he explained. "You know those guys who don't actually play the violin? They just tell the violinist what they want to hear? Same with me. I say to my programmer, make the drums go ba-boom ba-boom and he sets the computer up to do it. I sing the chords I want to the piano player and hum a rhythm to the bass player. Pretty soon we got a song."

He was also an orchestrator of parties. His hits were climbing up the charts, so he needed a place to dance to them. He began holding weekly jams at a midtown Manhattan nightclub called the Red Zone. (The DJ spot was held down by a DJ named Funkmaster Flex.) The party became so popular it was almost a second job for Puffy. And with fights breaking out on the dance floor, the whole thing started to become too hectic.

"I didn't want party promotion to become the main thing in my life," Combs said. Especially not when things were going so well at Uptown. His relationship with Harrell grew into almost a father/son bond, with Harrell filling that void in Combs's life.

"My moms was driving me crazy,' Combs said. "Andre let me live at his house. Right before he moved out, I put a hole in the wall, which cost 30 grand to fix. Then he let me live at his house in Alpine New Jersey. I mean I was 20 years old, living in a mansion with a bad-ass pool."

Combs sometimes got wild, threw temper tantrums, and acted like a spoiled child. "The whole company hated me," Combs admitted. "People were like, 'Dre created a monster.' I was aggressive. I would trash the office. I'd call Andre a wimp and a house nigga." But Puffy's bad-boy behavior was indulged as long as the hits kept coming. Andre always seemed to understand where Combs was coming from, no matter what he did.

Magic Johnson shocked the world in October 1991 when he announced that he was retiring from basketball because he'd tested HIV-positive. In December of that year, Combs and Heavy D decided to organize a celebrity basketball game to benefit AIDS charities. The goal was to raise money and HIV awareness while promoting Uptown artists. It was a good idea, but things got way out of hand.

Heavily promoted on radio and by word of mouth, the game turned into a bigger event than anyone ever imagined. There were too many people and not enough police at the Nat Holman Gym at City College in Harlem. Organizers closed the doors in an attempt to sort out paying customers from those who still needed tickets, but it quickly became a bum rush.

"People started jumping down the staircase," said Combs. "People started piling on top of each other and glass started breaking in the doors. People started getting scared and running. Pushing and pushing. It was more pressure. And we started seeing some scary shit."

By the time it was all over, nine people were dead. Combs had blood on his hands—literally—from trying to save people who had been trampled, as well as attempting to revive some victims with mouth-to-mouth resuscitation. "I'm seeing my girlfriend bugging out because her best friend is there not breathing and I'm trying to give her mouth to mouth," Combs recalled. "And I start to feel this feeling in the breath I'm getting back that people were dead. I can feel the death going into me. Later I went home and I kept saying to myself that it was all a bad dream. That I was going to wake up. But I never woke up."

As Combs panicked, Harrell flew back from his vacation in Barbados, hired famed attorney William Kunstler, and helped his young apprentice regroup. While no criminal charges were filed against the organizers, Combs was haunted by the incident. "I started to lose it," he said. "I felt like I didn't wanna even live no more. I was so fuckin' sad. The lawyer's advice was not to go anywhere, not to talk to anybody. But I wanted to go to the wakes and the funerals and try to provide some comfort, even though I knew my presence probably wouldn't have given comfort. But what I was going through with the blame and stuff was nothing compared to what the families were going through. "

Combs was sustained by the knowledge that others had it worse than he did. "If they had the strength to go on," he said, "I had the strength to go on and handle people looking at me, thinking whatever they gonna think."

He poured his pain into his work. On the surface, it might have looked like denial. But Puffy had made himself two promises: To do a better job of building his own empire, and to remember that life had to be lived to its fullest because nothing was promised. But before he could think about his own empire, there were still Uptown artists who needed his attention and expertise.

Mary J. Blige, a beautiful but tortured young woman from the same rough-and-tumble section of Yonkers that reared the Lox and DMX, had all the vocal chops in the world but no control, musically or otherwise. She sang beautifully, with a fierce attitude that was part church, part house party. Her voice spoke of a tough childhood and perhaps a broken heart along the way. When photographers asked her to be more open, more sexual, Blige toughened up like a tomboy. She wore boots and pulled her bent-brim baseball cap low over her eyes—masking shyness and vulnerability with an air of brooding toughness.

Instead of trying to soften or dilute that attitude, Puff embraced it and turned it into Mary's trademark. Combs helped Blige become the patron saint of ghetto girls. She sang for all the 16-year-olds pushing baby strollers and the girls stuck doing nails and braids when they should have been finishing high school.

Her first song was "You Remind Me," a cut from a soundtrack album that was the only memorable thing about the movie *Strictly Business.* The single shot to No. 1 on *Billboard*'s R&B chart, and cracked the Top 40 on the pop singles chart while she was still living in the projects.

Her first single, the one that pumped all summer long during the summer of 1992, "Real Love," had a familiar backing track: the drums from Audio Two's seminal 1988 rap classic "Top Billin'." The sample was a line in the sand. This was hip hop soul—not R&B with a little hip hop "flavor." Instead of rapping over a breakbeat, Mary would sing over it. She had the sneer of a hardcore MC but the voice of an angel.

Puffy's genius was in melding the two in such a way that one genre did not subvert the integrity of the other. Her subsequent album, *What's the 411?,* featured cameos from Busta Rhymes—who was just beginning to emerge from his group, Leaders of the New School—and a title track with Grand Puba from Brand Nubian, on which Mary actually rapped. The hip hop beats on Mary's album felt organic, not like a sales gimmick. Perhaps that's why they did sell—moving two million copies at a brisk pace.

Both the Jodeci and Mary J. Blige albums were complete departures from the spit-and-polish "new money Negro" image that Andre Harrell had crafted for his company. They were also massive smashes, making Uptown a major force to be reckoned with, the jewel in MCA Records crown. By the time Combs was 21 years old, he was named the vice president of A&R—the youngest boss in the industry. He had money, ghetto fame, and a white BMW to match.

But he was nowhere near satisfied. The problem with Uptown was that, even with all those R&B hits, none of the records Puffy was responsible for truly reflected the reality of what was going on in the clubs and the streets. He felt left out—and rightly so. Hip hop was in the midst of one of its most exciting

A teenage Wallace rocking the mike at a street-corner jam in Brooklyn. Though he called rap a "hobby," Big slaughtered all competition.

periods ever. Dope MCs were popping up like dandelions, and Puffy wanted to start weeding them out. He didn't yet have the juice, but he had an idea: Bad Boy Records. Bad Boy would be a satellite of Uptown, a sub-imprint where all the grimy niggas that didn't fit into Andre Harrell's idea of what an artist should be would find a home.

"I don't like no goody two-shoes shit," Puffy said when he was forming his company. "I like the sense of being in trouble. It's almost like a girl, y'knowhatumsayin'? Girls don't like no good niggas. Girls like bad boys."

Puffy wanted to make real street music, with real hardcore MCs, but stuff that would have a universal appeal—a mixture of thugs and hugs. It wasn't just about making compelling gangsta rap records—lots of people could do that. It was about an MC that represented the full package. It was about finding the next Big Daddy Kane or Rakim. Someone who had undeniable skills and true street appeal, but at the same time who could be marketed to the masses. Someone who sounded hard even when he was rhyming on a pop radio record. Combs had the vision thing all worked out. All he needed now was that mystery voice, that person who could set things off and put his fledgling company on the map.

Then Matty C. walked into his office one day with the tape that would change his future, and that of hip hop.

Puff didn't waste any time with small talk. He wanted to know if Matty had heard any new artists who were truly dope.

"Listen to this kid Biggie Smalls," is what he said.

As soon as the first song began, Combs knew he'd have to close the deal fast.

"He sounded like no other human being I ever heard in my life."

GIMME
THE LOOT
(I'M A BAD BOY)

CHAPTER 4

" Goodness gracious the papers!
Where the cash at? Where the stash at?
Nigga pass that... **"**

Mister Cee walked the three blocks from his apartment on Gates to the corner of Fulton with the frenzied enthusiasm of a man who has to pee and suddenly spots a restroom. He couldn't get there quick enough.

Wallace was standing on the corner as usual, in the middle of a Cee-Lo game, an L hanging from the corner of his mouth. D-Roc lamped against the wall, arms folded, watching everything and everybody. Wallace looked up from his dice-rolling crouch and smiled.

"Puffy liked the tape," Cee said.

"Puffy who?" Wallace asked.

Cee reminded Wallace of the March 1992 issue of *The Source*—the one that contained his "Unsigned Hype" write-up. In that same issue Heavy D had penned a guest editorial expressing remorse over the deaths that occurred at the celebrity basketball benefit he and Puffy had organized. More important—for Wallace's purposes—Puffy was the man who could get him a deal at Uptown Records.

"Uptown?" Wallace said, shaking his head. "Heavy D and the Boyz? Guy? Jodeci?" He took a hit from the L and exhaled a thick cloud. "They ain't gonna know what to do with a nigga like me."

"Puff says he wants to try something new," Mister Cee insisted. "He wants to do hardcore shit. He was diggin' you, man."

Wallace stared at Cee for a second and then shrugged.

"Well, you know, I ain't gonna be doing no talkin' in the meeting," he said in a low voice. "You gon' do all the talkin'. I don't really know Duke and I ain't talking to him. *You* talk. You make everything happen."

True to his word, Wallace barely opened his mouth at the meeting.

Puffy Combs sat behind the desk in his smallish office with a few plaques on the walls while Mister Cee did most of the talking. In the other chair, dressed in standard Brooklyn guerrilla gear—army jacket and Timberland boots—sat Wallace, looking toward the window, toward the corner, everywhere but at Combs.

Combs, meanwhile, couldn't take his eyes off Wallace. He'd wondered what this Biggie dude would look like and now he knew. He was tall and a bit heavier than husky, with sullen but expressive eyes and rounded features. It wasn't a pretty face, but, as they say, beauty fades. This was the kind of guy whose silent presence would make people nervous coming out of the subway at night. But then again, Wallace had this mysterious charisma about him. What made him scary also made him appealing. He did not, at first glance, possess the "fuck-ability" Andre Harrell preferred his artists to have, but this cat had something else. Combs couldn't put his finger on it, but maybe Biggie could help him figure it out.

"Yo, man, could you kick a rhyme for me right now?" Combs asked.

"Yeah man, you want me to kick a rhyme?" Wallace said nonchalantly.

Combs assured him that he did, then got up from his desk and closed the office door. Rocking a demo was one thing, but an MC's voice, flow, and presence would have to translate live and direct if he had any chance to become a real star.

And then Wallace started rhyming.

As soon as he opened his mouth, Christopher Wallace *became* Biggie. Sitting there silently, he seemed almost shy. But when he rhymed in that thick commanding voice, his shoulders lost their hunch, and the eyes that once looked at your shoes now pierced your soul. The transformation was instantaneous and breathtaking.

"I didn't want him to stop," Puff recalled afterward. "He just sounded so good and so refreshing."

But Wallace did stop, and Combs gulped. He tried his best to maintain a poker face. It was the only leverage he really had in this negotiation.

"I could have a record out on you by the summer," Combs said, sounding calm. "Would you be cool with that?"

Mister Cee smiled and Wallace just sat there, as cool as Combs wished he could be. This part of the game was like dating—the more you played hard to get, the more money would get spent in the long run.

"Well, you know, you know," said Wallace, mumbling offhandedly, "just talk to Cee, know what I'm sayin'? Whatever he wants to do, I'm down with."

It wasn't a resounding vote of confidence Combs might have hoped for, but it would have to do.

"I was thinking, Now how am I gonna market *him*?" Combs recalled. "My many looked like a liquor store robber. But damn he could *spit*."

There was only one more hurdle before Wallace could join the Uptown Records family: a meeting with the Big Man himself, Andre Harrell.

A few weeks later, there they all were—Harrell, Combs, Mister Cee, and Wallace—at Sylvia's on 125th Street. "I figure a big man likes to eat, let me give him some soul food," Combs recalled. Over a plate of short ribs and collard greens, Mister Cee talked about how Biggie was the future of hip hop. Harrell liked the demo, but he was still on the fence. And the artist was not helping matters at all. "He didn't eat," Combs recalled. "He didn't talk. He just sat there real quiet."

Lunch ended on an undecided note and then they all piled into a black Lincoln Town Car. While riding the 50 blocks back down to Uptown, Harrell decided to put Wallace to the test.

"Yo Money, I want you to rhyme right now, in the car," said the CEO.

This time around, Mister Cee was prepared. "Can I put a beat in?" he asked.

"Sure," said Harrell. Cee passed him the cassette; he put it into the car stereo, and then Biggie started rhyming. The sullen Wallace persona was replaced with raw MC power. Harrell witnessed the transformation firsthand, and he was unable to keep his composure for more than a minute.

"Okay, Puffy will draw up the paper work, and we'll get everything going," Harrell said. The business at hand was suddenly urgent.

Combs wasted no time hooking Biggie up to rhyme on the remix to Mary J. Blige's smash hit "Real Love." When Puff got hired to remix "Dolly My Baby" by the Jamaican dancehall don Super Cat, he had "Big Poppa" close the song with 16 bars of uncut Brooklyn funk. Wallace's friends on the block couldn't believe it—their boy was on the radio! It was all good, except for one thing: He wasn't making any ends. He wasn't so sure about the music game.

"It seemed like everything took forever," Wallace complained. "I was doing whatever I had to do, paying my dues with all the stuff they wanted me to do." When it came time to do his album, they'd have to do it his way. But even for these one-off jobs, the money was incredibly slow to come. And the real money, the money he expected to receive when he finalized his album deal with Uptown— that would take much longer. Meanwhile he was expected to wait by the phone, hoping that Puffy could work it all out so he could sign up and get that paper. Summer came and went, and Wallace still didn't have a record deal. He kept calling Puffy, keeping the pressure on. But he needed to figure something out, because he was about to get hit with a whole new set of pressures.

Voletta Wallace was sitting back on her bed, trying to relax after a long day at school when Christopher came into her room. It didn't matter how big her son grew, his large, expressive eyes always made him appear childlike to her.

"Yo, Ma."

She looked up at him. He looked like he wanted to say something but couldn't find the words.

"What," she said. "*What*, Christopher?"

"Jan's pregnant."

"I beg your pardon?" She sat up, blinking her eyes.

"She's pregnant."

"I thought you broke up."

"We did."

He sat on the edge of the bed, saying nothing more. After a lingering silence, he turned to look at his mother.

"Is that your baby?"

"She say it's mine," he said. "It's mine."

She exhaled. "Christopher, can you afford a baby emotionally?"

"Of course I can," he said. His eyes glimmered with a sudden pride. Then, childlike again, he added: "If I can't take care of it emotionally, you can."

She stood up, her temper flaring.

"Christopher," she began, "What the hell are you going to do?"

"What you mean, what the hell am I gonna do?"

"When I was about to have you, I don't think I was ready to be a mother. But at least I had a job. I started planning for your future. What do you have?"

Wallace bristled. "I got a deal."

"Where is this deal? For weeks, you talk about this deal. It's not cemented yet. You have to do something. Do you know what you're going to do?"

Wallace knew what he had to do—although he wasn't going to tell his mother. He would go get his hustle on for real. He didn't want to do it, but he just wasn't cut out for a "May I take your order, please?" type existence. Yes, he was a high-school dropout, but he didn't want to live like one—and he wasn't about to let his daughter want for the things that she needed. From his perspective, the street was the only place where he could hope to take care of all those issues.

Jan was happy about the record deal. But she also knew he was thinking about making moves—the kind of moves that might have been okay for a boy-friend, but were risky for a father.

"We've gotta prepare for this baby's future," Jan said one afternoon.

"You think I don't know that?" Wallace said. "She's gonna be okay. She's my girl."

"So what are you doing?"

"You don't know what I'm doing to prepare for this child's future," he snapped. "Stop beating me in the head with that."

"So what are you doing?"

"I don't have to tell you everything I'm doing. Just trust in me to know that I'm making sure she's gonna be okay. I'm doing everything I'm supposed to do."

Although he had been arrested for drug possession during a trip down South the previous year, the opportunity for fast money was just too good to pass up. On the streets of Brooklyn, where crack was readily available, it was a buyer's market. If you didn't like the price on one corner, you went to cop somewhere else. Wallace had spent many a day in the rain or in the cold, lucky if he earned a few hundred dollars on the corner. It was hard for any street-level dealer to make big money—you had to move up the food chain for that.

In North Carolina he was a much bigger cheese. And it was a seller's market. Crack was still somewhat exotic down there, and the fiends bought in bulk—like they were never gonna see those rocks again. There wasn't a central strip. It was all word of mouth. Some fiends traveled 30 miles to score. Plus getting out of town was the only way he could provide for himself and his family while preventing Combs from knowing too much about his business.

He wasted no time heading back to Raleigh and the money was coming fast. Biggie and Zauqael were making $30,000 every two weeks. But he kept getting pages from up in New York. Somehow Puffy had found out where he was.

It wasn't hard for Combs to figure out what Wallace was doing.

"Believe it or not, he did not wanna mess with Puffy at first," Zauqael said. "He was like, 'Yo, I ain't fucking with this nigga. He be bullshittin'. I don't like the way he work. He be putting me on hold. I'd rather do this.'" Biggie's friends didn't push him at first, but the calls kept coming. Biggie's mom even called to say that this Puffy person was trying to reach him. But Wallace wasn't interested. "We were doing our thing," said Zauqael. "When we went to the club, we had celebrity status in a different way. But if I'da known it was gonna be all that, he woulda been kicked outta the house and you'd be talking to me as his manager."

The one Monday morning, the phone rang again and Wallace took the call.

"What the fuck are you doing!" Combs yelled into the phone. "I thought I told you about that shit!"

"What?" Wallace said, playing dumb.

"I know why you down there, nigga. You know that is only gonna lead to jail or death. But you don't need to be down there. I just got a call from your lawyer. Deal's closed, man. You can come by the office Tuesday morning. I got a check waiting for you, ready to cash, right here."

"Word?"

"Word."

"I'ma come back, but if we don't hit off big, I'ma be mad," Wallace told him. "Cause we getting ready to do our thing down here."

Wallace told Zauqael he was going back to N.Y.C. to sign a recording contract.

"Congrats, yo," he said, genuinely happy to see his partner succeeding in a legal profession. "When you gonna bounce?"

"Day after tomorrow," Wallace said.

But the more he thought about it, the more he wanted to get to New York as soon as possible. What if something happened with the train and he got there late? He didn't want anything fucking up his payday.

"Something told me, Yo, let me just leave Monday," Wallace later explained. And that's what he did. Good decision.

"Don't you know Monday night, police ran up in the house that we were staying in and locked those niggas up?" Wallace said.

"Big left that morning and we got arrested that afternoon," Zauqael confirmed.

Wallace took his miraculous good luck as a sign he was on the right path. When he got to New York, there was no looking back. He appreciated the opportunity he had been giving. Wallace left the hustling life behind and decided to give this music business thing a shot.

"He was one hundred and fifty percent focused on rap," said D-Roc.

The $125,000 budget Uptown gave him wasn't a lot of money—recording costs and many other expenses would have to come out of that.

"The original deal was a standard, very cheap deal," said Mister Cee, who had his lawyer broker the contract through his production company. All the same, Wallace was happy. He had a little cash in his pocket and some legitimacy. Now the only thing he had to do was write some dope rhymes and record them.

His creative process really evolved from hanging out. Wallace would sit in his room and watch music videos, studying Ralph McDaniels's *Video Music Box* and *Yo! MTV Raps*. He'd always been a fan, but now he was listening to every rap record he could get his hands on.

Lil' Cease, who was fifteen at the time, had dropped out of school and was getting caught up in the Fulton Street scene. Wallace, who always admired his character, pulled him off the Avenue and into his new rap world.

"I'd go to the payphone and call him," Cease recalled. "He'd tell me to come to the front window. He'd drop down $20 and I'd go get a bag of weed... That was like the normal schedule once we got cool like that. We'd go in the crib and we'd kick it. And he'd just work on his music."

The "One Room Shack" that Biggie would later refer to in the song 'Juicy' was Wallace's bedroom—funky yellow walls, a bed and a chair, clothes and assorted junk all over the place, a TV with a VCR, and two big party-size speakers. It was in that room that Biggie Smalls the rapper worked out his rhymes.

"That was the shack," Cease recalled fondly. "Ten, twenty niggas in there, and it was yay small. Small as a motherfucker, where it was some niggas hangin' in the closet. Just to be in there. That's how it was back in the day in the 'hood. That was all a nigga needed."

No matter how rowdy it got, there were rules. This was Ms. Wallace's apartment, and some of the toughest roughnecks on Fulton Street cowered in her presence.

"I wasn't an ogre," she said. "But there's just certain principles I maintain in my home. You cannot wear a hat inside my house. It's a form of respect. Take your hat off. Tie your sneakers. Do not walk into my house with some laces flying all over, your shirt open, your 'hood on like you're a bum. You come into my house with your shirt into your pants and your sneakers tied, and take your hat off. And yes, you can sit in my living room, but you do not put your feet on my coffee table. You know, rules are rules and ethics, principles are principles and manners is manners. You come into my home, you respect my home."

Wallace and his friends played the music loud, kept the windows open, and were quick with the Lysol spray if he sensed his mother was coming.

"Turn down that noise!" she'd say.

"One of these days," he said with a smile, "that noise is gonna make you rich."

When he finally got a chance to record a song of his own for Uptown Records —rather than just appearing on somebody else's remix—he tried to recreate the energy of those bedroom sessions. His first opportunity came in 1993 when Combs was putting together a soundtrack for the hip-hop comedy *Who's the Man?* The song was "Party and Bullshit" produced by Brooklyn's own Easy Mo Bee.

Easy Mo Bee was the last producer to ever work with Miles Davis and the first to work with Christopher Wallace. Being a lifelong friend of Mister Cee, he heard about Big before everyone else in the industry did.

"Mister Cee was like, 'There's this cat I want you to hear,' " Mo Bee remembered. "And I was like, you know, I think the cat is nice. But I never knew that we would hook up."

Once Big got signed, they seemed to gravitate toward each other. After hours of auditioning beats, Wallace heard some of Mo's tracks and liked them. Mo never forgot the voice. The match between them was organic.

"I used to come over there and pick him up and we'd ride around, you know,"

Mo said. "The guy used to lean my car over on one side, man. I didn't care, I just liked riding around with him."

The idea for "Party and Bullshit" grew out of just listening to music. Mo Bee had a cassette copy of the Last Poets' self-titled debut that he'd scored off a Nostrand Avenue street-table tape vendor. If he was educating the young MC to the origins of hip hop, the Last Poets were a good place to start.

The Poets emerged from Harlem's Black Arts Movement, a radical cultural groundswell that took place during the late '60s and early '70s. The goal was to channel the progressive spirit of the Black Panthers through the arts, in hopes of reaching people who wouldn't dig the speeches. Revolutionary playwrights included Amiri Baraka, Ed Bullins, and Richard Wesley; the musical component featured Gil Scott-Heron and the Last Poets.

With its insistent bongos and its chorus addressing "Niggas... all niggas," the Last Poets' "Niggers Are Scared of Revolution" used sarcasm, frustration, and humor to make the point that not enough young black people were taking the struggle for equality seriously. As much as folks loved talking about Malcolm X, when it came to putting his words into action, they'd rather play basketball or shoot pool.

"Niggas will party and bullshit, and party and bullshit," complained Poet Umar Bin Hassan. "Some will even die, when the revolution comes."

The rest of it may have gone in one ear and out the other, but Wallace gravitated toward the line "party and bullshit."

"Yo, Mo, we gotta use that," Wallace said. "You gotta put that in something."

Much as he would later steer New York hip hop away from revolutionary themes and toward the gangsta party, Wallace flipped the revolutionary anthem into a punch line that people could dance to. In the process he totally subverted the song's message, transforming a line from "Niggas Are Scared of Revolution" into its very antithesis—a party record.

"I was a terror since the public school era," Biggie rapped. "Bathroom passes, cuttin' classes, squeezing asses. / Smoking blunts was a daily routine since thirteen/A chubby nigga on the scene."

The song was brilliant on many levels: the flow, the casual way that Wallace showed what a detail-specific MC he could be. On first listen, the song was supposed to be about how he was just another buck-wild kid who loved to bring guns to parties and start trouble. But on further reflection, the lyrics contained their own powerful post-crack social commentary. All the rhetoric of Public Enemy, Brand Nubian, and X Clan had not truly altered the reality of the streets. There was a whole new generation of cats raised in the drug game whose only love was paper—and Wallace would be their spokesperson.

As Mo Bee remembered, the recording session for that song was almost as wild as the song itself. That was the day he discovered that "keep it real" wasn't just a catchphrase when it came to Wallace's art.

At the end of the third verse, you could hear the sound of a fight breaking out in the party Biggie has been describing, just as he's about to leave with a young lady. ("Can't we just all get along," he says afterwards, with a sly reference to Rodney King's post-L.A. Riots lament, "so I can put hickies on her chest like Lil' Shawn?") That fight wasn't in the original plan. While rhyming off the top of his head, Wallace just came up with the idea for a sonic transition—and had the spontaneous creative energy to make something new.

"I remember after he did the second verse he stopped all the music," Mo Bee said. "He called all of us—me, Chico, Cee. We all go in the booth."

"Yo, we gonna do this little interlude," Wallace told them. "This what I want y'all to do. We gonna take the chairs, the mike stand, everything; we just gonna throw mad shit around in the booth." It was an unorthodox idea, but Mo Bee went with it, recording all the frenzied pushing and shoving as they mashed up the booth. The final result sounded exactly like one of those fights that break out at hip hop parties. As interludes go, this one was unusually effective, giving the song a sense of realism and immediacy.

"If you listen to the background in the song, you can hear me real low, like, Yo, what happened to the music?" Mo Bee said with a chuckle. "I had never seen nobody do that before. Never. Then he came back, 'Can't we just all get along?' Dude is creative, man. I was just trying to get the hang of him, right there. I was like, 'Okay, he got something up his sleeve.'"

In the final mix, Combs took time on the closing overdubs to announce "Bad Boy" and "Junior M.A.F.I.A." as future concepts. Neither entity actually existed yet—but they soon would.

"Who's Junior M.A.F.I.A.?" Lil' Cease asked when he heard the song.

"That's y'all," Wallace said, as if he should have known.

"Everything with him was all about 'my niggas,'" Mo Bee said with admiration. Wallace was that rare individual whose dreams about making a better life extended beyond himself. "He used to always talk about Junior M.A.F.I.A., Junior

Biggie Smalls throws up an M to represent Junior M.A.F.I.A. while the Blastmaster KRS-One and ace producer Easy Mo Bee show love.

M.A.F.I.A., Junior M.A.F.I.A."

The crew was thick, and every record that he appeared on—"Dolly My Baby," "Real Love," and "Party and Bullshit,"—was a hit. His name was getting out there, and he was beginning to earn fans beyond the streets of Brooklyn.

"You heard this shit yet?" asked Tupac Shakur, punching the rewind button on the car's tape player. It was the first time director John Singleton had heard "Party and Bullshit," but he would hear Biggie's song many more times while on location in Los Angeles for his 1993 film, *Poetic Justice*. Shakur was the film's romantic lead, starring opposite Janet Jackson. When he wasn't on camera, he kept playing the song over and over again, laughing every time.

"Tupac loved that song," said Singleton. Even though some people warned him that Tupac was trouble, the Academy Award–nominated film maker chose Shakur for his follow-up to *Boyz N the Hood*, one of the first films to cast a rapper (Ice Cube) alongside professional actors (Laurence Fishburne, Cuba Gooding Jr.) Although Singleton and Shakur had some spirited disagreements, the director was enjoying the experience of working with him. One of his fondest memories was the weekend he and Shakur spent in Atlanta during the black spring break celebration known as Freaknik, chasing girls and promoting the film. They rented a limo and cruised up and down Peachtree Street, blasting the song by this guy Biggie all the while.

Neighborhoods all over the country were pumping Biggie's voice, but Christopher Wallace's life still wasn't without problems. Trouble seemed to follow him like a cold wind.

He and D-Roc were walking down Gates Avenue one night, having just left D-Roc's grandmother. "We was talking about how we would buy 4Runners if Big went gold," D-Roc recalled. "All of a sudden the police rolled up on us." They took off down the block, and as they ran Wallace threw away the gun he was carrying. The cops caught up with them, and after a brief search, the unregistered gun was found. The two men sat in an interrogation room at the 79th precinct.

"There's two of you, but only one gun," the arresting officer said. "Take some time and figure it out." He left the room.

The two friends looked at each other. They both knew it was Wallace's gun, but he was already on probation for gun possession and an old drug case. Another violation would mean serious time in jail—at least a few years. He had a baby on the way, and he'd lose his record deal if he took the charge.

Wallace didn't have to say anything. "I'll take the weight," D-Roc said. Wallace shook his head.

"You got too much on the line. I'll take it. Just look out for me when I get out."

With tears in his eyes, Wallace accepted his friend's display of loyalty. It was a sacrifice he would never forget.

D-Roc was sentenced to four years. Wallace had his freedom, and his future. He was wanted in the studio and to make promotional appearances. He shot a video for the "Dolly My Baby" remix with Supercat. He was invited to appear on Heavy D's upcoming album, *Blue Funk,* on the posse track "A Buncha Niggas." Money was finally starting to flow.

But the wind was still blowing.

One night while Jan was still pregnant, she and Christopher had an argument in his room. She hadn't seen him for a while, and she assumed it was because he was off enjoying his new life as a budding rap star. He had other reasons.

"You don't have any idea what I'm going through," he said heatedly.

"What *you're* going through?" she responded.

Jan was met with silence. She was surprised to look up and find him crying. "What's wrong?"

Wallace collapsed in sobs. "It's Ma. She has cancer."

"I saw a different side of him I had never seen," Jan said, still moved by the memory. "And to see him like that made me cry. He felt so helpless."

"She just came home from the hospital," Wallace told her. "She's so weak, she can't even lift a tissue off the night table," he said.

"Why didn't you tell me?"

"She didn't want me to tell anybody," he said. "She just doesn't want anybody to know."

In the end, Voletta Wallace had 20 lymph nodes removed. She didn't have to undergo any chemotherapy. Christopher was overjoyed as he watched her slowly regaining her strength. His mind was clear enough to get back into the studio and began the first tracks of what would eventually become his debut album.

His mother soon had enough energy to take her annual vacation back home to visit her family in Jamaica. When she came back, she was a grandmother—a reluctant grandmother.

"Ma, the baby's here," Wallace told his mother on her return. "You should see her. She's beautiful."

Voletta shook her head. She was still mad at her son for becoming a father in the first place.

"I don't want to see that baby," she said.

"Why not?"

"I just don't," she said severely. "You made the baby. You've been planning for the baby. You're a grown daddy. Go be a father. Take care of your family."

She could be just as stubborn as her son—but rather than being put off by his mother's harsh words, he persevered.

"When you see her, you're gonna fall in love with her," he said. Every time he saw her, he'd say the same thing, slowly working her.

"Fine," she said one day. "I'll go see her. Just to get you off my back."

"I saw that ugly little thing," Ms. Wallace recalled, smiling with a grandmotherly glow. "I fell so in love with that little girl. The tears were rolling down my eyes. It wasn't because I was happy. I was crying because there was such innocence, she was such a gift, and we didn't know what was in store for this kid."

Look at you, she thought as she watched her son play with the little girl, rubbing noses with Tee Tee. *You're a bum. You don't even have a job. You're not a lawyer. You're not a teacher. You have nothing. No profession. And you bring this innocence into this world.*

She said a silent prayer that her son would be able to take care of the new life that had been entrusted to him.

But Wallace was having enough trouble taking care of his career. In July 1993, just weeks before Wallace's daughter was born, Combs was fired from the job at Uptown by his mentor Andre Harrell. It was the story of Wallace's life: one step forward and two steps back.

It wasn't that Combs was doing a bad job—he was fired because he was too good. His success with Jodeci and Mary J. Blige had made him arrogant. It didn't matter that he had the track record to back up his attitude—he was just beginning to get on people's nerves.

His days of wearing polka-dot ties and saying, "Yes, Mr. Harrell," were long gone. Now he had millions of sales under his belt. Kids all over the country were dressing like Jodeci, because Jodeci was dressing like them. Anytime he went to a club, he was sure to hear one of his remixes. He sensed that he was standing on the verge of something really big.

"At first I was shy," Combs said, "then one day I realized that shy shit ain't gonna get me nowhere in this world."

So he started making himself known. Strutting around with his silver briefcase, showing off his company logo, talking to anyone who would listen about Bad Boy. He had his "street team" hit the pavement with fliers of a photo of his godson, in a diaper, one hand grabbing his tiny nuts, with a caption announcing "THE NEXT GENERATION OF BAD MUTHAFUCKAS."

But all the bravado began to backfire. The beginning of the end for Combs was Mark Siegel, the white general manager Harrell hired while Combs took a brief leave of absence following the City College tragedy. It was a classic showdown of the bean counter and the boy wonder. The boy wonder of course, didn't like being told that he was spending too much money on studio time, on street promotions, on all of the things that made Puffy Puffy.

"I felt like I was busting my ass for four years to be behind a black company," Combs said, "so I told Andre that I wasn't gonna be respectin' the man he brought in because I didn't feel he knew the music and respected it."

Maybe it was Puffy's appearance in a Karl Kani advertisement. Maybe it was his penchant for saying his name on all the remixes. Maybe it was the way he played his stereo louder than anyone else in the office, stated his opinions with more disdain than anyone else, showed open disrespect toward Harrell and Siegel—or anyone else who got in his way. Maybe it was a perception that he took credit for more than he really deserved. Or maybe it was just his spending habits. For whatever combination of reasons, Puffy was pissing off the corporate brass at MCA, which had acquired a 50 percent stake in Uptown.

When Combs was fired from Uptown, he worked hard to convince Wallace that his future was in good hands. "I'm a visionary," Combs said. "You have to trust me."

"He was a disruptive force in the system that was just too much of a headache," said Harrell's old partner Alonzo Brown. "Grabbing for power, grabbing for power, and Andre was like, 'Let me get you the fuck up out of here.'"

"There can only be one lion in the jungle," Harrell told Combs. He explained that making hit records was not the whole picture. Harrell was trying to expand Uptown into television. "Besides," he said to his young protégé, "you're ready. Go make it happen. You're ready to fly."

Combs was escorted from Uptown's offices the same day he was told to pack. "Dre can be like that," Combs said later. "Real cold. He doesn't cry at anybody's funeral, but I told him he was gonna cry at mine." Combs shed a few tears himself that day. "It was like leaving home," he said. "I wish that I'd never left."

But Harrell didn't shut Combs out completely. He agreed to extend his payroll and those of his staff for a limited time. Still, there was a lot at stake. Combs had signed his artists to Uptown, and had financed their recording sessions with the label's money. A number of tracks had been recorded for Biggie's debut album, and now it was quite possible that they would never see the light of day.

There was another artist too—this kid from Long Island named Craig Mack. Both projects were now in jeopardy.

The songs that the executives did hear they didn't like. "They didn't know what to think," said one MCA insider. "Biggie's songs were violent." Somehow the president of MCA's secretary had gotten a copy of the lyrics to "Dreams." Also known as "Dreams of Fuckin' an R&B Bitch," the tune was a wickedly ribald freestyle over an old James Brown loop on which Big fantasizes about sexing every female singer in the business: "Sade—Ooh, I know that pussy's tight / Smack Tina Turner give her flashbacks of Ike." That tune alone may have ensured that Uptown would never have anything to do with the unruly rapper's project. "A lot of people were really offended," said the MCA employee. "Some of the artists he mentioned were on the label."

Wallace was depressed about the fact that his album might never come out. If he had never released a single, he would have been okay with it. But to get so close to his dream only to see it taken away bothered him to no end.

The job of keeping Wallace encouraged and on the straight and narrow path fell to Howard alum Mark "Gucci Don" Pitts.

"I was with him 24-7, always by his side," said Pitts, ever the businessman. "We lived in Brooklyn, I came and picked him up. I made sure he got up, I was just there with him every day, We just got tight."

It was Pitts who made sure that Wallace didn't fall back into the drug game during this period of hiatus. Pitts was the one with the relationship with Wallace's parole officer, the one who made sure that he was doing the things he needed to do. When Wallace got impatient, Pitts knew how to calm him down.

"I was the pain-in-the-ass big brother, you know what I mean?" Pitts said. "I would threaten him sometimes. It was tough love at times. I had to do what I had to do. Because he had a promising career ahead of him and I ain't want to see him mess it up."

Whether he admitted it or not, Wallace appreciated the attention and the care.

"Mark used to come to my crib and I'd be like 'Fuck you, I ain't doing shit.' But he would take a hot rag, wipe my face and help me up," Wallace said with a smile. "I can ask him for anything, at any time. That's why I call him the manager extraordinaire."

While Combs spent the summer of '93 trying to get a new situation together, he also made a trip out to Brooklyn that fall to reassure his impatient young star that their luck was going to change. Wallace's close friend dream hampton remembered a dinner the three of them had at Junior's, a Brooklyn institution famous for its cheesecake. Combs tried to assuage Wallace's concerns, doing his best to assure him that his future was in good hands.

"I'm a visionary," Combs said. "You have to trust me."

Combs's ego might not have been affected by being fired, but he was running out of time. All he had was his Beemer, his chutzpah, and big plans for remaking the whole rap world in his image.

"Andre taught me that music could be a movement or a lifestyle," he said. He hadn't fit into the Uptown lifestyle, so Combs decided to build his own empire, the sort of place a Bad Boy could call home.

He gathered his troops—Howard University–era cronies like Harve Pierre, Mark Pitts, Nashiem Myrick, and a few others—and began running his own thing from an extra bedroom in his mother's Mount Vernon house, as well as a home studio in Scarsdale, New York.

"I don't think I ever worked that hard in my life," said Pierre. "Every day, all day." Combs had everyone in the crib up at eight in the morning, filling out daily reports. Eight A.M. may not seem that early for most folks, but in hip hop terms, those are the 4 A.M. milk-the-cows, feed-the-chickens hours of a farmer.

"That was the inception," said Pierre. "One computer, four or five people working every day, going back and forth to the city." Biggie, Craig Mack, and the female vocal trio Total would travel to Scarsdale every other day and record in the studio that Myrick had built there. "That's where we started Bad Boy—just recording in the house, having the artists writing, the same way we have these studios now, we were doing them in a house in the beginning."

Combs's lawyer, Kenny Meiselas, began brokering meetings, trying to find Combs some overhead money and a distribution deal. Combs, meanwhile, had to figure out what the Bad Boy "movement" was going to be.

It started off as a logo, and a cool thing to say on a remix. Now he had to convince a major white conglomerate to invest in his vision—and at the same time prevent them from interfering with his creative process —and wreaking havoc on what was so cool about his vision in the first place.

"I was scared to death," said Combs. "I knew I wanted to get to a point of Berry Gordy and Quincy Jones, but I wasn't thinking of how they got to that point. I was forced to handle a situation, and then I had to grow up real quick." He was fortunate to be understood by an old white man whose ears had always been attuned to young black artists: Clive Davis, the head of Arista Records.

A Harvard Law graduate and former CBS attorney, the man behind Santana and Janis Joplin rose through the record-industry ranks in the late '60s. He was smart and charismatic enough to sign some of the most talented artists of his generation—the Grateful Dead, Chicago, Bruce Springsteen, Billy Joel, and

Aerosmith, to name a few—while they were still young, hungry, and relatively cheap.

Like Combs, he was also fired by his parent company—Columbia Records—for spending too much. He was let go in 1976 after being audited for submitting exorbitant expense account fees—and was later cleared of any wrongdoing. By then Davis had moved to a failing label—Arista Records—negotiated a 20 percent personal stake, and signed the likes of Barry Manilow, Neil Diamond, and a resurrected Aretha Franklin. When Aretha's former backup singer Cissy Houston revealed that her daughter Whitney had talent, Davis was in the right place at the right time once again.

And like Combs, Davis had a healthy ego. Some in the industry joked that he thought the CD was named after him. Others pointed to the fact that A&R man Gerry Griffith was actually the one who signed Houston.. He quit after Davis had him cropped out of a magazine photo.

"I'm a noteworthy figure," Davis had explained. "The picture would be somewhat diminished by an unknown A&R man."

With Whitney, Arista became an R&B powerhouse. Davis signed label deals with some of the hottest names in R&B: L.A. Reid and Kenny "Babyface" Edmonds, and Dallas Austin. But he could see that the company's one weakness was that there was no pipeline into the emerging hardcore hip hop scene.

"Clive was old school, but he knew a hit when he heard it," said a former Arista employee. She remembered Davis playing the video for Naughty By Nature's "O.P.P." during a weekly meeting when the song was still quite new.

"This is what I'm talking about," Davis said. "This is what I want to see. This has all the elements of a hit. The song is hot. The lyrics are great. There's a catchy hook. This guy Treach is a star."

Clive wasn't stupid. Rap may not have been his personal taste in music but he understood that a hit was a hit. Would it sell records—that was the question.

That's where Combs came in.

When the two men met in the Arista offices, they were mutually impressed: Combs with Davis's stature and smarts, and Davis with Combs's ambition and perspective. A deal was struck: Davis gave Combs a $1.5 million advance and complete creative control. Combs immediately used the money to buy back from Harrell the tracks that had already been recorded for Wallace's album, plus negotiated the release of Total, Faith Evans, Craig Mack, and a few other artists.

With the distribution plan in place, Christopher Wallace could focus on what he did best—creating an album that would rock the whole hip hop nation. His vision was simple but powerful: "It's gonna be some real ghetto shit," he declared.

"It ain't Brooklyn shit. It's the shit that niggas in Houston can get with. Shit that niggas in Idaho can get with. It's just reality laid out on the table."

The blueprint for what would become *Ready to Die* was laid out, inadvertently, at Matty C's apartment during the fall of 1992. Capoluongo, who lived around the corner from Wallace, often saw the rapper after the "Unsigned Hype" column appeared in *The Source,* and the two became friends. Both men were connoisseurs of good weed and potent beats. And as an editor at *The Source,* Matty C had access to records months before they came out. One of the records that he had, before anyone else, was Dr. Dre's masterpiece, *The Chronic.* Its influence on Biggie was immediate and long-lasting.

"The first time he heard *The Chronic,*" Matty C recalled, "he listened to the whole thing, then he was like, 'I gotta go home and write!' "

The Chronic not only changed the kinds of records being made, it also altered hip hop's business landscape. All of a sudden the only records that sold on a national level were gangsta rap records. It wasn't all Dr. Dre's fault—equal blame goes to the man who made the record possible in the first place.

Marion "Suge" Knight Jr. had always dreamed about things no one else around him dared to even think about.

"When I was a kid in Compton the other kids would say, 'When I grow up, I want a Chevy," Knight once recalled. "I would say, 'I want a Porsche or a Rolls-Royce.' I wanted something other than what I saw in the ghetto.

Born in Los Angeles on April 19th, 1966, Knight was raised in Compton, a middle class area that, like Bedford-Stuyvesant, fell on hard times when the white folks left and black folks' jobs disappeared. On the surface there were plenty of neatly mowed lawns and working families, but there were also gangs like the Tree Top Pirus and the Southside Crips fighting over different segments of a small area. Sunny, cloudless days were often riddled with the sound of gunshots.

Knight was lucky enough to be raised by two doting parents, Marion Knight Sr. and his mother Maxine, who gave him his nickname—short for Sugar Bear. Knight was a big kid who played football just like his father before him. His skills as a defensive tackle allowed him to bypass gang membership without anyone calling him a punk.

"He was always involved in sports," said Manuel Johnson, an ex-Crip turned football coach for Compton High School. "As long as you're in sports, no one will mess with you."

Knight excelled at Lynwood High School and then El Camino College, transferring to UNLV in 1985. The quiet soft-spoken guy off the field was a monster on it. Number 54 would punch, kick, scream, and do anything he had to break through the line and get the quarterback.

"Most of all he was a good player," remembers the late Bigga B (a.k.a. Bill Operin), a UNLV teammate, who would go on to work in the music industry before dying of a heart attack at age 34. "He was real quick off the ball and his favorite move was the head slap, even though that's illegal. But he used to always try to get away with that. He tried to be real physical, to intimidate guys on the field. He was a dirty player. He did whatever it took. And coaches loved him."

Knight was named a defensive captain. He had dreams about playing for the NFL, but he was cut from the L.A. Rams after the 1987 season. He was arrested in Las Vegas later that year for attempted murder, grand larceny with an auto, and the use of a deadly weapon—charges that were later dropped.

"Ain't nobody perfect in this world except God," Knight said about the incident. "We all make mistakes."

While Knight was trying to make moves with the L.A. Rams, another Compton native was making serious moves in the rap game. Former drug dealer turned record entrepreneur Eric "Eazy-E" Wright founded Ruthless records in 1986 with a $7,000 investment of his "retirement" earnings.

Wright recruited hot local DJ Andre "Dr. Dre" Young, and his "World Class Wreckin' Cru" partner Antoine "DJ Yella" Carraby to produce for Ruthless. Dre in turn recruited a friend of his cousin Sir Jinx named O'Shea "Ice Cube" Jackson. Wright picked local rappers Lorenzo "MC Ren" Patterson and Tracy "D.O.C." Curry to round out the group, who would be Compton's answer to Run-D.M.C.

The idea was to make raw, violent records that would never be heard on radio airwaves. Records that would combine the bawdy humor of Richard Pryor's comedy routines with true stories of the violence taking place on the gang-infested streets of South Central L.A. Ice Cube handled most of the lyrics, all set to Dre's high-octane beats. It was a new sound and it sold like hotcakes. The lyrics seemed so "real" that the separation between fantasy and reality felt thinner than ever.

Eazy was pressing his own records, owning his own masters, and collecting every penny of the profits from Ruthless Records. At the pressing plant, he met former Creedence Clearwater Revival manager Jerry Heller, who said he thought Eazy's song "Boyz N The Hood," was "the most important music I had ever heard." Heller became Eazy's partner at Ruthless, helping him secure distribution through Priority Records, a fledgling company owned by former K-Tel executive Bryan Turner. While Wright and his partners focused on the dough, Dre came up with the concept for what would become the biggest Ruthless release.

"One day Dre and Eazy picked me up in the van and they was like, 'You know what we gonna call the group? Niggaz With Attitude," Cube remembered.

"Niggaz With Attitude,," he replied. "Nobody gonna put that out."

"We'll break it down to N.W.A and wait till people ask," Dre told him.

It sounded like a plan.

The album, *Straight Outta Compton*, was released in 1988. It cost only $8,000 to make and took just six weeks to complete. The FBI was so concerned about N.W.A's song, "Fuck The Police," that a federal agent wrote to Priority Records to express disapproval. The notoriety only served to make N.W.A hotter. They hit the road in 1989 and sold out venues across the country. The tour netted over $650,000 in gross receipts.

The money changed everything. Ice Cube, who had written the lion's share of the lyrics, asked why he had no royalties or publishing. He refused the $75,000 flat fee that everyone else in the group accepted. Cube soon went solo, and D.O.C. came off the bench as the group's chief lyricist.

When D.O.C. started doing shows in the L.A. area, Suge Knight went with him, having transformed from a football player into a bodyguard. Knight found that being a bodyguard was a lot like being invisible: half the time, people didn't even acknowledge his presence. Plus you got to go everywhere—lunches, dinners, attorney meetings. Knight's size worked to his advantage for two reasons—no one would ever mess with him, and people didn't mind talking around him because they assumed he wasn't smart enough to know what was really going on. He didn't smoke. He didn't drink. He didn't do anything but watch.

"I was out there, looking and learning," he said. "I'm hearing it all."

Knight was part of Bobby Brown's entourage but he also became close with Dick Griffey, the owner of S.O.L.A.R. (Sound Of Los Angeles) Records, the former label of Shalamar and of The Deele, L.A Reid and Babyface's R&B group. Knight learned about how people got paid in this business, about getting "points" on record sales, and about publishing. He learned that the real power was behind the scenes, not in the spotlight.

From bodyguard, Knight progressed to manager. He began managing D.O.C. as well as D.O.C.'s friend from Dallas, rapper/producer Mario "Chocolate" Johnson. Suge founded a publishing company, management firm, and record label Funky Enough Records.

"In the beginning they thought, 'He must be a dummy,' " Knight said. "They were arrogant towards me. They didn't respect me as a man. But they underestimated me. They didn't know I had a briefcase full of tricks."

Had the D.O.C. not fallen asleep at the wheel of his jeep on August 20th, 1989, it's doubtful that Knight would have delved into that briefcase, or that

N.W.A would have broken up, or that Death Row Records would have been founded.

The fateful accident cost D.O.C his rap career when he was thrown from the car and his larynx was crushed. Knight was one of the first people at the hospital after D.O.C. was brought in. He was shocked to learn that D.O.C. couldn't pay his medical expenses. Despite having a million-selling album, he was broke. Suge got a copy of D.O.C.'s contract and soon understood why.

"If they fuckin' with mine," D.O.C. said, "you know they fuckin' with Dre too."

"Suge Knight was the only brother that I ever knew who loved to see black men get paid," said a former associate. "He never used to player hate nobody about making money. He made it happen."

Meanwhile, Chocolate, the producer Knight managed with D.O.C., had written a number of songs for a white kid named Robert Van Winkle from the suburbs of Dallas. Chocolate—who used to dis Van Winkle when they were both rappers in Dallas—wrote and produced "Stop That Train," 'Life Is A Fantasy", and most importantly, "Ice, Ice, Baby."

"They paid me $1500 for the two songs that I was supposed to do," Chocolate said. "And when I got there I ended up doing five more songs. I did ["Ice, Ice, Baby"] for free, and ended up leaving from Dallas coming to California. Next thing you know, a year later, the song blew up. That's when I called Suge and told him, Look man, that's a song that I did."

As Chocolate's manager, Suge was entitled to a percentage of Chocolate's earnings. Anybody messing with Chocolate's money was also messing with Suge's.

Knight and the people close to him say that he used only legal means to get what was owed to his client. Vanilla Ice, in an infamous TV interview, implied that Knight came to his hotel room and coerced him to sign over his rights. No matter who you believe, the bottom line was that Chocolate got half a million dollars.

"To be straight with you, Suge was the only brother that I ever knew who liked to see black men get paid," Chocolate said. "He never used to player hate nobody about making money. If I didn't have Suge, on the real, I wouldn't have got all my money. He made it happen. He was on it every day. I respect that about him."

With his percentages of Chocolate's $500,000 production and publishing deal with Sony, Knight had the seed money for his next venture.

Knight had Dick Griffey look into Dr. Dre and D.O.C.'s Ruthless contracts.

"They had had the worst contacts I had ever seen in the history of the record business," Griffey said. "If I said 'draconian,' that would be a kind word."

Dr. Dre, who was only getting pennies on the dollar from Ruthless Records after producing records that sold over 8 million copies in a six-year period, wanted a change. He considered Eazy-E to be his partner and closest friend, but didn't realize how much the deal he had brokered on the strength of trust favored Eazy.

"Suge bought it to my attention that I was being cheated," Dre said. "I'm not no egotistical person. I just want what I'm supposed to get. Not a penny more, not a penny less. There was some sheisty shit, so I had to get ghost."

Knight got Dre, D.O.C, and some other artists released from their Ruthless contracts. Eazy-E contended that he negotiated under threat of a beating with metal pipes. Not only did he file a claim in Los Angeles Superior Court in August of 1991, he followed it up with a civil suit.

People who knew Knight wouldn't comment on the allegations, on or off the record. But everybody agreed that he was the wrong man to piss off.

"Suge is cool. He's just temperamental," said one friend. " He's the type of brother who can' t take No. He just feel like he gotta always have that last word." But sometimes words were not enough. "Don't get me wrong—Suge'll smack the shit out of you. In a heartbeat. I done seen niggas get the shit beat out of them. Believe me. I seen a hallway of niggas at the Palladium get cleared out by that nigga. I done seen him make two niggas slap each other. He ain't no coward. I'll tell you that. That nigga'll demonstrate in a second."

Once Knight had Dr. Dre, and Dre's younger half brother, Warren G hooked him up with Snoop Doggy Dogg and Nate Dogg, Suge had the nucleus of talent that would become Death Row Records. The single "Deep Cover" was the first salvo, a story of killing undercover cops set to a beat so seductive it rocked the East and West Coast simultaneously. Folks fell in love with Snoop's voice. The Long Beach rapper possessed a flow that was countrified yet as intricate as anything a New York freestyle champ could have come up with at the time.

Bolstered by the positive reception, Suge and Dre's next move was to record an entire album that was calculated to cement their position in the rap game. But they didn't want to get into another situation where they would have to fight for their sovereignty. As much as he would criticize him in later years, Knight learned a valuable lesson from Eazy-E: full ownership meant everything. The secret was to do like the white boys did—own your masters, stay independent, and plug into a major distribution network that could pump your records nationwide.

"I knew the difference between having a record company and having an organization," Knight said. "First goal was to own our masters. Without your master tapes, you ain't got shit. Period."

The album they wanted to make would cost about $250,000 to record. For years, they would claim that that money came personally from Suge's bank account, from his share of Chocolate's perpetual Vanilla Ice publishing settlement deal. But a lot of that money was tied up. The lawsuit that Eazy-E filed was draining Knight's resources—court dates and motions were expensive.

But there was talk of a silent partner; famed defense lawyer David Kenner started showing up at S.O.L.A.R. Records for some of Dre's recording sessions.

Among other big-time drug dealers, Kenner represented cocaine kingpin Michael "Harry-O" Harris. Harris, a Bounty Hunter Blood, was known for being just as smart with his legitimate earnings as he was his illegal money. He had heard about Knight, the young ambitious man who was going places fast. Kenner had the juice to set up a meeting between the two men at the Metropolitan Detention Center in downtown Los Angeles. Harris had some money to invest, and he was looking for a partner on the outside who could make it grow.

Dr. Dre and company stayed in the studio. The bills got paid. Kenner remained a consistent presence, eventually becoming Dr. Dre's own criminal attorney. And the album that would come to be *The Chronic* got finished. And after months of being turned down by major labels that neither believed in the music, nor in granting Knight and Dre's demand that they own their own master tapes, Death Row Records finally signed a $10 million deal with Jimmy Iovine and Ted Fields at Interscope Records that met all their demands. Everything was in place.

"I know you've heard all the stories," Knight said. "But you have to realize one thing: results. People don't always like it, but one thing about me, I'm 12 o'clock. That's a street saying. It means that I'm straight up and down. If I promise you I'm going to do something, you can believe it's going to happen. Mark my words, Death Row is going to be the record company of the decade."

The Chronic hit the rap world like a 10-megaton bomb on December 15, 1992. It wasn't just Dre's production, so heavily influenced by Parliament-Funkadelic, but Snoop Doggy Dogg's nimble-tongued vocals. It was the casual way they painted their violent pictures and the morbid, tongue-in-cheek attitude with which death was depicted: "Rat tat tat tat / tat-ta-tat like that," Snoop rhymed. "And I never hesitate to put a nigga on his back."

The records were so hard that Snoop and Dre didn't even have to curse and they still sounded gangsta—yet at the same time, songs like "Nuthin' But A G

Thang" and "Let Me Ride" were so smooth, the mainstream pop audience had to pay attention. Not only did the album go multi-platinum in a matter of months, the videos crossed over into regular rotation, the first time a non-corny rapper had ever accomplished that feat.

There was just something about that Cali style that Wallace loved, a new musical attitude. East Coast rap at that time was very much on the positive tip. A Tribe Called Quest, De La Soul, Brand Nubian, Public Enemy, and Pete Rock & C.L. Smooth were the biggest stars. Philosopher thugs like Nas and the Wu Tang Clan had yet to fully emerge. Meanwhile, the hardcore lyrics propagated by the Kool G Raps and the Pretty Tone Capones of the world were too far underground to make much of an impact outside the Tri-State Area.

Wallace wanted to make the kind of ribald, violent, darkly humorous hit records that Snoop was making out west or Scarface was making down south—but he wanted to do it with East Coast flavor. From his perspective as a former dealer, he knew he could bring a new level of realism to his rhymes about the game.

Previous gangsta rap records talked about drug dealing, of course, but always from the fictional standpoint of the "Don." The lifestyle epitomized by Ice-T was one of flash and big dollars—boats, planes, and all types of crazy player shit. Wallace wanted to break the game down to a more realistic perspective. He would depict the stress of a street level dealer standing out on the corner, to show how treacherous the game could be—from stickup kids and undercover cops to betrayal by friends. He would even address the self-loathing that comes from making a living as a merchant of death—whether the death of the users or the murderous competition among traffickers and sellers. "When I die, fuck it, I want to go to hell," he would rhyme on "Suicidal Thoughts," the rawest track on what would be a thoroughly hard-boiled album. "I'm a piece of shit it ain't hard to fuckin' tell..."

The album's rather morbid title, *Ready to Die*, was Puff's idea. Biggie wanted to call it *The Teflon Don*, evoking John Gotti, whose ability to escape scrapes with the law was dominating the New York news media at the time. Puff thought the reference was too regional. "We can't do that," he insisted. "We gonna hit 'em hard, but we gonna do it in a way where we're gonna represent for the masses." After a long discussion, Big agreed to do it Puff's way.

But before he could get started telling stories, the beats had to be tight. That's where Mo Bee came in. Since he was a Bed-Stuy neighbor, Wallace would often come over to Mo's place and listen to instrumentals—not only the ones that Mo came up with, but demos by other producers as well. Wallace was meticulous—before he could write it, he had to feel it.

"We'd load up beat after beat," Mo Bee said. "He'd be like, 'No, no, no.' He was real picky . We'd go through a hundred beats and he didn't like any of them."

One beat that Wallace did like was actually meant for another "Big" rapper—Big Daddy Kane. Based on an Isaac Hayes sample, it was slow, brooding, and rippled with menace. Mo Bee nicknamed the beat "Raising Kane," but when Kane passed on it, Biggie grabbed it. The song became one of the first that he recorded for his new album, a paranoid narrative of greed and betrayal called "Warning."

After a beat passed Wallace's screening process, it was off to the studio. The sessions, Mo Bee remembered, were all pretty much the same. He would play the track through the giant studio monitors, and Wallace would sit there in the room, smoking weed and nodding along with the pounding drums, seemingly lost in his own world. And then, just when you thought that all these hours of listening had been wasted, Wallace would stand up, walk into the booth, and perform an entire song off the top of his head.

Wallace's working method in the studio involved long hours of smoking weed and listening to a beat. Then he'd stand up, walk into the booth, and perform an entire song off the top of his head.

"He ain't take no long time to do no song," Mo Bee said. "When Big went in the booth, he usually knew what he was going to do. All the other times he's sitting over there in the chair looking big and fat. He just be cutting his eyes left and right, looking at everybody, sitting there mumbling to himself. Breathing hard, just mumbling. Then he'd say, 'Mo, I'm ready.' And he'd just go in there and knock it out."

And the things that Wallace would "knock out" were sometimes surprising to Mo Bee. It wasn't just his talent for visual detail, or his genius at evoking a menacing aura—it was the fact that he was scared of nothing. He would say anything in a rap song, the more outrageous the better.

His first encounter with this side of Wallace came when they recorded the very first song for the album— the title track, "Ready to Die."

"Fuck the world, fuck my Moms and my girl / My life is played out like a Jheri curl," he said right before the chorus. "I'm ready to die."

Mo Bee looked up from the mixing board.

"You know what you just said?" he asked, sounding upset.

"Yeah, man," Wallace said, stepping out of the booth.

"Fuck your *Moms*?"

"I'm just trying to say that I'm ready to die for this shit," he explained. "This is urgent. You got to be willing to do whatever you got to do to make this paper."

Mo Bee just kind of nodded. He knew he was in for a hell of a ride.

The producer didn't speak up again until they were recording another song, "Gimme the Loot," a song that would later be considered a hip-hop classic.

The track was a lyrical tour de force with Wallace rapping from the perspective of two different stick-up kids arguing about who to rob next. Rapping in different voices was nothing new—Slick Rick, rap's master storyteller, had done it all over his 1988 album, *The Adventures of Slick Rick*. But Wallace took the technique one step further. Not only did he rap in two different voices—each voice had a completely different rhyme style and personality.

"Slick Rick played different characters, but the characters sounded the same," Wallace explained. "And with 'Redman Meets Reggie Noble,' he played two different people, but both the characters sound the same. I wanted to make them two completely different dudes, to the point where someone could wonder, who was that rapper with Big on 'Gimme the Loot'?"

The deeper voice Wallace used on the track—the more reasonable of the two— tries to coach his eager young partner on how to rob. "You ain't got to explain shit," the higher-pitched voice replies. "I've been robbing muthafuckas since the slave ships, with the same clip, and the same .45 / Two point-blank a muthafucka's sure to die."

The verse was a brilliant display of all of Wallace's gifts—crisp visual detail, dark humor, and subtle culture-specific references. "Since the slave ships," linked Wallace's stick-up kid to Stagolee, the original "bad nigga" who had been immortalized in song and fable since the days of slavery. Later in the song, he describes a victim's mother singing "It's so hard... " This was a coy reference to Boyz II Men's remake of the tearjerker "It's So Hard to Say Goodbye to Yesterday," the death theme for the character Cochise in the film *Cooley High*. Boyz II Men's revival of the tune had become a popular request at funerals for black men and women who died before their time.

Wallace's "calm" character, to prove his worth, tries to outdo the younger character, proving how hard he is, too. "Then I'm dipping up the block, and I'm robbing bitches too / Up to herringbones and bamboos / I wouldn't give a fuck if you're pregnant / Give me the baby rings, and the #1 Mom pendant."

The lyric gave Mo Bee pause, but he kept his cool. (Puffy would later have the line edited out on the final mix of the album.) It wasn't until Wallace recorded "Dead Wrong" that Mo Bee felt he had to stand up and say something.

"Hail Mary full of grace / Smack the bitch in the face," began one verse. Then: "Move over Lucifer / I'm more ruthless / Leave you toothless..."

Wallace came out of the recording booth to high fives and catcalls. As offensive as some of the lyrics were, the power of his performance made them sound good. That was the whole point of the song, to be "Dead Wrong": to come up with lyrics that were so outrageous, even the most jaded listener would be shocked.

Like Wallace's mother, Mo Bee was a devout Christian. The line about the Virgin Mary was too blasphemous for him to let slide. He was nobody's father, but he felt he had to say something. Combs stood behind the mixing board next to the engineer. Wallace sat in the back of the control room, listening to the playback, swigging from a 40-ounce with Lil' Cease. Mo Bee looked at Combs.

"You sure you want to release that?" Mo Bee asked him.

Combs raised his eyebrows. "What you think?"

"The women's right organizations, the churches, all that shit, they gonna come after you after this shit comes out."

Mo Bee turned his head when he heard a huge chorus of laughs from the other side of the room. It was Wallace, flanked by Lil' Cease and other members of what would soon become Junior M.A.F.I.A. Cease was laughing the hardest.

"Mo, you sensitive, man," Cease said. "Mo's too sensitive."

The whole room was laughing at the producer. Wallace walked over to Mo Bee, letting him know that even though they were cracking on him, he still had love.

"I'm serious, man," the producer said.

"Nah, nah," Wallace said. "We just having fun, man."

"Big ain't stress it," explained Lil' Cease. "Big was like, It's just a rhyme. I guess he was testing his waters, like, Let me go write some outlandish shit. Cause when you got that type of mind where you intelligent like that and you really got that pen sharp? You can talk about anything. He was just experimenting."

And so it went, beat for beat, and blunt for blunt, until they had enough tracks to choose from. As choosy as Wallace was about beats, Combs was about which tracks would make the album, and which wouldn't. Some songs, like "Dead Wrong" and "Come On, Muthafuckas," a duet with Brand Nubian's Sadat X, didn't make the final cut. Combs had other concerns besides street-level appeal. With almost two years of recording going into the album, and the huge sums that he spent buying back Wallace's tracks from Uptown, Combs knew that Wallace's album had to have a few commercial hits.

The Chronic had laid out the blueprint for video and radio breakthrough. You had to come with something slower and funkier—but maintain enough of a gangsta edge that the song would still be considered "real."

The songs that he and Wallace had completed up until this point would wrap up New York City—no doubt. But Combs knew he needed something that could rock anywhere. Imagine *Thriller* with "PYT" but no "Billie Jean" or "Beat It." Following the Quincy Jones–Michael Jackson model, Combs needed a lead-off single that would knock everybody out the box.

Wallace and Mo Bee wanted the first single to be "Machine Gun Funk." It was funky, upbeat, and attitude to spare. But Combs wanted something smoother.

Wallace wanted to fight Puffy's decision, but he knew Combs had an uncanny feel for the crossover. If he wanted to get paid, that was the man to listen to. He was sure Combs wouldn't let him do anything to play himself.

"Puffy tells me, Yo, do your thing," Wallace said of their collaboration. "I'm gonna get busy. You can give my little limitations, but when I get a track, I ask him, 'What do you want from this, you let me know.' And he might be like, 'You need to be partying on this joint—you don't need to be killing nobody's mother on this one. Take it easy.' "

This time Combs wanted a party joint. The kind of song that would make women shake their hips while and sent men to the bar to buy fancy drinks.

Such was the evolution of songs like "Juicy" and "Big Poppa." When Combs couldn't entice Mo Bee into something as simplistic as looping Mtume's "Juicy Fruit" or the Isley Brothers' "Between the Sheets," he found other people to make the hits that he heard in his head.

Puff, as Wallace had seen, was less a knob- and drum-programming producer than he was someone who tried to re-create a lifestyle. It's about being in the mix, and from Combs's perspective, the sound of the mix. "We may be all in a club one night," Wallace explained. "Me, him, and a couple producers. And he'll see people dancing to Diana Ross's 'Upside Down.' He'll see that come on in the club and he'll see how everybody just jumps up on the dance floor. He'll see how a 31-year-old lady is rocking to this joint, and a seventeen-year-old lady is dancing to this joint. And he'll be like, 'Yo, I want to hook that up.'

"He'll tell one of the producers, they'll track it, and I'll rap to it. Then we'll give it to Puffy and Puffy will give it that gloss. It's the way he EQs it and the way the snares hit. People look at him like he's not a producer; to me he's a producer because he takes a hundred percent record and takes it to two hundred percent."

Despite putting his heart into songs like "Machine Gun Funk" and "Everyday Struggle," Wallace slowly came around to the fact that he had to entice a new audience with his album. If he didn't have a radio joint, he might not be able to expose that audience to his "gutter" joints.

"That's when he started learning how to make records, toward the end," said Mark Pitts about Wallace's musical evolution. "He started making records for a hit, and hooks for the radio."

If Wallace lost the battle for the A-sides of his singles, so be it—as long as he got to do whatever he wanted on the B-side. If he lost the street, he lost everything, and having a "gutter" joint that would keep the Ron Gs, Kid Capris, and other underground mix-tape kings happy was the only way to go.

There was only one person to call.

DJ Premier sat in a corner of D&D Studios, his head bowed down, nodding over his MPC60 drum machine.

The beat reverberated throughout Studio B—a smoldering complexity underneath a sparse, spare rhythm, like a shark swimming underneath the surface of a calm sea. Wallace wanted a hot underground joint, so he visited the master.

"I just need that gutter shit," Premier remembered Wallace asked him. He was almost done with his album, he finally had a September release date, but Wallace felt as if he just needed one more thing, one more final touch that would send the album over the edge. And he needed it quick.

"You talking about having it done in, like, two days," Premier said.

"I know you can do it," Wallace said. "I don't give a fuck. Just loop "Impeach the President."

"For real?"

"Flip that and just do some shit to it," he said.

"Alright," Premier said. "Meet me at the studio."

And a day later, he did. Instead of sampling the Honeydrippers' classic Nixon-era breakbeat, Premier programmed a variation of the beat—making the drums a little more synthetic, a little more spaced out. Flipping it, so to speak.

Premier had gotten into his favorite workshop, D&D Studios' "B" room, and had been working the whole thing out since 5:30 in the afternoon. Wallace showed up a few hours later, entourage in tow.

"It's a smash," Wallace said when he first heard it. He offered Premier a suggestion about using another rhythm to counter the main rhythm, to give the track a jittery feel. Primo nodded and got back to work.

Wallace mostly sat in the back of the room, saying nothing, writing nothing down, just nodding his head and mumbling to himself, over and over again.

Then he disappeared into the lounge.

Premier felt a tap on his shoulder. It was Dave Lotwin, one of the two D's who co-owned the studio.

"Do you know what's he's doing back there?" Lotwin asked, his eyebrow raised.

"What?"

Lotwin leaned close and whispered in his ear, "Go check it out."

Primo got up and opened the door in the middle of Studio B. He walked down a short corridor. The vocal booth was just off to his right, and a little bit farther back was the Studio B private lounge, a little place that at one time was probably a storage room.

He opened the door.

Wallace was there, leaning back on the couch. His pants were open. Two attractive women had their heads between his legs.

"Yo, Preme," Wallace said. "You want some of this?"

"Nah, I'm good," he said. Primo closed the door and chuckled.

Wallace eventually came out and sat in the room. It was getting late and they still hadn't even tracked his vocals. He sat around listening to the track over and over again, saying nothing.

"We had been in the studio for the longest time doing nothing but listen to the track," Premier said. "I was getting worried. We still smoking and drinking, and he ain't writing nothing."

Wallace looked up. "I'm ready."

No notepad, no notes, nothing. Premier watched him step into the booth, the same booth where he had watched Nas a few months earlier do the exact same thing for "New York State of Mind." Just step up to the mike and do it.

Premier hit the button on the board. And Wallace closed his eyes, nodding his head for a few seconds, letting the rhythm play for a few beats. Then he started rapping: "Live from Bedford-Stuyvesant, the livest one / Representing BK to the fullest, Gats I pull it / Bastards duckin' when Big be buckin' / Chickenheads be cluckin' in my back room fuckin'..."

Premier sat there amazed. Even what just happened in the back room of the studio had made its way into his lyrics. It was like he picked the rhyme out of thin air and assembled the pieces in real time, at will. Within less than an hour, the whole song was recorded, three perfect verses.

They didn't have a song title, but Wallace had an idea for the chorus, based on the last line of each verse, where Wallace says, "unbelievable." They could scratch in the vocal hook from R. Kelly's single, "Your Body's Calling."

"You sure that's gonna fit?" Premier asked.

"Yeah, it's gonna sound just right. Don't worry about it."

Premier picked up a copy of the R. Kelly 12-inch at Rock & Soul Records a few blocks from the studio. Much to his surprise, when he scratched it and looped it, the hook did fit perfectly. The bigger surprise came a few days after the final mix-down: Premier and his brother were driving back to Brooklyn late after a recording session when they heard another car booming the track. Premier caught up with the car at a stoplight, irate that the song had already been boot-legged.

"How'd you get a copy of that!?" he yelled, rolling down his window.

"It's on the radio," said the driver, who rolled up his window and sped off.

Premier idled at the curb, shocked. The song wasn't even a week old, and it was already getting radio play. That had never happened to him before.

Within a year, he'd also have the first gold single RIAA plaque of his career. Somehow "gutter" became "butter," and Wallace was the cause.

He was getting Big, now. Notoriously so.

Just as "Juicy" hit regular rotation on BET and MTV, "Unbelievable" was becoming the hottest track in clubs. The only thing critics and fans in New York City could talk about was the Notorious B.I.G. Though his earliest releases used the name Biggie Smalls, he was forced to adopt the Notorious B.I.G. (He sometimes said the acronym stood for "Business Instead of Game," though Cease said the crew would sometimes flip it to mean "Bullet in the Gut").

"I changed the name because there was a little white boy on Atlantic Records named Biggie Smalls," he explained. "His lawyers stepped to me, and were like, I can't use the name or I'll be sued. But I still say Biggie Smalls in my rhymes. I just have 'The Notorious B.I.G.' as a stamp on the front of the record. Everybody knows who the real Smalls is."

If the Wu-Tang Clan was the new super group, Nas was New York's savior, and Black Moon the darlings of the underground, the Notorious B.I.G was poised to become, as he put it, "the black Frank White," Christopher Walken's starring role in the movie *King of New York*. And *Ready to Die* would remove all doubt.

From beginning to end, the album was a revelation. Not so much in content as in function. People have asked what happened to the black protest novelists, people like Chester Himes and Donald Goines and Richard Wright, who used to tell stories that exposed the reality of what was happening in the ghetto. That art form didn't die as much as transform itself. Rapping rather than writing became the most effective medium for getting the word out about anything. The history of popular music, of any race, has always been shorter, flashier, faster. Why spend 300 pages to make your point when, with the right beat and the perfect lyrics, a comparable emotional impact could be delivered to a larger audience in three minutes?

In the introduction to *Native Son*, Richard Wright described the real-life men who shaped his fictional protagonist, Bigger Thomas—the tough guys and "bad niggers" who would never bow down to anyone, black or white. "His rebellious spirit made him violate all the taboos and consequently he always oscillated between moods of intense elation and depression," Wright wrote. "He was never happier than when he had outwitted some foolish custom, and he was never more melancholy than when brooding over the impossibility of his ever being free."

It's not clear if Wallace ever read *Native Son,* but *Ready to Die* was the musical personification of everything Wright communicated in that novel. The character Wallace portrayed as Biggie Smalls walked the razor's edge, gat in hand, a self-described menace to society (and sexual dynamo). But the man of action also has a conscience, and he is haunted by his own propensity for heartless violence and self-destruction. The album was a pitch-perfect depiction of the desperation of life in the Brooklyn ghetto—*Manchild in the Promised Land* as street opera.

The album's introduction neatly summarized the evolution of a street thug, from delivery room to domestic violence to doing dirt. Then the music kicked off with "Things Done Changed," one of the most powerful depictions of modern-day life in the 'hood ever recorded. The song recalls the innocent games of youth and describes in dramatic fashion how they were transformed into shattering displays of violence when crack cocaine was introduced to the neighborhood. Jump ropes have been replaced with yellow crime-scene tape, plastic bottles of juice with 40-ounce bottles of malt liquor, games of skelly with gun battles.

"Back in the days, our parents used to take care of us," he rapped. "Look at 'em now. They're even fuckin' scared of us. / Calling the city for help because they can't maintain. / Damn, shit done changed."

Rather than being a distant narrator, Wallace peppered the song with details from his own life: "Shit, my mama got cancer in her breast. / Don't ask me why I'm muthafuckin' stressed. / Things done changed."

The album's next three songs served as a showcase for his lyrical gifts. The stories depicted on "Gimme the Loot," "Machine Gun Funk," and "Warning" were bloody yet sarcastic. Like the filmmaker Quentin Tarantino, Wallace managed to make profound statements about the nature of violence by depicting it as random, brutal, and terrifying. In "Everyday Struggle," death lurked around every darkened corner, either at the hands of a corrupt cop, or another stick-up kid like himself, itchy to write his name on the wall with someone else's blood. Nobody could accuse Wallace of glamorizing a life of crime. If you listened to his album from start to finish, al the gangsta trappings of money and fame ring as hollow as the sound of a bullet casing bouncing off the pavement.

Despite the funkiness of "The What," the disarming poignancy of "Me and My Bitch," and the freestyle master class that was "Unbelievable," the album's most memorable moment was "Suicidal Thoughts." Nothing could prepare listeners for a song in which Biggie apologizes for the wrong turn his life has taken, then blows his brains out. The sound of the crisp gunshot and the phone receiver dropping to the ground is chilling, reckless, and yet compelling.

The most important thing about *Ready to Die,* was that it displayed Wallace's talent as more than just being a skilled word slinger. He could drop a potent message rap if he wanted to, yet he didn't want to be considered preachy. Biggie reveled in the good life in a way that was infectious no matter how one felt about sex or violence. And yet it was now impossible to listen to others rapping about the excitement and riches to be had in the drug game without recalling the self-loathing despair of "Suicidal Thoughts."

There was no way Uptown Records would ever have put out this album, because there was no way to predict the audience's reaction. But "Puff Daddy" anticipated that the public was looking for something new, something raw. And he provided them with an album that would make some people party, make some people mad, and that just might make some people think.

Christopher Wallace stood near the stoop of the apartment building he grew up in, a lit blunt in his mouth, his eyes looking toward Fulton Street. On the surface, if someone from the neighborhood had been watching him, it would have seemed like nothing had changed.

Yet everything had changed. Every single car that passed was blasting a different song from *Ready to Die.* These days, the outsiders who came to the neighborhood with notepads in hand weren't detectives but journalists. And instead of serving up crack, Wallace stood on the very same corner as before serving up quotes about his perspective on life.

Meeting him for the first time on a blistering Tuesday afternoon in late September, it was easy to see why folks called him the Mayor.

"I run this, dog," he explained. "I mean, I've been doing this for the longest. Everybody know Biggie. There ain't a nigga out here that don't know me. From down in that area they call Park Slope to all the way up in East New York, you know what I'm saying? And they all go through me. If they don't know me, they know of me. And they give me my respect—a lot.

He just stood there and people found their way to him, some to say hello or to give him a pound. Some would stand just within earshot, just to hear him talk. Some had other ideas.

Two short kids, eyes red from an afternoon of smoking blunts. walked up to Wallace in the middle of our interview. The rapper had been telling stories about growing up in the neighborhood, selling crack, dodging bullets, and some of the other things that directly influenced the content of his album.

Wallace acknowledged the kids with a nod. They were Trife and Larceny, part of a crew of youngsters Wallace called "The Snakes."

"You got that deuce-deuce?" Trife asked him.

"Why, what's up?" said Wallace, curious what use his friend could have for a .22 caliber pistol.

"We gonna throw this nigga down for his VCR, kid," said Larceny. "That shit is butter."

"Take it!" Wallace said. "I don't know where my shit is, though. Fuckin' Moose has an M-1, though."

"Nah, that shit is too big," Trife said, shaking his head.

"What about that Eight?" Wallace said, referring to a .38-caliber pistol someone had.

"Never mind," Trife said. He nodded his head and Larceny followed him down the street.

"I know exactly where that gun is," Wallace said with a mischievous glint as soon as the two were out of earshot, "but I'm not gonna be a part of that shit there. Fuck that!"

He wasn't concerned with concealing what had happened from the journalist standing next to him. Yet as he watched the two young men walk away, he expressed his need to help things change, even if it was only one step at a time.

"You've got to understand," he said, "you got a group of niggas over here who are fifteen and sixteen years old, and ain't doing nothing out here. Their parents look at them like they're doomed, but I can't let them do that, because I didn't do that. Either get some kind of hustle, or roll with me, but don't be sitting there just smoking lah and giving your life over to the weed."

"Even if niggas don't go to school, you're going to be doing something," he insisted. "You ain't just going to be sitting there disappointing your parents. You're going to get some kind of paper. Try to play some ball. You're going to do *something*, man. You can't just sit there because that's what really hurts parents the most, to just watch their son give up and not do nothing to fix it."

Those who focused on the negativity of *Ready to Die*—from the bleak-sounding title to the album's closing track, "Suicidal Thoughts"—missed the fact that it was a fundamentally an album about survival, as summed up in the line "Another day another struggle." Wallace used this very line as he talked about his young friends in the grind, and I asked him to explain what it meant to him: "A struggle in my eyes is living," he said with a meaningful pause. '*Living.* Waking up is a struggle for some of these niggas man. For a lot of these niggas—eighty-five percent. They between the ages of fourteen and eighteen and they got single parents. That's the struggle right there. Just waking up dead-assed broke."

One of the by-products of Wallace's newfound success was to realize his dream of having a group of his own put a record out, his Junior M.A.F.I.A. The goal was to give the kids in his crew something to do—even if some of them couldn't rhyme. Blake and Banger were already rapping a little. And Cease's sister had a friend named Lil' Kim who could kick serious rhymes. (She'd soon be kicking it with Biggie as well). Big Poppa wanted to put everybody on: Chico, Lil' Cease, Klept, Nino, Trife, Larceny, and Gutter. They would have an opportunity because he had an opportunity—and he would use another brother from the neighborhood to form his own record label and make that dream a reality.

Lance "Understanding" Rivera was that brother, a heavy-set dude with impeccable street credentials. Rivera's younger brother Justice was one of the first people to recognize Wallace's talent, circulating some of the tapes he made with 50 Grand to people he knew in the industry like Kedar Massenberg, who would one day rise to be the president of Motown, working with the likes of Erkyah Badu, India.Arie, and D'Angelo. (Massenberg later admitted to Rivera that the worst decision he ever made in his career was having a young Christopher Wallace on his couch and not signing him.)

"My brother had wanted to be in the music business since he was little," Un said. "But I ain't never really paid any attention to it."

Justice, of course, brought Wallace to Un, and Un was impressed with Wallace's style, but not enough to take the plunge.

"I used to sell drugs and shit and I was getting some money," Un said.

Un "understood" the game and was smart enough to recognize opportunity. Because of his brother, he was in the right place in the right time, right before Wallace blew up with the success of *Ready to Die*. He was always there to loan money to Wallace when he came up short, to make sure that everyone in the crew had pocket money.

But it wasn't until he met Sean "Puffy" Combs for the first time that he realized exactly how he wanted to be involved. Wallace invited Un to a Jodeci video shoot and Un sensed that Combs was intimidated by his massive presence.

"Puff pulled up across the street and he called Big over," Un remembered. "I seen him talkin'. Then I seen Big put his head down. Something told me they was over there talkin' about me. So when Big came back across the street he just looked at me, and he ain't want to say nothin'. I was like, 'You ain't got to explain.'"

Un was insulted. Combs hadn't even tried to find out who he was. He just took one look at him and decided that he was trouble. As he left the video shoot, he vowed to make Combs pay for this slight. And he would not get his revenge on the streets, but in the board room.

"I got on the phone and called my brother," Un said. "I told him, 'I want to be in the music business because I want to become a thorn in Puff's side.'"

"I knew the nigga Big was dope," Rivera reasoned. "And I knew the nigga Puff needed Big. So I would get in the middle of they shit, not to really be disruptive, but to manipulate certain situations."

Wallace like having Un around because he put money in his pocket when he didn't have any. More impor-

tant, he was "real"—he had a credibility in the streets that Wallace respected and looked up to. As much as Wallace wanted to lead a bigger, better life, outside of Brooklyn, he was just as afraid to change his lifestyle.

"Ain't no real Brooklyn niggas blew up to the point where they could be considered a superstar, and stayed," Wallace said wistfully. "Everybody moved. I'm gonna get me a spot one day, but I have to be surrounded by my niggas. I'm afraid of how my shit's gonna sound if I don't fuck with my niggas. That's the reason Chubb Rock fell off. He live in the Hamptons. There's no 'hood out there."

Wallace took in his surroundings for a moment. "How real can your music be if you waking up in the morning hearing birds and crickets?"

And what would he rather hear instead?

"A lot of construction work, the smell of Chinese takeout, and someone banging a different track from my album," he said. "Brooklyn is the love borough."

His love for Brooklyn, however, didn't prevent Wallace from being paranoid. Quite the contrary. He knew the mindset of people who lived by taking things away from those who had much. Now he was on the other side. On one hand

Combs helped Wallace understand that he was selling a product with his music. But as much as Wallace wanted to get money, he was reluctant to change his lifestyle.

he enjoyed his success. On the other, he realized he had something to lose.

When Touré went to Wallace's house to profile him for the *New York Times*, he peeped the security protocol. "Every time the door opened, somebody would look down to see who it was," the writer said. "Even little girls just coming back with milk were interrogated, like, Who are you? That street sense that they had to watch out for everything and everybody never went away." Toward the end of the interview he watched as Lil' Cease went to Wallace's bedroom. "He just calmly reached under the mattress and pulled out a pistol and put it under his fuckin' pants like it was nothing," Touré recalled. "I was like, Wow, these niggas are still mobilized for street warfare."

Throughout all his interviews, Wallace always seemed to have a hard time envisioning himself living to a ripe old age.

"I ain't gonna lie to you," he told a writer from *Rap Pages*. "I really never pictured even being like 35, I guess 'cause I was always living day to day, and there's always so many things that coulda just snuffed me out. The way niggas be trippin' out here, I can't really plan that far ahead. And when you plan, shit be going wrong anyway. We just living day by day."

That didn't stop him from making permanent moves. By the time I met Wallace on September 27, 1994, barely two weeks after the release of *Ready to Die,* he was already married to a backup singer and songwriter, who up until that point no one had ever heard of, named Faith Evans. Just the mention of her name made Wallace smile sheepishly.

"When you start hustling, you get introduced to shit real fast," he said. "You be getting pussy real quick, because you be fuckin' the users sometimes. I done had every kind of bitch. Young bitch, old bitch, users, mothers, grandmothers, dumb bitches, every kind of bitch I done fucked and I *never* ever met no girl like my wife," he said with pride.

"She talks to me like nobody else on earth talked to me before. The conversations be striking me like no other honey I ever fucked with," Wallace said.

"So where is she?" I asked.

Wallace smiled.

"She ain't speaking to me right now, but it's all good."

That's how the whole thing started between the two of them. Just a little harmless conversation followed by a whole lot of drama.

He first saw Faith at a Bad Boy promotional photo shoot in June, 1994. "She was killing me with those eyes," Wallace recalled. "I rolled up to her and said, "you're the kind of girl I would marry." And she said, "Why don't you?" So I was like, 'Fuck it then—it's on!' " Faith remembered being introduced to Wallace by the female rapper Hurricane Gloria, who was close with Redman, another mutual friend. "During the lunch break or whatever, he asked to see some pictures I had," Faith said. "And obviously he was really slick 'cause he got my phone number off the envelope."

Born in Lakeland Florida to a black mother and an Italian father she never met, Evans moved to Newark, New Jersey as a child, and was raised by her grandparents. They made sure she was in church, which is where she honed a voice that was deep, powerful, and poetic. Faith was a hybrid of influences: Mahalia Jackson's power, Aretha's soul, and Sarah Vaughn's nimble touch when it came to phrasing. She won talent pageants, sang at weddings and funerals, and after graduating from Newark's University High, she went to Fordham University.

She dropped out a few months later and ended up in the New York music scene. Her boyfriend, Kiyamma Griffin, produced tracks for Christopher Williams, an Uptown artist who was working with Combs at the time.

Combs and future Bad Boy executive Kirk Burrowes met Evans through her boyfriend. "He was working on Usher's album and we were pursuing him to be a Bad Boy producer," said Burrowes. "He bought along his pregnant girlfriend, and we didn't have anyone to do a background vocal. He said, 'My girlfriend can sing.' And she did. Puffy said her voice sounded like rain."

Faith signed to Bad Boy as an artist and composer. She had to support herself and her daughter Chyna, so she did background vocals on Mary J. Blige's *My Life* album, writing songs for Blige and Color Me Badd as well as composing tracks for herself. Combs believed that she would be a big star, and wanted her introduction to be perfect.

"Faith is very complex," Combs said. "She's a true diva. A lot of people that be kicking that shit aren't divas. True divas don't act like divas. They don't say they're divas. They're just interesting and they're fly."

Wallace thought so too. Evans remembered being introduced to him by the female rapper Hurricane Gloria. "During the lunch break, he asked to see some pictures I had," Evans said. "And obviously he was really slick 'cause he got my phone number off the envelope."

Evans was intrigued by the heavyset dude with the suave demeanor. "He was pretty quiet then," she recalled, "but he had a certain charm about him. I was talking so much I don't know really what attracted him to me. I was kind of familiar with the name Biggie Smalls, but I really wasn't that much into hip hop at the time, so I didn't know that was him." Biggie didn't even know Faith was an artist signed to Bad Boy. "He thought I was a background singer or something," she said with a smile.

"I gave him a ride to Brooklyn from the photo shoot and we just ended up"—she paused and smiled—"you know... He said he was gonna call me. He did, and of course it was a very short courtship." They were only apart for a few hours before Wallace asked her out to a movie. Evans doesn't remember what they went to see at the Newport Center Mall in Jersey City, only that Wallace kept making her laugh. They walked around the mall talking and holding hands.

"We just kind of hung out doing all fun stuff," she said. "We went to a couple of parties, then after like a week or so he told me he was gonna marry me, and I said okay."

The whole thing wasn't as crazy as it might have seemed. Faith and Biggie had a lot in common. Both were artists on Puffy's hot new label, and both had been through the frustration of working on projects for years only to see them languish as Bad Boy Records made the transition from Uptown to Arista. Both were studio rats—perfectionists willing to spend hours upon hours in the lab to get a song exactly right. Both were close to their mothers and haunted by fathers they never knew. Both were Geminis—needy free spirits who hated to be held down, yet at the same time extremely jealous and codependent. Both adored their daughters—Wallace had T'Yanna, and Faith had Chyna, her little girl from a previous relationship, She loved to cook. He loved to eat.

Faith found herself attracted to Biggie not because of his money—he was flat broke at the time, and, ironically, she was the one with more financial stability, having already written songs that were recorded by people like Mary J. Blige. Faith also liked the fact that Wallace had so much game—his whole approach, from the way he got her phone numbers, down to the way that he called her that night for a date that never really ended.

"Let's get married," he said one night. They were in Faith's car, which is where they spent a lot of their time. Like Quincy Jones and Spike Lee before him, Wallace never learned how to drive, and was famous for convincing people not only to pick him up but take him anywhere he wanted to go. This time they were on the way to pick up some Chinese food, near Wallace's apartment on St. James.

"Are you serious?" Faith said.

"I'm dead ass," he said.

"All right, okay," she said, smiling warmly at the memory. And the funny thing was she had no doubts about it.

"Absolutely nothing occurred to me like, *Hello, you don't really know him. You just met him*," she said. "It was a different feeling. I felt the same way that he did. I had never met anybody like him."

Wallace told everybody who would listen that he was getting married. And like the boy who cried wolf, nobody believed him.

"I'm getting married, Ma," Wallace told his mother one evening. She laughed at him. He pouted.

"Mark ain't believe me. Puffy ain't believe me. Ma, I'm getting married on Monday." This conversation was taking place on a Friday night.

"Congratulations," she said, her voice brimming with sarcasm. "Who's the lucky one?"

"Ma, I'm serious. I'm getting married. I found this honey, Mom. This is the one. This is the one."

Ms. Wallace began to lose her temper.

"Christopher, cut it out!" she scolded him. "Every second you come in you found one. Please, no, you found one hundred. Get a life!"

Wallace called Jan. The two of them had been separated for several months, but they still had feelings for each other. Jan even thought there was a small possibility they would get back together, based on the fact that he was just as flirtatious as ever. Those hopes ended when he told her he was getting married.

"For real?" she said, her voice suddenly small.

"Yeah, for real."

"I only have one question," Jan said, collecting her thoughts. "If you had the chance to let me go, why didn't you let me go? You brought me back for this?"

"If I let you go, I thought I'd lose my baby," he said. "I was being selfish."

Jan promised him that she would never keep T'Yanna from him. She said she just wanted him to be happy.

"Damn, that was too easy," he said. "I was expecting you to trip, and you didn't."

"I'm not gonna trip," Jan said, though the news hurt bad. "If you're happy and that's what you want to do," she said, "then I'm happy for you."

Kim was another story. Her lovers' quarrels with Big were growing more frequent and more heated.

Knowing that he wasn't going to lose T'Yanna was all Wallace needed, He left with Faith for Rosslyn, New York, a small town in upstate New York. One of his boys from the 'hood, Gutter, stood as his witness. On August 4, 1994, the bride and groom got dressed up to stand in front of the justice of the peace.

"*Kind of* dressed up," Faith corrected. The groom wore jeans and a button-down shirt. The bride wore a simple dress. There was no cake, and no time for a honeymoon. In ten minutes they were married, and within hours she dropped him back in Brooklyn so he could go to the studio and she could pick up her daughter.

He came home later that night, tired from the drive and the session. His mom was still up. "Guess what," he told her as soon as he arrived home. "I did it."

"Did what?" Ms. Wallace said, suspecting nothing.

"I got married today."

Ms. Wallace stared at her son for a minute, with no expression. "It was like hearing a ten-year-old telling you he was getting married," she would say later.

"Does she have a name?" Ms. Wallace asked.

"Faith," he replied.

"Faith? Lord have mercy. We both need faith."

Wallace still pouted. His mother didn't believe him; neither did Combs or Pitts.

Ms. Wallace still didn't believe him until she got a phone call at work from her sister Melva a day later.

"Are you listening to the radio?" she asked. "Christopher got married. He was just on the news saying hello to his 'wifey.' "

That's when Voletta came home and confronted her son. "Christopher," she asked, "are you really married?"

He rolled his eyes.

"You don't believe me when I talk to you, do you? Puffy don't believe me. Mark don't believe me. Nobody believe me. I'm married."

"I wanted to slap him," Ms, Wallace remembered.

"What is she like?" she asked, horrified. He went into his room and came back with one of her promotional photos.

"Is she white!?" Ms. Wallace asked. No, he explained to his mother, she just had a very light complexion.

It was weeks before Faith got up the nerve to go meet Ms. Wallace. Or maybe it was Christopher who had to work up his courage. He told his wife to avoid his mother. Meanwhile, Ms. Wallace just got angrier.

A few days later, Ms. Wallace called Mark Pitts, whom she trusted to give her the straight story. "She's a very nice girl," he told her. "She looks like she's very decent. She's somebody that I think you'd like."

It was weeks before Faith got up the nerve to go meet Ms. Wallace. Or maybe it was Biggie who had to work up his courage. He told Faith to avoid his mother, and Ms. Wallace got angrier and angrier at the daughter-in-law she never met. "What kind of a woman would marry a man knowing that he has a mother," she asked herself, "and not even want to meet her?"

One night, a few weeks after their wedding, Faith called 226 St. James, and

Ms. Wallace picked up the phone. "May I speak to Christopher?" the voice on the phone asked tentatively. "It's Faith."

There was a long pause. Ms. Wallace exhaled, trying her best to keep cool.

"Do you have a mother?" she asked.

"Of course," Faith said.

"How would your mother feel if you ran and off and got married?" she asked.

Faith was apologetic, almost to the point of tears. "Ms. Wallace, I'm so sorry, but Christopher told me to stay away from you. I know you're very upset right now, and I know exactly how you feel, because my mother would feel the same way you do, and that's how I would feel."

The two began their conversation as adversaries and ended it as friends. The door opened. Christopher came home.

"Ooh, I wanted to kill him," Ms. Wallace said. "I had fire coming out of my ears."

"How dare you tell that little girl to stay away from me!" she said.

Her son looked at her.

"Ma, you are furious. Aren't you?"

"Christopher!"

"Ma, look. I love you and I love her and I know you're mad. I just didn't want you to say anything because, Ma, you're a little bit opinionated. You know what I mean? And you might say something to hurt her feelings. So, I just told her to stay away from you right now."

She shook her head. What could she say? He was right.

When she and Faith finally did meet, they liked each other right away. Christopher was going on one of his promotional tours, and Faith came by their home and picked up the rest of his furniture to put it into the duplex that they rented in Brooklyn's Fort Greene.

"It was a beautiful apartment," Ms. Wallace said. "I went over, but I just let them live their life, you know. I said, 'God, at least somebody's going to take care of him.'"

But the newlyweds hardly had a chance to enjoy the apartment or each other.

"I wouldn't even give it two weeks, a week maybe of him and I both being there at the same time," Faith said. "We got new furniture, and then he started going on his promo tour with Craig Mack." He was on the road and she was in the studio and even when she went to visit him, there was never any real time to be together. There was always pressure from one career or the other.

"It was really crazy," Faith said, looking back. "I even think about the times when I did go and visit him on the road. I would have to leave the next morning or I'm getting a call from somebody as if I'm doing something wrong. Like,

'What are you doing?' What am I *doing*? I'm with my husband."

Her husband was blowing up. It was what they both wanted. And they would have to adjust their marriage accordingly. "It wasn't like it took a long time," she said. "He just blew up. Like boom."

Ready to Die sold 500,000 copies in its first week alone. Suddenly the video for "Juicy" was all over MTV, the radio was playing his song three times an hour, and it seemed like everywhere he went, people knew who the Notorious B.I.G. was.

By November, not only was Wallace a success, but Bad Boy Records was no longer considered a fledgling label. People were beginning to know who Sean "Puffy" Combs was, and what he was capable of. Craig Mack's "Flava in Your Ear" was No. 1 on the *Billboard* rap charts for three straight weeks. "Juicy" backed by "Unbelievable" entered at No 5.

And there was Puffy, in the middle of it all. Racing from the set of Biggie's video shoot for "Big Poppa" at Nell's nightclub in New York, then down to a party in Philadelphia on Saturday, back up to New York for another video shoot for "Warning" on Sunday, then catching an hour's worth of sleep before going to a Mary J. Blige video shoot on Monday.

"Sleep is forbidden," Combs said. "When most are sleeping, we are working."

Puff still consulted with Harrell on some of the biggest acts at Uptown, Jodeci and Mary J. Blige. Combs reveled in the fact that he was scaring the competition. Within a year, he went from being fired to being in a position to knock both Def Jam's Russell Simmons and his best friend Harrell off the map. He had a penchant for making young men look like old men, and by embracing the street, made his rough-and-tumble artists the East Coast's platinum standard.

But Harrell was too busy to worry about Combs making him look bad. Suge Knight had been hanging around Uptown artists like Mary J. Blige and Jodeci of late, insinuating himself into their contract negotiations.

"I saw that Jodeci weren't being paid right, and I did something that's never been done before: I went to MCA, their label, and renegotiated a contract on a record that was already out . MCA gave the group a $2 million advance, and doubled their point spread. Then I went to Uptown, their production company, and told Andre Harrell to give the group $75,000 a week. It didn't matter how he felt about it.," Knight said. "It needed to be done. Same thing with Mary J. Blige. I told Mary to speak her mind, that she didn't have have nothin' to worry about. Then I told them they was letting her out of that fucked up deal. And they did."

There were persistent rumors that Knight had physically intimidated Harrell in the Uptown Records offices. Both Knight and Harrell denied the talk, but Harrell did hire the Fruit of Islam to guard his offices soon after the renegotiation. Both Blige and Jodeci denied any threats, instead basking in the attention Knight lavished on them.

"I know Suge's got this reputation for being a guy who goes around strong-arming," said Jodeci's Devante Swing, "but I think those rumors just come from jealous people. The thing is he won't let anybody walk over him or any of his artists—and a lot of people really resent that."

"I have had so many people take advantage of me that it's nice to finally have someone on my side," Blige said. "Suge's like that guy in the movies who goes around getting the bad people—Charles Bronson, right?"

Knight even turned up at one of Wallace's recording sessions at the Hit Factory, a quiet but powerfully menacing presence. Combs wasn't sure what his intentions were, but he couldn't worry about that right now. He was focused on his own vision, and it was a beautiful thing.

"My artists are bad boys, bad boys for life, and they basically depict that type of image," Combs said. "It's the confidence they have about themselves. We just got a little bit more flavor. That's what the kids want: the realism, the lingo, the attitude, the bounce."

"That's what separates me from Russell and Andre," Combs added, feeling himself. "I live for the music. I think they live for the money. I stay up longer than either one of them; I can be out in the street a lot longer."

Despite friendly relations with Combs, Harrell—who was godfather to Puffy's first son Justin, born in August 1994—went out of his way to belittle his former charge.

"He's not a competitor yet, but he's got a great start," Harrell told a reporter from the *New York Times*. "It's not enough to have a hit record, you have to have a hit career."

Yet Combs was well on his way. *Ready To Die* was climbing the charts, and Craig Mack's "Flava In Your Ear," was also doing damage. It was just like after City College. When they thought he was down, he came back stronger than ever.

Though the money was slow to come at first, by late 1994, Wallace was starting to enjoy the first fruits of Biggie's fame. The butter leather coat, the Land Cruiser. Still he wanted security for family.

He threw himself a party at Roseland on the night of September 11, 1994, was large in a style that could only be described as "Puffyesque"—a term that folks would be hearing a lot more in the years ahead. It was also the first major party he had thrown since the tragedy that was City College. Video monitors featured Combs dancing in the background of videos. Many of the songs that played were hits that he cultivated for Uptown and Bad Boy, everything from Fine Young Cannibals and Doug E. Fresh, to Mary J. and now Biggie and Craig Mack.

The party, more than anything else, was an announcement: We're here—and we ain't going nowhere.

Wallace was in the VIP lounge, of course. And there he held court with one of his closest friends in the rap game, an established star who identified with Big since the first moment he heard "Party and Bullshit": Tupac Shakur.

The two of them had been tight for just over a year. Every time Tupac was in town, Wallace and his friends brought the weed and they would all hang out. The two were both kindred spirits and physical opposites. Each saw in the other something he lacked. In Shakur, Wallace not only saw an elder in the rap game, but also someone who had survived the tumultuous childhood and abject poverty that Biggie rapped about but never actually lived. And in Biggie, Tupac recognized an artistic genius as well as someone who rolled with real thugs—gun-toting outlaws with two feet in the street life.

Shakur was at Combs's party taking a break from a highly publicized rape trial, and he was shocked to see some of the very people he held responsible for his predicament hanging close to Wallace. Wallace, who understood the New York streets, did his best to warn his friend about the shady figures he had offended, telling him, ever so subtly, to watch who he was rolling with. But it was a party, there were blunts to be smoked, champagne bottles to be popped, and even in this slightly tense environment, a good time to be had by all. For Bad Boy it was the birth of a nation, for Wallace, a first taste of superstardom, and for Shakur, the last fun night he would ever have in New York City.

WHAT'S BEEF?

CHAPTER 5

66 Beef is when I see you
Guaranteed to be in I.C.U. **99**

The first time Christopher Wallace met Tupac Shakur they clicked right away. The year was 1993, and the Bad Boy team was traveling to California for the first time. "Tupac knew Biggie was coming," said Sybil Pennix, who was Combs's assistant at the time. "He really respected him as a lyricist. He brought us to his house and barbecued for everybody. After that they were, like, immediate friends."

Lil' Cease remembers Wallace talking about meeting Shakur after doing a show in Maryland with Puff to support his first single, "Party and Bullshit."

"Big went out there to perform that song," Cease recalled. "He said Pac was loving that shit. He stepped to Big like, 'What up, Big? I like your shit.' " Big respected his work too and they hit it off.

The morning after the party, at around 8A.M. there was a knock on Wallace's hotel room door. He opened it and there was Shakur, smiling, with a bottle of Hennessy cognac in his hand.

"What up! Nigga, let's it kick it."

They made for an odd pair—so different in size and appearance—but these young men had more in common than met the eye. "Pac and Big, they really connected," Lil' Cease said. "They both was Geminis, so they both had the same personality, the same persona. They kind of looked at shit the same way." They were both book smart—and both went to great extremes to downplay the fact with their homeboys. Both men loved weed and Hennessy, and both had a spontaneous, powerful gift for storytelling. Moreover, each of them represented something that the other—in his own perverse way—envied.

The son of black activist Afeni Shakur, Tupac really did come from the kind of impoverished background that Wallace would later fabricate on the introduction to *Ready to Die*. Between being blacklisted for her revolutionary past, periods of homelessness, and sporadic drug use, Shakur's mother had seen the worst that life had to offer—and wasn't always able to shield her children from those horrors. While she was in jail during the New York Panther 21 case—accused of plotting to blow up various buildings throughout New York—she had to fight for eggs and milk to care for her unborn son.

Shakur recalled many times when his family had nothing to eat and no money. He would get picked on and teased because of his raggedy second-hand clothes. To Big, this represented a realness that he had never experienced. Shakur grew up without Colecovision, designer clothes, or expensive stereo equipment. Every day really was a struggle.

Shakur, on the other hand, respected Wallace's street pedigree. Although he had known hustlers in New York and Baltimore, he wasn't really a street guy. Shakur was a student at Baltimore School for the Arts, where he studied with Jada Pinkett. He also suffered from the same problem that the Black Panther Huey P. Newton once had—he was so handsome, he had to fight that much harder to make people fear and respect him on a street level. Wallace, with his huge girth and lazy eye, didn't have that problem—some people would cross the street when they saw him coming. And despite his middle-class upbringing in a cultural sense, Wallace had a certain authentic wildness hardened by his years as a hustler on the Fulton Street strip. Wallace was the real deal and Shakur knew it. And Wallace sensed the same thing about Shakur, who had the advantage of being a veteran of the rap game, and could warn Wallace of the ups and downs he had yet to experience. In some strange way they completed each other, almost like a hip hop yin and yang.

Wallace came back to Fulton and told Cease all about Tupac, who was a big star to them. "Dawg is real," Wallace said. "I gave him my number, and told him when he come up here we'll kick it, or when I go out there we'll kick it. We're gonna keep in touch. He's supposed to come up here and do a movie." Cease said they used to talk every other day. "That was Big's homie."

During one trip to California Wallace stayed with Tupac and slept on his couch. Another time Shakur visited Fulton and Washington with much fanfare. "He came through the 'hood, and I was respecting that shit," said Lil' Cease. "That's gangster. He was big to us." Shakur arrived in a stretch limousine to pick up Wallace for a show he was doing at the Ritz that night. "A white limo pulls up on the block," Cease recalled. "Pac jumps out. The 'hood's going crazy."

Wallace, Cease, and the rest of the crew took Shakur downstairs underneath a pizzeria on Fulton that doubled as an underground gambling spot. Cease was surprised that a rap superstar who wasn't from the neighborhood had no problem rolling up his sleeves and shooting Cee-lo with the rest of them.

"Tupac was down there and everything," Lil' Cease said, "keeping it gully."

Later that night, Wallace and Shakur performed onstage together at the Ritz. Cease watched them rock the crowd side by side, East meets West–style.

"They'd just feed off each other," said Cease. "You couldn't really take them apart. Them niggas was together every day. He had to prove something to Big and Big had to prove something to him. Pac was that thug nigga in the industry. And Big was the next thing to come from the 'hood that was gonna fuck niggas' heads up. And they were building, together. That shit was looking strong. They was really looking out for each other, and they did records together."

In September 1993, Pac was doing a show at the Ritz and he invited Big to come open for him. "Big's out there doing his song and everybody was giving him love," Cease recalled. "Big got so hyper that he fell and bust his ass right on stage! The whole crowd saw, but he kept on goin'. It amazed me cause nothing stopped his flow. He was on his back still rhyming. The crowd thought it was part of the show and they went crazy."

Their most memorable show together was the legendary performance at the Budweiser Superfest in October 1993. Biggie and Pac shared the Madison Square Garden stage with Big Daddy Kane, Kane's dancers Scoob and Scrap Lover, and Shyheim the Rugged Child, alongside DJ Mister Cee. Big electrified the crowd by demanding "Where Brooklyn at?" before ripping a rhyme about his "seven Mac 11s, about eight .38s, nine 9's, 10 Mac-10s / The shits never end..." Pac cheered his friend's masterful verse and then took over microphone duties. "No matter how you try / Niggas never die," Pac proclaimed, "We just retaliate with hate until we multiply." It was a seminal event in rap history, a session that solidified Shakur's East Coast fan base while introducing Wallace as the hottest new MC of the moment.

Backstage at that show Wallace introduced Shakur to his neighbor Easy Mo Bee, who would later produce most of the tracks on Shakur's *Me Against the World*. Mo Bee also produced the first duet between Wallace and Shakur, "Runnin'," which was meant to appear on Shakur's first Thug Life album. When it was shelved at the last minute, "Let's Get It On," a song Big and Pac did for Eddie F & The Untouchables with Mount Vernonites Heavy D and Grand Puba, became their first official joint release in 1994.

Shakur and Wallace also recorded a song for *Ready to Die* along with Randy "Stretch" Walker of the Live Squad, a New York based gangsta rap trio. But Puffy thought the song was too raw for the direction he wanted to take Biggie, and the song was never released.

In some interviews, Tupac said that the plan was for Wallace to be an unofficial member of Thug Life. Their cliques began politicking at the "Runnin' " session—Wallace, Shakur, members of the Outlawz and Junior M.A.F.I.A. all hung out together smoking trees. "It was a cool vibe—he was a real nigga," Lil' Cease said. "It was our team and they team, but we were all together as one. That shit used to be fun."

Just about any time Shakur was in New York, he and Wallace would hang out. If Pac needed weed, protection, anything, Biggie was there for him. "We used to make sure he was good," Cease recalled. "What you need? Whatever it is. You got it. Big can't make it. he'll send lil' niggas up there. Yo, go take him these two nines. Put 'em in a bag, get on the train, go drop 'em off. We used to do that type of shit for the nigga up here. We taking our chance to do it for another nigga. But that's' cause we was thorough niggas. He was cool and we was fuckin' with him. Big about to get out there, he out there poppin'. Shit was lookin' right. So a nigga was doin' it for him out of love."

Shakur spent his time traveling between New York, the Bay Area, Atlanta, and California. Wallace stayed with him once on a trip to California. The two communicated daily. But when Shakur came to New York in late 1993 for the

Gemini brothers Wallace and Shakur blowing up the Palladium, New York City, 1993. "They'd just feed off each other," said Lil' Cease. "You couldn't really take them apart."

filming of *Above the Rim*, he started making new friends.

Jacques Agnant, a.k.a. "Haitian Jack" was a music promoter and all-around player with all the respect, admiration, and fear that comes from being a "real street nigga." Shakur met him while researching his role Birdie in the movie *Above The Rim*.

It might seem contradictory for a gangsta rapper to have to research a role on how to play a street thug if he was truly "keeping it real," as he said on his records. But to question Shakur would be to misunderstand his seriousness as an actor. Tupac Shakur had more in common with a young Dustin Hoffman than with other rappers who made the transition from recording studio to movie screen. A star pupil in the Baltimore School for the Arts' prestigious acting program, Shakur was taught that acting is telling the truth under imaginary circumstances. He was familiar with the Method—a way of making a character real by going beyond the script so as to understand not only what a character was doing and saying but why. The only way Shakur felt he could do that was to walk around the world in the character's shoes—to get close enough that one could understand his soul.

One School Of The Arts teacher who was particularly close to Shakur through-out his life, Donald Hicken, had long discussions with his former pupil about the separation between Tupac the person and 2Pac the artist. Hicken believed that authenticity of performance was different from authenticity of life, that what made an actor credible was his ability to make the journey between those two worlds. If you lived the life you portrayed, he felt, there was no journey.

"[Tupac] had a completely different take on it," Hicken said. "His point of view was that he didn't want to be a phony. He needed to be authentic. He needed to be real. And in order to that, he needed to live what he said. What he wrote was what he lived."

"I know how to play a West Coast bad boy," Shakur explained. "But I don't know how to do that whole East Coast thing. I was hanging around the real thing—that's how I do it: that's how I did it with *Juice,* that's how I do it with everything. So I'm hanging around these dudes—and I'm picking up their game. I didn't have to dress with a hoodie to be a thug. So I was dressing like they were dressing. They took me shopping, and that's when I bought my Rolex and my jewels. They made me mature. They introduced me to all these gang-sters in Brooklyn. They was showing me all these guys who I needed to know to be safe in New York."

Shakur was seeing a whole new world—big-time dealers, the kind of guys with money-counting machines, not "shoebox" money. Agnant and his friends chided Shakur for hanging out with the young rap crowd. They were going to be his introduction to a whole new world—the "upper echelon." Shakur said Agnant promised him, "We're not gonna let you get into no trouble."

Agnant took him to Nell's, where he first met 19-year-old Ayana Jackson. And it was there on the club's dance floor that Shakur said Jackson had oral sex with him before leaving with him to have sex. Then, on the night of November 18, 1993, Ayana Jackson came to the rapper's $750-a-night suite at the Parker Meriden Hotel. Shakur said Agnant fixed drinks for everyone after she arrived. Wallace was reportedly there too, chilling with Shakur and planning to go with him to a show at a New Jersey club. But Wallace decided to leave soon after Jackson showed up.

The unspoken gangster code about women was that unless you claimed one as your "girl" they were to be shared with the whole crew. Always aware of his street rep, Shakur made a decision he would later regret.

Jackson and Shakur retired to the bedroom, where they got comfortable.

"That's all I'm thinking about—getting another blow job," Shakur said. But before anything could go down, Agnant and Pac's road manager Charles "Man" Fuller entered the room. Shakur said nothing. The unspoken gangster code about women—especially those who were considered groupies—was that unless you claimed one as your "girl," they were to be shared with the whole crew. Holding out would be considered a sign of weakness. And Shakur, always aware of his street rep, made a decision he would later regret.

"How do I look saying 'Hold on'?" Shakur reasoned in his interview with Powell. "That would be making her my girl. I'm not making her close like that." Shakur said he left the room, sat down on the couch, and fell asleep.

His next memory, he said, was of being woken up by Agnant. He felt groggy. The lights had been turned up.

"The whole mood had changed," Shakur recalled. "When I woke up, it felt like I had been drugged. I didn't know how much time had passed."

Jackson was screaming and crying. "Why did you let them do this to me?" she demanded of Shakur. "I came to see you! You let them do this to me! This is not the last time you're going to hear from me," he recalled her saying.

Moments later, Shakur received a call from his publicist to come down to the hotel lobby. As soon as he stepped out of the elevator, police pounced on him.

Shakur, Agnant, and Fuller were arrested on the spot. They would be bailed out that same night, but Shakur refused to use Agnant's lawyer, who was affiliated with the PBA, a police union.

Shakur's lawyer, Michael Warren, had lots of questions about Agnant but Shakur refused to tell him anything. "I wouldn't give up no information about these guys," he said. "I thought they were criminals; I needed to protect them from the world."

Shakur's lawyer now believes that Agnant was a confidential informant working with police. Warren said that he had a long rap sheet in different states, but never seemed to do any time. Agnant was able to have his case separated from that of Shakur and Fuller, and he pleaded guilty to sexual misconduct, receiving probation. As Pac's case moved closer to trial, communication between the men dwindled. Shakur and Agnant would never speak again.

Shakur spent the morning of Tuesday, November 29, 1994, at 100 Centre Street in courtroom 677, where the Honorable Judge Daniel P. Fitzgerald was presiding over his trial for sodomy, sexual abuse, and weapons possession. Shakur sat next to his codefendant Charles "Man" Fuller with an impassive expression as he listened to Assistant District Attorney Melissa Mourges argue why both men deserved the maximum, 25 years. Today was judgment day: after closing arguments by both sides, the jury would convene and then deliver their verdict. Though he was usually restrained in court, Shakur saved his bold statements for the horde of press waiting outside the courtroom for a juicy quote. As witty and verbose as Muhammad Ali in his prime, Tupac seldom disappointed. "No matter what happens," he told the pack of reporters that afternoon, "innocent or guilty, my life is ruined."

Even before the verdict was read, Shakur's reputation suffered as a result of the rape charge. His friend, director John Singleton, who had cast him opposite Janet Jackson in *Poetic Justice*, was forced to drop him from the movie *Higher Learning* at the urging of Columbia Pictures execs. Shakur was furious, and the two former friends fell out over it. Pac's biggest crossover hit was "Keep Your Head Up," a heartfelt tribute to black women, which took brothers to task for disrespecting them—asking, at one point, "Why do we rape our women?" Now, in the press and on the street, black women were taking him to task.

"This trial is all about my image. It has nothing to do with me," said Shakur. "This is what I do for a living. I'm selling records. Don't get it twisted. This is not my life." Shakur steadfastly maintained his innocence from the start. He made no apologies for connecting with many of the women who threw themselves at him from coast to coast. But why would he need to force himself on anyone when there were so many women willing to do whatever he asked? Almost nobody who knew Tupac before he was became 2Pac believed he was guilty of rape. But they worried about his judgment when it came to his friends—friends who didn't always have his best interests at heart. But Shakur could be stubborn.

"I had already got a call from Mike Tyson saying, 'Pac, don't hang with Jack, he's bad news,' Shakur said. 'But I thought Tyson was being paranoid, so I was like, 'I'm not going to leave Jack until I see it for myself.'" But when Agnant had his court case separated, Shakur had a change of heart. "I was angry," he said. "I put it in the newspapers."

A "hanger-on" is what Shakur called Agnant in an item that appeared in A. J. Benza's popular gossip page in New York's *Daily News*. At the time the celebrity grapevine was buzzing about Shakur dating Madonna and hanging out with Mickey Rourke. But those in the know read the quote about Agnant and anticipated trouble. Word was out on the street—they had beef. "This was the first time I had ever said anything against him," Shakur said. "So I was nervous, waiting for him to attack."

At this point Big and Pac were still cool. Pac had understood when the song they recorded together did not make *Ready to Die*. But he was disappointed that he wasn't even thanked in the album's liner notes. "I heard a lot of Pac in that album," said Money B of Digital Underground, the Oakland crew that gave Shakur his start in the rap game. "He was not even mentioned, no shout-out, nothing. I was like, Pac's gonna be mad."

Mad or not, that didn't stop them from hanging out. "We'd get on the train and go meet him at whatever hotel he was staying in," remembered D-Roc. In March 1994, journalist and filmmaker dream hampton captured one such session on a video camera purchased by Shakur. The men smoked blunts and drank Hennessy in Shakur's hotel room at the Royalton in midtown Manhattan.

"I'm staying right here in this little-ass room," Shakur said. "Nigga got to stay out of trouble."

Shakur pulled out a tiny wireless microphone he had just picked up from a spy store. "From now on, bitch wanna fuck with me, I'm getting it all on tape," he told Big, laughing. "Whatchusay? You wanna give me some pussy . . . repeat that? What's that? You want to engage in consensual sex in my hotel room?"

He pondered aloud whether he should use the device to record his so-called friends, to see if they would plot against him while he was out of the room. He imagined coming back into the room Chow Yun Fat–style, guns blazing, *"Blaow! Blaow! Blaow!"*

All jokes aside, Shakur showed visible concern for his safety. Before leaving the room, he changed shirts, and then slid into a bulletproof vest.

"Good luck catching a cab," Wallace said, giving Shakur a quick embrace.

"That's all I got is good luck," Shakur said.

But Shakur's luck was running out. He and Fuller were still the only ones on trial for raping Jackson.

Weeks later, Shakur ran into Agnant at Puffy's party at Roseland. He was shocked to see him among Christopher Wallace's entourage. " I was hurt," Shakur fumed. "I was like, I'm going to trial, I'm probably going to get convicted, and this nigga's showing up at a party with champagne, hanging with Biggie. I was like, Damn, he's just bouncing from rapper to rapper."

Wallace greeted Shakur warmly at the party, introducing him to Faith. As soon as they had a few moments alone, Wallace pulled Shakur aside.

"You still kicking it with Jack?" Shakur recalled Wallace asking him.

"No."

"Don't," Wallace told him. "Be careful." Shakur was struck by the

Inside the studio Junior M.A.F.I.A. was recording "Players Anthem." The mood in the room was celebratory. Wallace was nodding his head to the beat when Cease said, "Yo Big, I just seen Pac outside."

fact that two different people with strong Brooklyn roots—Biggie and Iron Mike—had each warned him about the same man.

"We knew of them, but we didn't know them like that," said Lil' Cease of Agnant. "That was Pac's friend. Those were his people. We did our own separate thing with Pac."

At the party Shakur simply ignored Agnant, never acknowledging his presence. This was a serious no-no. Even bitter rivals, when caught in public but neutral territory, were supposed to recognize each other with eye contact and the briefest of nods. But Shakur kept on talking to Wallace, never looking in Agnant's direction.

"Even though I didn't like them, I used to pretend," Shakur said. "But now I couldn't pretend no more, because I knew they were snakes. When I saw them with Biggie, that's what let me know they were snakes. I was like, 'Damn, they just bounce to the next nigga.' They weren't sending me any money. They weren't trying to help me through my charges, even though it was them that set me up. I was through with these niggas."

As Shakur's trial dragged on, he was becoming desperate for cash. Because of the trial, he couldn't leave the city to do any performances. Even if he could, few people would book him due to the perceived security risks. Despite his skills as an actor, no completion bond company would insure a studio for his contract, which virtually blacklisted him from feature film work. He had been talking to Andre Harrell, executive producer of *New York Undercover,* about appearing on the TV show, but Harrell knew that it would take a lot of convincing to get Dick Wolf and the Fox network to approve an appearance. "They don't want to get involved with too many people that have controversial issues going on," Harrell said, "like open rape cases."

Shakur's back was against the wall. One of the few outlets left for Shakur to express himself and make some money was the recording studio. Most of the earnings from his shows, and royalties from his last album, the multiplatinum *Strictly 4 My N.I.G.G.A.Z.,* went to cover various legal fees as well as supporting members of his family. When he wasn't in court, Shakur spent much of his time in the recording studio, pouring his frustration into his next album, *Me Against the World.* Shakur did not specialize in the nimble cadences and intricate internal rhymes that were Biggie's forte. But what he lacked in technique, Tupac made up for in raw emotion and naked emotional truth. Songs like "Dear Mama" and "If I Die Tonight" were masterpieces of pain and frustration.

"Pac was going to court by day most of the time," remembered Mo Bee. "When he'd come out of court, it'd be six or seven o'clock by the time he got to Unique Studios. Then BOOM! Tupac would bust through the door and be like, 'Mo Bee, throw me some weed!' He used to be stressed-out, so when he came in the studio, he was ready to spit. He would do everything in one take. When we did 'If I Die Tonight,' all of that anger and everything—I just seen it, man."

Shakur was so quick on the microphone—and was having such trouble getting film parts, due to legal troubles and bad publicity—that whenever he needed money, he'd go to the recording studio. His system was cash on delivery. As long as the producer had his money ready, he'd come record a freestyle.

November 29—the evening of his jury deliberations—was one such night. Shakur needed cash. He needed an escape. And he also felt the need to drop a hot tune since he knew it might be a while before folks heard from him again. His first stop was to visit the uptown apartment of mix-tape king Ron G. For another DJ, a Tupac session would run several thousand dollars, but Shakur did his verse for Ron G on the strength. A hot cameo on a Ron G tape could be worth its weight in gold, waking up New York's rap underground and helping Pac reconnect with his East Coast roots.

While he was finishing up with Ron G, Shakur's pager went off—Little Shawn's manager was calling. Again. The rapper, who had become well-known for a novelty record called "Hickies on Your Chest," had asked Shakur to appear on a song with him and Biggie. Despite his reservations about working with anyone who was friends with Agnant, Shakur needed the money.

Pac called back and set his price. "You get me seven G's and I'll do the song."

"All right," the manager told him. "I got your money."

Shakur took his time after finishing the song with Ron G. They picked up some food and hooked up with a couple more friends and stopped at a weed spot. After an hour or so, the studio paged him again.

"Where you at? Why you ain't coming?"

"I'm on my way," Shakur said. They got in a car drove down to the studio.

While they were in the car, Shawn's manager called again to say he didn't have the money.

"If you don't have the money," Shakur replied, "I'm not coming."

The manager called back within minutes. "I'll give you the money out my pocket," he said. "I'm gonna call Andre and make sure you get the money."

They parked the car near Times Square, and all four men—Shakur, Walker, his friend Freddie Moore, and Zane, the boyfriend of Pac's younger sister—walked to Quad Studios. As they drew near the building they heard a voice from above.

"Yo, Pac!"

Shakur looked up and saw Lil' Cease high on a balcony at Quad Studios, a blunt burning between his lips. He waved at Shakur. Shakur waved back. Behind his bloodshot eyes, the 24-year-old rapper was fatigued, stressed, and paranoid. But he seemed happy to see a friendly face.

"Yo Cease, what up?" he hollered. "What the fuck you doing?"

"We up in the studio." Cease replied. "I'ma come down and get you and bring you upstairs." Seeing one of Wallace's closest friends put Cease at ease too. But it was the last pleasant exchange the two men would ever have.

Cease came off the terrace to back inside the studio where "Players Anthem," the first big hit from the Junior M.A.F.I.A. album, was being recorded. Wallace was running the session, nodding his head as the chorus blasted: "Grab your dicks if you love hip hop." The mood of the room was celebratory and the Junior M.A.F.I.A posse was excited. This was the first song they had ever recorded, and for some was their first time in a big time studio. They had finally arrived.

Lil' Cease walked towards Wallace.

"Hey, Big, I just seen Pac," said Cease.

"Pac's outside?" Wallace asked.

"I'm gonna go downstairs and get him," Cease said.

"Bring him up here," Wallace said.

A few floors down from the Junior M.A.F.I.A. session, Mark Pitts and Sean Combs sat in the lounge, talking to Andre Harrell.

Combs had just finished shooting his portion of the Hype Williams video for "Warning," a shot of him driving down Seventh Avenue, the lights of Times

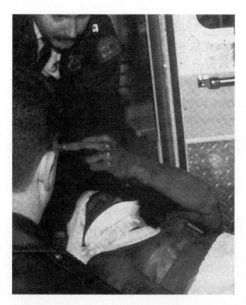

Square reflecting off the car. He saw a member of his Bad Boy Records staff heading toward Quad Studios. He knew Wallace was working with Junior M.A.F.I.A. that night, but didn't realize the session was so close by.

Combs had originally decided to stop by the studio to check on Big, but when he got off the elevator, he saw his old boss, Andre Harrell.

Harrell saw Combs and smiled. Even though they'd had their differences, he was happy to see his young protégé doing well for himself. In fact, everything going on at Quad Studios was the realization of a dream Harrell had had since he was a young boy growing up in the Bronx. There were four sessions going on in separate studios, each representing the future of black music: SWV was on one floor, Deborah Cox on another, along with the harder sounds of Mobb Deep, Junior M.A.F.I.A., and Lil' Shawn. So

After being beaten, shot, and robbed in the lobby of a New York recording studio, Shakur was sure he had been set up. He became mistrustful of everyone, even old friends like Wallace.

many people were dropping in on each other's sessions that the whole studio complex felt like one big party. For a while.

"Puffy just came up the elevator and everyone was happy to see him," said Harrell. "We was just sitting there, and everybody was just kind of reminiscing. From my era going all the way back to the current era with the new generation of young producers and music executives. Hope was in the air and success was all around. So everybody was excited about Pac comin' in. We were starting to get antsy, like, 'Where's Pac?' It was just excited energy for him to arrive and see how this was getting ready to set off."

Shakur was not feeling the party vibe. As soon as he and his crew entered the studio lobby, he knew something was amiss.

"There was a dude out there with army fatigues with a hat low on his face," Shakur said. "And when we walked to the door, he didn't look up. I've never seen a black man not acknowledge me one way or the other, either with jealousy or respect. I get either one, always. But it didn't click to me yet, because I had just finished smoking chronic."

Shakur, Stretch, Moore, and Zane entered the lobby and looked around.

"While we're waiting by the door to get buzzed in, I saw a dude sitting at a table reading a newspaper. Both these guys were in their thirties. At first I'm like, these dudes must be security for Biggie. I could tell they were from Brooklyn from the army fatigues. But then when they didn't look up I said, 'Wait a minute. Biggie's homeboys love me.'"

Stretch also thought the guy at the door might have been a part of Wallace's extended Brooklyn family. He sensed nothing unusual when the man in fatigues walked into the lobby behind them. "He looked like somebody who was with Big, or somebody from Brooklyn," said Stretch. "I had just seen Cease and them upstairs, so I figured that it's probably crowded upstairs."

As he pressed the elevator button, Shakur turned around to tell Stretch that something didn't feel right—but by then it was too late. The strangers in camouflage pulled out two identical 9-millimeter semiautomatic pistols.

"Don't nobody move!" they yelled. "Everybody on the floor! You know what time it is. Run your shit. Run your shit!" Tupac just stood there.

Shakur turned to tell Stretch something didn't feel right—but by then it was too late. The strangers in camouflage pulled out two identical nine millimeter pistols. "Everybody on the floor! You know what time it is."

"All my homeboys dropped to the floor," Shakur said, "but I wasn't going to get on the floor. I'm thinking Stretch is going to fight because Stretch is so big he was towering over these niggas. And from what I know about the criminal element, if niggas come to rob you and they see the big nigga, they always hit the big nigga first. But they didn't touch Stretch. They came straight to me. Everybody dropped to the floor like potatoes. I'm the only nigga who didn't go to the floor."

From his vantage point on the ground, Stretch couldn't figure out why Shakur was still standing. He figured that it might have something to do with the fact that Shakur was the only one of the four men holding a gun.

"I'm the nigga that goes for mines," Stretch said later, "always forever. But I ain't no dumb nigga. Niggas run up to me with guns, and I ain't got no gun? What the fuck am I supposed to do? I ain't fighting no niggas with no guns. I can be towering over niggas, but I'm not towering over no slugs."

Shakur kept on standing. Less than thirty seconds had passed, but it felt like a whole hour.

"Take off your jewels," one of the gunmen said. But then the other seemed to be losing patience.

"Shoot that muthafucka!" he roared. "Fuck it!"

"Then I got scared," said Shakur, "because the dude had the gun to my stomach. All I could think about was piss bags and shit bags and all that shit. I drew my arm around him to try to move the gun to my side. He shot, and the gun twisted, and that's when I got shot the first time. I felt it in my leg. I didn't know I got shot in my balls. Everything in my mind said, 'Pac, pretend you're dead. Do not move no more so they don't shoot you no more.' It didn't matter. They started kicking me, hitting me. They wasn't touching nobody else. They were snatching my shit off me while I was laying on the floor.' That's when he felt a blow to the back of his head. "I thought they stomped me or pistol-whipped me, and they were stomping my head against the concrete. I just saw white, just white, and I didn't hear nothing. . . .And then they hit me again, and I could hear things and I could see things, and I knew I was conscious again."

Cease and Nino Brown of JM rode the elevator downstairs to meet Pac. Cease was excited; he admired Shakur and enjoyed his music. It still tripped Cease out to be in a recording studio working on his own Junior M.A.F.I.A. record. If Wallace hadn't blown up, he might still be on the corner selling drugs.

But those pleasant thoughts were interrupted as soon as the elevator door opened. They saw Shakur and Walker laying down on the floor. At first Cease thought they were playing around, drunk. But as soon as they stepped a foot closer, Cease and Nino saw two men in fatigues, one standing over Shakur and taking off his $40,000 pieces of jewelry.

"Get the fuck back on the elevator," one of the men in fatigues said. They did.

The assailants promptly ran out into Times Square. There was momentary silence in the room as everybody tried to figure out what had just happened. Walker saw blood running from a wound in Shakur's head. They needed help. Shakur, Stretch, Zane, and Fred stumbled outside. A stripper who worked at the club next door was standing outside.

"Pac starts screaming for the police," Stretch remembered. "We asked this bitch, 'What did you see. Did you see something? Where'd the niggas go?' And the bitch was like, 'I don't know nothing. I didn't see nothing.'" They went back inside the studio building.

While one elevator took Shakur and Walker upstairs, Cease and Nino had already jumped on the other to alert the Junior M.A.F.I.A. session about what was going on.

"Yo, Big!" Cease said. "Pac downstairs getting robbed right now."

'You fuckin' lying," Wallace said.

"I'm serious. Homeboy's getting banged down right now and shit."

"Y'all niggas don't move," Wallace said, rushing to the elevator.

Fifteen minutes passed. No Big. Cease went down to see what was taking him so long. When the elevator door opened, a police officer stood there, his gun drawn and pointed at Big and Chico.

"Police was hemming us up," Lil' Cease said. "Taking down our information. They was saying he was dead. So that's what happened. But he was coming to the studio anyway. You know what I'm saying? He wasn't coming there to see us."

Just then the elevator door opened on the floor where the Lil' Shawn session was taking place. Shakur stumbled out. Bloody. Wounded. Pissed. Mistrustful of everything and everyone.

Stretch and Zane followed him out. Andre Harrell was there. Puffy was there. All in various degrees of shock. "You were the only one who knew I was coming," Pac said, mistrustful of everything and everyone.

During the wait for the police to show up, the studio began to thin out. "They immediately knew the rules," Harrell recalled. "They knew the type of police that was coming and what was involved. Since there was a head wound, the case would be investigated by the homicide guys in the suits." Unlike uniformed patrolmen, homicide cops had the right to frisk anybody. Everybody started whispering, 'Yo, Homicide is coming.' Everybody united on one front," said Harrell. "The inner-city young black male Public Enemy Number One front.

"The main thing all of them were concerned about was the frisk," Harrell continued. "Because people evidently had guns. I didn't see guns, but I realized niggas was starting to talk about stashing they joint. And Puff was standing in front of me and I looked in Puff's eyes, and Puff's eyes opened when he heard about the detectives coming. And I remember thinking, You mean *you* got a gun!? I didn't say that, but he was looking at me like, I don't want you to know I got a gun, Dre. And I was looking at him like, What you got a gun for?"

As Wallace said in the song, "Things Done Changed." Could this really be the same eager intern whom Harrell had taken under his wing three years ago? The same one who addressed him as Mr. Harrell and wore bow ties to work was now rolling with thugs and acting like a real "bad boy."

"It made me realize that the element of energy being young and black right now in the inner city is so violent that young people just feel the need to have that level just in case," Harrell said sadly. "If it goes there, they got the potential at least to make them back off, because they're prepared to have the final say. And you know, gun play is the final say."

Down in the lobby there was blood on the floor, police were everywhere, and yellow crime scene was tape going up. The police wouldn't let Wallace back upstairs to where Tupac was. Then the elevator door opened and Shakur was carried out on a flat stretcher by two paramedics. They had cut off his clothes, and he was wearing a neck brace. As he was being loaded in the ambulance, a photographer emerged from the shadows. Even in his weakened condition, Shakur managed to give him the finger.

Fading in and out of consciousness as the ambulance made its way to Bellevue Hospital, Shakur kept asking himself, "Who did this?" He was sure it wasn't a random robbery. "They were mad at me," Shakur continued. "I felt them kicking and stomping me; they didn't hit nobody else." "First I was thinking that it was the girl and her people, because we had an argument in court one day." But he kept thinking. The attack was coming on the day before the verdict, and soon after he'd dissed his former codefendant in the *Daily News*. He said that the assailants reminded him of "the type of niggas Jack was introducing me to."

Inside the trauma unit, doctors surrounded him, marveling that he was still alive, let alone conscious. "The doctors were going, Oh my God! Oh my God! They were scaring me," Shakur said. "I didn't feel no pain, really... They started cleaning and sewing me up. The whole time I'm talking and joking with people."

"You don't know how lucky you are," one doctor told him.

"What are you talking about?" Shakur replied.

"You got shot five times."

The next afternoon Shakur was rushed into surgery to repair a damaged blood vessel on his right leg. He was out of surgery by 4 P.M. and—against the will of his doctors—checked himself out by 6:45. He had been in the hospital less than 15 hours. "I haven't seen anybody in my twenty-five-year professional career leave the hospital like this," said his surgeon, Dr. Leon Patcher.

Shakur said the unfamiliar faces of doctors poking around him were too upsetting. And he didn't like that people knew where he had been taken. "My life was in danger," Shakur said. "I knew what type of niggas I was

After Pac was admitted to the hospital, Big tried to visit him, but he had already checked out, fearing for his safety. Wallace and Shakur would never exchange a friendly word again.

dealing with."

According to Cease, Tupac had a gun on him when he was attacked. It was stashed in a piano at the studio before the police arrived.

"Big went back to the studio, got [Pac's] burner, and took it to him at the hospital," said Cease. But Tupac had already checked out.

On Thursday, December 1, two days after the shooting, Shakur surprised everyone by appearing in Judge Fitzgerald's courtroom to hear his verdict. His entrance was characteristically dramatic, as he was rolled in with a wheelchair, his head swathed in bandages and covered with a wool Yankees ski cap. He sat there for four hours, until 2 P.M., leaving for Metropolitian Hospital Center on East 97th street, due to the numbness he felt in his leg.

"I knew I had to show up no matter what," he said. "I swear to God, the furthest thing on my mind was sympathy. I just thought, I want to show them that I'm standing up for my responsibilities. All I could think of was—stand up and fight for your life, like you fought for your life in the hospital. So I came to court."

The newspapers, however, read his appearance as a naked plea for sympathy and near jury manipulation. The timing of the incident made some skeptics believe that Shakur himself might have set it up. "What thug would want to shoot Tupac?" went the thinking. "Tupac is a thug hero."

No matter. Within hours of his departure, the jury found Shakur guilty of fondling the plaintiff against her will—but innocent of the much more serious weapons and sodomy charges. A few jurors had even argued for a full acquittal due to lack of evidence, but were outvoted.

Because of his medical condition Shakur remained free on $25,000 bond. He checked into Metropolitan Hospital under the name Bob Day. They told him nobody knew he was there, but he kept getting strange phone calls. "The phone was ringing and I answered it and a man would say, 'You ain't dead yet?'"

Still, Shakur couldn't bring himself to cooperate with the police.

"When the police said, 'Who shot you!' I was like, 'I don't know,'" Shakur said. "And I knew the dudes' faces as clear as hell. They'll never leave my head. But I didn't want to tell the police. I don't know why, but I couldn't even tell them about Jack and them."

Shakur checked out of Metropolitan and stayed at the apartment of actress Jasmine Guy, a longtime friend of his, under the care of a private doctor, and a security force made up of the Nation of Islam's Fruit of Islam security detail and his mother's friends in the Black Panther Party, revolutionaries who had known him his entire life.

While there, he had recurring dreams about being shot, hearing voices screaming, "Shoot that muthafucka." Waking up with sweats. Two weeks later, Shakur read a piece in the *Village Voice* called "The Professional: Tupac Shakur Gives the Performance of His Life." Touré's brilliant but scathing piece compared Shakur's life to an open-ended work of conceptual art. His lifetime practice of intermingling his life and his art had raised the question of whether he was truly in pain or just an actor giving the most brilliant performance of his life.

Toure called Shakur "a master performance artist whose canvas is his body, and whose stage is the world. If Tupac escapes jail time, he's the Teflon don, able to leap multiple convictions in a single bound. If he's locked down, he's the realest of the real, going back to his roots (remember, he was in jail as a fetus). Either eventuality carries the bonus of keeping him onstage, which for all its surface political insubstantiality gets at the heart of a very black male necessity: Through all the contradictions and posturing and bullshit, it's really about nothing more than never for a single moment being invisible."

After he read the article, Shakur said he closed the paper and cried "like a bitch. It just tore me apart. That's what helped me see that I had to be for myself."

In January of 1995, Shakur did exactly that. He went for self.

When Shakur agreed to meet with VIBE correspondant Kevin Powell in the visiting room at Riker's Island during the weeks while he awaited sentencing; in his mind his image, his integrity, and his life were on the line. He was alone, behind bars, unable to promote his upcoming album, and feeling as if he might be forced to spend his best years locked up, with the people around him powerless to do anything. Whether or not it was true, he felt certain that people in prison wanted to kill him—and might succeed. The bad press, the shooting, and all the frustration of the past two years had reached a boiling point. So he did what he'd done his entire life, for better or for worse.

He spoke his mind.

In one of the most controversial interviews in modern music journalism, Shakur let it all hang out. He named names about who he thought set him up—Agnant. (The magazine, for legal reasons, substituted the pseudonym "Nigel.") He accused Andre Harrell, "Puffy" Combs, Lil' Cease, and Christopher Wallace as being complicit because they were all present that night. He even implied that his road dog Stretch Walker might have been in on the set up. He went on to compare himself to Marvin Gaye and Vincent Van Gogh. Like them, he felt that his genius would not be appreciated until after he was dead. He also declared that Thug Life, the movement he had once championed (the name was an acronym for "The Hate U Give Little Infants Fucks Everybody) was now dead.

"This Thug Life stuff, it was just ignorance," Shakur told Powell. "My intentions was always in the right place. I never killed anybody, I never raped anybody,

I never committed no crimes that weren't honorable—that weren't to defend myself. So that's what I'm going to show them. I'm going to show people my true intentions, and my true heart. I'm going to show them the man that my mom raised. I'm gonna make them all proud."

Harrell, Combs, Wallace, and Walker, and others mentioned in the article were asked to comment before the Q&A was published, but they declined.

During a break in a studio session, Combs read an advance of the Shakur-Powell cover story that was circulating around the music industry like wildfire.

"We say nothing," Combs told Wallace. "Niggas come up to you, start asking questions, reporters start asking you shit . . . Nothing. Complete silence."

Wallace nodded.

Combs himself was heated, but his former mentor urged calm. Harrell focused on Shakur's statements toward the end of the article that reflected his growing maturity, not the rants and raves of a firebrand who had just been shot, and was confused and frustrated about his fate.

"This was a major issue for Puff, that he was being portrayed as a sucker," Harrell said later. "I looked at him and said, 'Nigga, you've said worse things about me. And me and you got an ongoing love affair. I don't give a fuck about all that. It will pass, nigga.' "

But it didn't pass. Instead, the accusations were about to become an all-out war. A few weeks after the piece ran, they all went on the record with Fab 5 Freddy to deny Shakur's allegations.

At the time, Christopher Wallace had other things to think about: his career. His record label. His marriage. His family. He didn't have time to stop and ponder why a close friend, who should have known he was innocent, thought he helped set him up.

"Why would Big do something like that?" Lil' Cease said. "[Tupac] knows where Big's mom lives. He know where Big stay at. I called you upstairs. You my nigga. Hell no, I didn't know about it. Why would I come downstairs if it was a setup? I wouldn't want it to be known I was there if that's what it was. Nigga, I saw you. I was calling you upstairs. I'm telling you to come to me. I ain't know you was coming to work. I just so happened to see you then told niggas you was gonna be downstairs. He wasn't telling the real story. Big got a record deal just like he got one. Big is promised the same career this nigga got. Why would Big want to set him up?"

Shakur repeated his accusations in other interviews, and they seemed to get more virulent with each retelling. "I used to share my experiences in the game and my lessons, and my rules, and my knowledge on the game with [Wallace]," Shakur said. "He owed me more than to turn his head and act like he didn't know niggas was about to blow my fuckin' head off. He knew."

"That's when I lost respect for him," Cease said. "He went against the grain on some real niggas that was holding him down. Big used to have us taking risks for that nigga, because that was the love that Big had for him." Lil' Cease searched for an explanation. "He was kinda paranoid and I think Big was just his target to take his frustrations out on."

"But damn, you supposed to be our nigga," Cease continued. "Why would you think a nigga would really do that to you? And then to really go with it and try to make you look like the foulest, punkest muthafucka out there. I thought that was foul. Nigga, we kept it to the utmost realness with you... And you really trying to destroy a nigga."

Wallace reacted to Shakur's scathing comments not with anger, but with confusion—and concern. He acted as if Pac was still his boy, and the whole thing was all a misunderstanding.

"You get shot and then you go to jail for something you ain't even do—that could twist a nigga's mind up," Wallace told Fab 5 Freddy. "But I want an apology.

"He knows that I was at the hospital with his mother when he got shot in that studio," Wallace would say two years later. "He knows me and Stretch was there. He knows after he left the hospital and went to his girl house uptown, me and Stretch went up in some weed spots to get this nigga a half ounce of weed, and bring him some weed to his girl crib. He know this."

"There was a whole bunch of shit that went down, man," Wallace continued. "Shit that I really can't talk about, that I was there for that nigga. That shit hurt me, man. It hurt me."

Wallace always figured that, over time, the paranoia and confusion of those tumultuous days would work themselves. He figured that he would run into Shakur sooner or later, sit down, and iron everything out. The situation was hot, but he was sure it would eventually cool off.

Wallace was wrong. Dead wrong.

MO MONEY,
MO PROBLEMS

CHAPTER 6

❝I be that cat you see at all events bent
Gats in holsters girls on shoulders
Playboy, I told ya...**❞**

By the summer of 1995, Christopher Wallace was no longer the same kid standing near the corner of St. James and Fulton wondering if he was going to rely on rap or crack to keep little T'Yanna in OshKosh B'Gosh. No longer did he have to try to convince his mother that yes, people did think he had talent as a composer and performer even though he couldn't sing. No longer was he merely "a chubby nigga on the scene"—as he'd put it on his first record, released just two years earlier.

Now he was a star.

Wallace had single-handedly dismantled the notion that the East Coast's rock-solid fan base would rather listen to a mix tape or buy a bootleg than purchase a full album by an artist they loved. "My album dropped on Friday the thirteenth, when I was on the road and niggas was betting on how much I was selling per week!" he bragged to his friend Bönz Malone in his first *Source* cover story. "I sold damn near a quarter of a million records in New York, dog! That's damn near impossible! Nothing gonna stop me from lettin' me or my family eat."

Ready to Die had gone double platinum and was still rocking the clubs. The million-selling remix to "One More Chance" would eventually knock Michael Jackson's "You Are Not Alone" out of the top spot on *Billboard*'s pop singles chart. By the end of the year, Michael Jackson would invite Wallace to record a rhyme on Jackson's song "This Time Around."

The makers of the rap documentary *Rhyme & Reason* captured the moment when Wallace unwrapped his RIAA-certified platinum plaque for *Ready to Die*. Dressed in a butter leather jacket, Kangol, and Versace shades, Big Poppa was characteristically laid-back, but at the same time visibly happy about his success.

"I'll have to prop these up," he said. "First Brooklyn nigga to go platinum, you know. It's all good. Got my gold joint from 'Juicy.' Straight out the 'hood, a nigga did good."

Videos like "One More Chance" and "Big Poppa" seemed to be on television constantly. Ever since Dr. Dre's *The Chronic* had so much success, MTV had begun to loosen its stance on playing rap videos outside the confines of *Yo! MTV Raps*. Snoop could now appear in heavy rotation next to the Metallicas and Pearl Jams of the world. White middle-class kids who were weaned on Vanilla Ice and MC Hammer now wanted the real deal—and they gravitated to hardcore rap. Dr. Dre created the formula with *The Chronic* and perfected it with Snoop Doggy Dogg's *Doggystyle*—pop songs that kept the hardcore attitude of the sound intact, rendered broadcast-ready by radio edits that, somehow, didn't castrate the groove.

DJ Enuff, who played the beats for Biggie when he went on tour, said Big openly admired these West Coast stars. "I remember Big always saying, 'I wanna be like Snoop, I wanna be like Dre and them. Like, I wanna get it the way they're getting it.' It was very important to him. That was the same kind of level he wanted." While it seemed that Snoop and Dre, Ice Cube, and Cypress Hill had the video and sales charts in a lock, Wallace was the first MC to bring mainstream acclaim back to the East Coast. And it was one of those Puffy songs that Big didn't want to record—the G-funk player rhyme "Big Poppa"—that was responsible for that paradigm shift.

The creative tension started back when they were selecting the first single from *Ready to Die*. Wallace wanted "Machine Gun Funk" to be his introduction to the world—a great song, but definitely aimed directly at New York's hoodies-and-boots hip hop audience. It might not have moved folks in Milwaukee. Combs tried to push the music in an R&B direction, knowing that Wallace's lyrical delivery would always have hardcore appeal. He urged Biggie to look beyond the borough of Brooklyn and take the chance of crossing over with "Juicy," a reworking of Mtume's 1983 electrofunk hit "Juicy Fruit."

"Puffy was on some, 'Yo, let's get rich' shit," remembered Wallace. "He said, 'If you put out 'Juicy' you'll have a gold single.' I wasn't even with 'Juicy,' but he's saying, 'Let's go get the money,' so I'm like, fuck it."

DJ Enuff witnessed the impact of Puffy's strategies firsthand on the road. "The early records, like 'Gimme the Loot' and 'Warning' and 'Unbelievable,' were all good records," he said. "But it wasn't until 'Big Poppa' and 'One More Chance,' the remix, that the rest of the country was, like, wow! this guy is dope. He's not just an East Coast MC." Still Biggie wasn't always comfortable in the crossover role. He knew how quickly rap's core audience could turn on a star who got too gassed up. "I remember Big huffing and puffing, like, I gotta do this 'cause Puff says so," Enuff recalled. "He wasn't really too happy about it.

Even though Biggie might say, 'Fuck what Puffy says,' when Puffy came around, he'd do exactly what Puffy told him to do, you know what I mean? 'Cause he knew it was right."

The compromise was the B-side. Wallace agreed to "Juicy" as long as it was back by his "gutter" joint "Unbelievable"—the best rap B-side since Public Enemy's "Rebel Without a Pause." The single went gold and Wallace got major airplay, yet he lost no credibility. "My niggas weren't mad at me," Wallace said, relieved, "so I was straight."

But the creative tension returned when Puff announced that he wanted to follow up with "Big Poppa." The last song that Wallace recorded for *Ready to Die* was also the last song that Wallace ever wanted to release as a single. But Combs prevailed again, and it was becoming clear that Daddy knew best. The smooth Moog sound and the Isley Brothers' "Between the Sheets" loop gave the song a West Coast feel, as if it was something off *The Chronic,* but Wallace's lyrics, even without the profanity, gave the song an East Coast underground feel. The single (backed by the chilling crime narrative "Warning") sold a million copies.

"It's a straight commercial joint," Wallace said. "But at the same time I'm talking about getting girls pregnant, I'm telling niggas I got infrared on my heat. I still spit that shit that makes niggas be like 'All right, he be kickin' some shit!' I think the mistake other niggas make is they say, 'Fuck it, we gonna come out with a radio joint too.' They get their little loop, but they just be so clean, it's corny. Put it like this: I coulda did the same song to a hard beat and you wouldn't have ever known. It was just the beat that made it commercial."

The video also expanded the song's commercial prospects. Hype Williams, with his slow motion tracking shots, beautiful lighting, and ingenious use of color filters, greatly expanded the look and feel of rap music video, helping the genre keep up with rock videos. The video for "Big Poppa" was no different. Not only did the clip change the way that the Notorious B.I.G. was portrayed, it altered the entire landscape of what was considered hip hop by offering a glimpse of a new lifestyle: ghetto fabulous.

"The power of images is like the power of the word—it conveys a thought," said Williams. "Whatever that thought is transcends having to take the time to elaborate. People can draw any particular conclusion they want from what they see." What the director gave them to see was young black men enjoying the good life: Wallace and his friends dressed to the nines, popping bottles of expensive champagne, rapping to gorgeous ladies in a chic nightclub. Combs spent the whole video soaking in a hot tub with his blond pony-tailed girlfriend Misa Hylton-Brim—the stylist who had first convinced him that Big was not too ugly to be a star. Nobody was aware of it yet, but a change was coming.

Hip hop fashion had gone through many phases—from track suits, Kangol hats, sneakers, and gold chains to jeans, work boots, and oversized hoodies. Before that video, no self-respecting hardcore rapper would be caught dead in a designer suit. But "Big Poppa" changed all that. "There was no Versace, none of that shit, before 'Big Poppa,' " Williams said. "Before he did that, Biggie was wearing camouflage. Nobody knew it was going to turn into an era of everybody wearing all this fuckin' jewelry and shit."

Sean Combs wasn't the only influence on Wallace's choice of clothes. Voletta Wallace could just as easily be blamed for the birth of ghetto fabulous.

"No rappers out there look good," Voletta Wallace would often tell her son. "I'm sure their clothes cost a million dollars, and their shoes are expensive, but they look like bums. Do not embarrass me on television. I don't want you going up there looking like a bum."

Her fashion standards may have been high, but Ms. Wallace was pragmatic. She saved her money and invested in things. Her credit was impeccable. Remembering her son's quick-money past, she worried about how he was handling his finances. "I'm reading things," Ms. Wallace said, keeping up with the rap press. "Okay, he's got a house. He got himself a car. He got two cars. Okay, he's fine. So Christopher, please, do you have any money?"

"Ma, I'll never be poor again," he told her. "Trust me, Ma. If I have a question about my money at five o'clock in the morning, I'm calling my accountant, How much money I got?"

"Okay, but if you read about Hammer, who was up there doing very well, he went bankrupt," she warned him. "Christopher, please, keep your money."

Even though they kept the apartment on St. James, Wallace worked on getting his mother a place in Florida. It was the closest thing to Jamaica. But she wanted to be closer to home, so he looked into real estate in parts of New Jersey. She finally settled on Pennsylvania and he began making plans to build her a house out in the Poconos.

As for himself, while Brooklyn was in his heart, Wallace realized that being on his old street with his newfound wealth made him a target for stickup kids even more than when he was in the crack game. "Call the crib," he had rhymed on his album, "Same number, same 'hood, it's all good." But he understood the hustler's mentality well enough to know that he wouldn't be safe there forever. Just a few years ago if he had seen someone like himself slipping, showing off the cash, he'd have been tempted to make a jack move. So first he and Faith moved into a Fort Greene duplex, and then, subsequently, into a gated community in Teaneck, New Jersey.

"To me, if you stay in the same spot as you were in when you were doing nothing and now you're doing something, that's not progression," Wallace told a *New York Times* reporter who asked whether rappers had to live in their old neighborhoods in order to maintain street credibility. Wallace had always thought so, but he was beginning to change his mind about what "keeping it real" was all about. "Being real is taking care of your family, your mother, your children, and doing things with your money," he said. "When you think of doing well, you think of mansions. Ain't no mansions in Brooklyn. You don't want to deal with subways and gunshots. You want to be comfortable and safe."

Although he was out of the drug hustle, Wallace felt safest with a lot of firepower nearby. Visitors to his crib were impressed by the elevator, the oversized Jacuzzi, the bedroom decorated with framed posters of Al Pacino in *Scarface* or Marlon Brando in *The Godfather*. But most of all, they noticed the guns. "He had two joints with infrared scopes," remembers a visitor, "couple joints on the wall. He kept pulling out all these guns. It was kinda hot seeing that. I was like, Wow! But I was also kind of scared. He was kinda like the Godfather in his world."

Financing the new lifestyle took money. And money, which had always been a major focus for Wallace, became an even bigger concern. For the first time in his life, he had something to lose. His albums were selling like hotcakes, but it still wasn't always enough.

"I still haven't gotten money from [*Ready to Die*] itself yet," Wallace told VIBE in October 1995. This was after the album had already sold been certified double platinum. Two million times $15 per CD meant Wallace's debut had generated some $30 million in gross revenue—and Wallace still hadn't seen a dime. And it wasn't that Bad Boy and Arista were going out of their way to jerk Wallace. This was standard operating practice in the music industry.

Artists typically do not make any money from royalties until after the record company has "recouped" all the dollars it has spent. Everything from photo shoots and music videos down to every last caterer's tray, airplane ticket, and hour of studio time—all of it gets charged to the artist. If any money starts coming in from album and single sales, the person whose talent made the whole thing possible in the first place is the last to get paid. So if $5 million went into the marketing and promotion of *Ready to Die,* and Wallace's royalty rate was maybe $2 per record—at best—he would have to sell almost four million copies before he started seeing checks.

In Wallace's case, he did spend a lot of money, especially on the recording itself. He voiced many of the songs at the Hit Factory, one of the most expensive studios in Manhattan, which cost up to $3000 a day. Instead of writing his songs before getting there, Wallace would spend hours smoking weed and vibing on the beat before spitting his lyrics. He was capable of recording songs in a single take, but he had a tendency to ruthlessly critique his own performances. The whole process could take anywhere from six to twelve hours. Even if every session resulted in a classic song, time was money, and the time added up. Added to this, of course, was the close to one million dollars Combs had to pay Uptown to release tracks that had been previously recorded for Wallace's album, in addition to the costs of the new songs under the Bad Boy deal.

"I spent a lot and the record company had to recoup first," Wallace said. "That's why I sold half my publishing to Puffy." Publishing is where the money is made in the music business. Companies like ASCAP and BMI track the sales and radio play of every single song in their catalog—and there's a fee that goes along with virtually every use of a song. Michael Jackson purchased the rights to much of the Beatles song catalog for $47.5 million in 1985, a catalog that is now worth almost $1 billion. Every time a Beatles song gets played in public, John, Paul, Ringo, and George got checks—but Jackson, now the "fifth" Beatle, gets his check first. When Biggie sold 50 percent of his publishing rights, he collected $250,000 for a few minutes of signing. I was broke and if a nigga could make a quick quarter of a million just from signing a few papers, you gotta let it go." It was a lot of money—just not enough for someone who spent money like Wallace.

And it was nothing compared to what he could have earned in the future.

At the time, there were few venues for rap songs to make money—the advertisers on Madison Avenue hadn't, in 1994, fully tapped the earning and selling power of hip hop music. But that was starting to change. Those publishing rights could net millions. "If I would step to niggas now," Wallace joked, "they'd be like, I'll buy your publishing and give you some head."

But meanwhile, to earn his "champagne wishes and caviar dreams" money, Wallace had to hit the road on the out-of-town hustle. Things had changed since the old days when he'd troop down south to move drugs. Now he'd show up in Podunk with his crew, rock a show, and get $20,000 cash for maybe half an hour's work—legal work.

Wallace also realized his dream of forming a record company when he set up Undeas Entertainment with Lance "Un" Rivera—a fellow hustler from his part of Brooklyn. He helped get Junior M.A.F.I.A. a deal through Big Beat/Atlantic. Not only was Wallace able to keep his promise to give his best friends a legal living, he also made money off of their hit records—as a label owner, writer, and producer. He was watching Puffy and learning that it paid to be the man behind the scenes.

Opportunity was everywhere, but there were drawbacks to all the work. He and Faith had been married only a short time, and they were constantly apart from each other. She had just finished her own first solo album and had to go out and promote it. Wallace had paid performances, television appearances, and promotional gigs to help build the type of loyal following that can sustain a long career, not just a novelty single. And with Junior M.A.F.I.A., his responsibilities were doubled. "You won't be around next year," warned Craig Mack on the first Bad Boy release "Flava in Ya Ear," and now Mack's own words were coming back to haunt him. He'd released more singles, but hadn't scored a significant hit. Wallace made up his mind that he wasn't going out like that. As much as his wife missed him, she'd have to understand that he had a job to do.

"Big understands what he has to do, and being on the road is a part of that," said "Hawk" Burns, one of Wallace's Brooklyn homeboys who became his road manager. So there he was, in the back of a broken-down tour bus with JM, Total, and other Bad Boy acts, smoking cheap weed and living off McDonald's. Every day was another concert or radio show, and always more hands to shake like he was a presidential candidate meeting the voters that could put him in office.

Meanwhile, at Clinton Correctional Center, the Dannemora, New York, prison that was once home to Charles "Lucky" Luciano, Tupac Shakur sat for hours in his cell, watching his career go nowhere.

His album *Me Against the World* hit stores on February 27, 1995, and shot to No. 1 on the pop charts on the strength of the heart-rending million-selling single, "Dear Mama." But Shakur also spent his share of money while recording the album, he hadn't recouped, and almost all of the money he did have went straight to his legal fees and his impending appeal. He couldn't book shows; he was in jail. He was the sole support of his mother and other members of his extended family.

All eyes were on him. And their hands were out.

For $1.4 million, he could be bailed out and back on the streets. Only problem was the same problem he'd had since he was a boy—he didn't have any money. He didn't save. Hell, he didn't think he was going to live past 25 anyway.

Shakur remembered the time when Shock G from Digital Underground, concerned about all the legal troubles he was having in 1993, offered him keys to his condo in Los Angeles. "This is for my condo," Shock told him. "If you ever want to be someplace where nobody knows where you're at, you got a place. There are threats out there."

"All I wanted to do," Shakur replied, "was have my voice on a record and be in a movie, and I've done that. All the rest of this shit, I don't give a fuck, so don't worry about me."

But he was wrong. What good did all of that do him in a place like this? A place where inmates could threaten his life. Where the guards went out of their way to humiliate him. What good was having a No. 1 record if he couldn't dance, travel, or do anything else he wanted to do? Write? He'd even have to ask them for a pencil. A cage was a place for an animal—not a man. And coming to jail showed him just how wrong he was.

It didn't matter to him that people whispered about him getting raped in jail. That wasn't going to happen. There were enough people in the Black Power movement, people with ties to Mutulu and Geronimo Pratt and his mother, who could prevent something like that from happening. It was the stuff that he couldn't control that messed with his head.

He could be messed with even when he met with his lawyers. Once, before he met with one of his attorneys, Stewart Levy, the guards gave him a rectal search. He conversed with Levy for six hours, in a locked room, under complete supervision, with no chance that anything, save some papers, could be passed between them.

But when he left he heard the voice, taunting him.

"Tupac! Tupac! It's time! It's time!" The guards were smiling, putting on plastic gloves, with mocking falsetto voices. They gave him a second prolonged rectal search.

The longer he stewed in jail, the more paranoid he became. Things he had once dismissed began to seem plausible. So what if Biggie had warned him about Agnant. What if that was just a smoke screen? Where were his friends now? Could he trust anyone?

It didn't matter to Shakur that Wallace, had no motive to harm him involved. He wasn't making any money off of Shakur—nor did they have any beef. *Ready to Die* was already selling massive copies, so there was no need for Wallace to eliminate any competition. Besides, Shakur had such a huge following, how could Wallace be considered competition?

Shakur was so angry about being set up he never questioned the motives of the people telling him these things. And he was in no position to verify anything.

Shakur overlooked, the fact that this kind of disinformation was exactly the kind of tool that certain people in law enforcement specialized in using. Through a campaign known as COINTELPRO, the FBI neutralized the Black Panthers by spreading rumors through paid informants and false letters. By inflaming tensions between Huey P. Newton and Eldridge Cleaver the FBI brought about a violent split in the party. Shakur's godfather, Geronimo Pratt, was still in jail for trumped-up charges. Accused of murdering a school teacher in Los Angeles back in 1968, he was actually at a Panther rally in Oakland hundreds of miles away at the time the murder was committed. The key witness against him was a paid informant—a fact that wasn't revealed until years later—and no fellow Panthers stepped forward. Newton had ordered them not to testify in Pratt's defense since he was a Cleaver loyalist.

It wasn't far-fetched that Shakur, because of his rebellious spirit and his influence over young people, could be considered a target. Politicians from Dan Quayle to Bill Clinton had spoken out against his music. The Los Angeles rebellion that broke out after police we cleared of criminal charges in the beatings Rodney King of April 29, 1992, freaked out a lot of white people in power. Crips and Bloods ended years of violence against one another and joined together in unity. Members of the Los Angeles Police Department feared that the gangs might unite and take on the cops—and there were reports of some cops actually trying to heighten tensions between the sets to prevent that kind of unity from happening.

A handful of rappers had more sway over this element of the youth culture than any politician—Shakur especially. Not only did he specialize in so-called thug records, he had also called for black youth to rise up against the cops. "Fuck Tha Police," got N.W.A on the FBI's map—but some considered Shakur even more dangerous because he didn't just talk the talk, he walked the walk.

Tupac was charged with shooting at off-duty Atlanta police officers Mark and Scott Whitewell on Halloween night 1993. Though the charges were later dropped, Tupac's stepfather, Mutulu Shakur—who had considerable firsthand experience when it came to these matters—worried that Pac would become a prime target for police reprisal.

"When Tupac stands up to a white cop, shoots it out, wins the battle, gets cut free, and continues to say the things he's been saying—the decision to destroy his credibility is clear," Mutulu said.

"I worked for the PBA for ten years," said Paul Brenner, the lawyer who helped Agnant beat his case. "I know the police. The police are friends of mine. But Tupac had no friends in the police. I couldn't find a policeman who had a good word to say about Tupac." Brenner suspected that cops might have planted guns in the Mutulu, meanwhile, months after Shakur's acquittal from his case with the cops, was transferred from prison in Lewisburg, Pennsylvania, to the toughest prison in the country, a "supermax" Prison in Florence, Arizona, because, in the warden's words, of Mutulu's "outside contacts and influence over the younger black element" a.k.a. Tupac.

With so many family members in jail or dead, it made sense for Tupac Shakur to be paranoid and distrustful. But his imprisonment made him bitter—and made him suspect that anybody at Quad Studios that night must have known something was going to go down and didn't tell him because they weren't true friends—no matter what they said.

People were talking a lot of shit—even saying that the B-side of the single "Big Poppa," a track called "Who Shot Ya," was a direct taunt at him. It didn't even matter to Shakur that the song was recorded in September of 1994, months before the shooting—he thought it was disrespectful that the song would even be released for people to speculate that it *might* be about him.

He saw the video for "Big Poppa" with Biggie, dressed in leather, hanging out at the club that Jack introduced him to, Nell's. Big was around when he got that first Rolex and now he was living Shakur's dream while he was stuck in here, rotting. "I couldn't believe that everybody was treating Biggie like the biggest fucking star in the world," Tupac said. "I couldn't believe that people was buying into the player image. Biggie is not a player."

No visits. No phone calls. No letters. It all began to build in his mind.

Doing all the push-ups and sit-ups in the world and reading until he needed glasses couldn't get rid of the time.

He read VIBE, with the responses from those he held responsible for the Quad Studios shooting. Something that Combs said stuck in his head.

"If you gonna be a muthafuckin' thug," Combs said, "you gots to live and die a thug, y'knowhatumsayin'? There ain't no jumping in and out of thugism. If that's what you chose to do, you gots to go out like that."

Being a revolutionary, and dealing with movement lawyers was only going to keep him in one place—jail. He appreciated the letters from friends like Jada and Jasmine, even strangers like Tony Danza, but none of that was action.

He was haunted by nightmares about the shooting. Maybe he was in hell.

"Hell is when you sleep, and the last thing you see is all the fucked-up things you did in your life," said Shakur. "And you just see it over and over again, cause you don't burn." Maybe hell was jail.

He needed to get out of here.

Only one person he knew had $1.4 million. It was the same guy who asked him to jump to his label while recording the *Above the Rim* soundtrack. The same man who gave him $200,000 for one song, one goddamn song on the soundtrack—"Pour Out a Little Liquor"—as if it was nothing. The one man who could move like he moved, ride like he liked to ride, and have his back so that even his worst enemies would have to think twice about stepping to him.

Marion "Suge" Knight, the CEO of Death Row Records, was that man. Other people sent him flowers. Suge sent a bullet-proof vest.

By the time the August 1995 Source Awards rolled around, there were two superpowers in hip hop: first Death Row, and now, Bad Boy.

While people loved Sean Combs; they feared Knight. His reputation preceded him. The 6'4", 315-pound former defensive end rolled like a freight train, the kind of man you loved to have behind you would never want to cross. Stories circulated about Suge beating people down for everything from cheating him out of money to unauthorized use of a telephone. He openly flaunted his ties to the Bloods street gang, wearing red suits in every photo shoot and even stipulating that rap magazines use red type when he appeared on their cover. It was said that even Dr. Dre, the musical mastermind behind Death Row's success, faced punishment if deadlines were not met. There was also, of course, the story of how he improved the royalty rates for Puffy's Uptown artists Jodeci and Mary J. Blige by hanging Andre Harrell out of a window (or, depending on who was telling the story, parading him around the Uptown Records office at gunpoint, naked). Andre and Puffy never commented about the stories except to deny them.

But there were other stories. About how his artists had some of the highest royalty rates in the business. How he bought them Ferraris and Range Rovers, expensive jewelry, condos, and houses. How he worked 24-7-365. And how he showed tremendous loyalty to those people who were down with his team. When Snoop Doggy Dogg was charged with the murder of Phillip Woldemariam on August 25, 1993, Knight not only guaranteed the rapper's million-dollar bail, he also made sure that his legal defense was the best that money could buy. In November 1993 Snoop's solo debut album *Doggystyle* would debut at No. 1 on the pop charts, the first gangsta rap album to achieve this level of success.

"Did you see what Snoop was wearing?" Knight pointed out to a reporter, referring to an expensive diamond-encrusted dog-bone pendant. "I bought it for him. Anyone who's my artist, they say 'I want,' I say, 'You got it.' The people who started with me, they end up with me."

Knight, it seemed, didn't care what anybody said one way or the other. "I leave my judgment to God," he said. "The rumors are helpful, but not true. They get me additional respect, and this business is about getting the respect you deserve so you can get what you want. I don't worry about all of the talk."

And whatever you thought about the man, you couldn't question the results. Getting Dr. Dre out of his contract with Eazy-E's Ruthless Records, by using metal pipes as a negotiating tool paved the way for Death Row, clearly the most successful rap label the music world had seen since the rise of Def Jam. In less than three years, the label had sold over 10 million records and made over $100 million—numbers that took Def Jam nearly a decade to reach. With Dr. Dre and Snoop Doggy Dogg, Daz and Kurupt, and the Lady of Rage, he had an arsenal of talent that the East Coast had to respect—and the multi-platinum sales of Snoop and Dre's records proved that many did have respect for "the Row." There was only one label that came close to matching its success—Bad Boy.

When Knight and the rest of his Death Row posse came to New York for the 1995 Source Awards, there was electricity in the air. Collecting a trophy would be nice, but what they really wanted was respect. Of course, you had to respect their dough, but New York MCs were always reminding cats from the rest of the country that N.Y.C. was the birthplace of hip hop. It was as if they looked down at rappers from the rest of the country. Now that they had their own hometown champions in Wallace and in Combs, they wouldn't bow down the way Death Row thought they should.

Knight and Combs knew each other well. In 1992 and 1993 they would hang out with each other whenever one was visiting the other's hometown. Combs respected Knight's balls and business savvy—the way he made the mainstream respect his music, and his determination to maintain control of his lucrative master recordings. Knight might be loath to admit it, but he respected Combs's knowledge of his fan base, his hustle, and his genius for self-promotion. Nonetheless, Knight would belittle Combs every chance he could.

But these Source Awards were different. The stakes were high and getting higher. The rap business was worth more money than ever before, and now the factions were aligning along coastal lines. Knight wanted the world to know there could only be one king, so he threw down the gauntlet.

On the evening of August 3, 1995, Knight confidently took the stage at Madison Square Garden. It was the first time that many in the audience had ever seen the man who had been whispered about so much. Holding the mike with a diamond bracelet sparkling on his right wrist, he gave the audience something to remember.

"Any artist out there that want to be an artist and want to stay a star and don't want to worry about the executive producer all up in the videos, all on the records—dancing, come to Death Row!" His sarcastic remarks were clearly a broadside directed a Puffy.

The audience gasped in shock and there were a few scattered boos. People couldn't believe Knight had the gall to disrespect Combs that way, openly trying to scoop his talent in his own backyard. In truth, some on the East Coast felt the same as Knight did about Combs's attention-grabbing ways. But it was bigger than that now. By virtue of the fact that they were in New York City, they had to stand by Combs—and they did.

By the time Snoop Dogg came onstage, the audience rained down a chorus of boos. Snoop—who had paid tribute to Slick Rick on his debut album—had always gotten nothing but love from the East Coast. But now he reverted to his Long Beach Crip roots, the timbre of his voice changed and his eyes were blazing.

"The East Coast ain't got no love for Dr. Dre and Snoop Doggy Dogg? And Death Row? *Y'all don't love us!?*" He wore a blue kerchief around his neck and brandished a machete in his right hand, swiping the air next to his leg for emphasis. "Then let it be known that we got no love for the East Coast then!"

It was on.

When Sean Combs came to the stage with Faith and Chris Webber to present an award, he tried his best to calm the crowd, but it was already too late. "I'm the executive producer that a comment was made about a little bit earlier," said Combs sheepishly, his face low and close to the podium, and his hat turned backwards.

"Contrary to what other people may feel, I'm proud of Dr. Dre and Death Row and Suge Knight for their accomplishments. I'm a positive black man, and I want to bring us together, not separate us. All this East and West, that need to stop. One love!" Combs even presented Snoop with the award for Best Solo Artist.

But Wallace had won awards for Best New Artist, Best Live Performer, Best Lyricist, and Album of the Year—a virtual sweep. But the scent of beef hung over the ceremony like a dark cloud. It got even darker after the Dogg Pound got on the stage to perform, and Dat Nigga Daz, surly as ever, looked out at the crowd and said, "Yo, from the bottom of my heart, y'all can eat this dick!"

By the time the news hit the ghetto grapevine, and the mix-show DJs and magazines started discussing it, the friction played out at the awards show took on a life of its own. A few weeks later Quincy Jones organized a summit meeting at a New York hotel to help ease the tension and discuss the future of hip hop. Though Shakur was did not attend—he was still in a jail cell—Knight and Dr. Dre were there, as were Combs and Wallace along with the likes of Colin Powell and Minister Conrad Muhammad. "Speaker after speaker talked about power as a form of responsibility," Jones wrote in his memoirs, "about being guided by the inner conscience, even if anger is the initial motivator for your actions." But it was no use, rumors of war were in the air.

On September 24, 1995, they went from rumor to reality. Knight and Combs both were invited to a birthday party for Jermaine Dupri, founder of So So Def Records in Atlanta. Atlanta police allege that during an after party thrown at the Platinum Club, members of the Bad Boy crew got into some friction, woofing about what Knight said at the Source Awards. The cops suspect that one

Biggie virtually swept the 1995 Source Awards, but his victory was obscured by the bicoastal bickering.

of Combs's bodyguards, Anthony "Wolf" Jones, shot Jai-Hassan Jamal, a.k.a. Jake Robles, but Jones was never arrested. Robles was a Def Jam executive who happened to be one of Suge Knight's closest friends. For a week he lay in critical condition, paralyzed by the bullet. And then he died.

Even though Combs clearly wasn't the shooter, Knight maintained that he was responsible. Combs denied having anything to do with the incident. "At the time there wasn't really no drama. I didn't even have bodyguards," Combs said. "I left the club, and I'm waiting for my limo, talking to girls. I didn't see Suge go into the club; we didn't make any contacts or anything like that. All I heard is that he took beef at the bar. I see people coming out. I see a lot of people that I know, I see [Suge], and I see everybody yelling and screaming and shit. I get out the limo and I go to [Suge], like, 'What's up, you all right?' I'm trying to see if I can help. Then I hear shots ringing out, and we turn around and [Robles]—God bless the dead—gets shot, and he's on the floor. My back was turned; I could have gotten shot and he could have gotten shot. But right then [Knight] was like, 'I think you had something to do with this.' I'm like, 'What are you talking about? I was standing right here with you!' I really felt sorry for him, in a sense . . . he was showing me his insecurity." A snowball of hatred was rolling downhill, gaining mass and momentum. And nobody was doing anything to stop it.

Meanwhile Wallace stayed on the paper chase, traveling from city to city, appearance to appearance, trying to keep getting money. And after each show, he had an opportunity to meet interesting people from different parts of the country, like in Sacramento, California.

Months earlier Big had given an interview to a free magazine called *Peace!* in which he was asked to rate different rappers on a scale of one to ten. He had been drinking before the interview took place, so he was extra candid in his ratings. When asked about the Sacramento rap mogul E-40, Big said, "No rating! Zero! I don't fuck with duke at all."

After rocking the crowd in Sacramento, Big and his six-man crew were returning to the hotel when they noticed they were being followed by several cars. At first they assumed the cars were full of groupies looking forward to an after-party. But when they reached the hotel, they realized that the cars were tricked-out low-riders. People in New York didn't have rides like that. They'd never seen such vehicles outside of a Snoop video. "And it wasn't one car," said DJ Enuff. "It was five, six, seven cars—and four dudes in every car. So the cars do this big circle thing, circling the entire parking lot, then everybody gets out of their car and we see they're all gangbangers."

Twenty or thirty riders closed in around the seven out-of-towners. Only one of them spoke. "What's up, Big?" he said. "You in Sacramento now." Then he handed Wallace a cell phone. E-40 was on the line, wanting to discuss Big's magazine interview. "You know what's the craziest part?" Enuff recalled, "Big didn't even look fazed. They're all flashing their guns and shit and Big is talking slick to E-40 on the phone. None of us were suckers, but there were seven of us with no guns, no knives, no mace, no sticks, nothing."

"My people is here," E-40 told him.

"Yeah, I see them," said Big.

He went on to explain that his comments in the interview referred to E-40's music only—after all, they'd never met, and for all Big knew, E-40 might be a wonderful fellow. And so a potentially nasty situation was avoided.

"As soon as that's done," Enuff said, "the same motherfucker who stepped to us was like, 'Can I have your autograph?'" The DJ was a bit shaken by the whole experience, but eventually found the whole thing funny. "Hip hop is so much like high school," he observed. "Everybody wants to test."

Despite the occasional run-in with unfriendly locals, Big was having the time of his life on the road. But Faith, who stayed home working on her own album, was missing her husband. And he missed her too—sometimes.

"Not seeing him at all was terrible," Faith said. "A few months after our anniversary, it seemed like he was getting caught up in all that 'Big Poppa' stuff." One line from that song goes "Money, clothes, and hoes, all a nigga knows . . . " And at the moment, that's how Wallace was living.

"That star shit didn't really hit me until like a couple of months ago," Wallace told VIBE's Mimi Valdés, who joined him on the road during the summer of 1995. In Raleigh, North Carolina, as he performed "Player's Anthem" with the rest of Junior M.A.F.I.A., women in the audience rubbed their breasts on beat as he got to the chorus, "Rub your titties if you love Big Pop." A riot damn near ensued after Biggie's hype man Money L threw two hundred one-dollar bills into the crowd during the song "Get Money." The money throwing was Biggie's idea. He used to do it himself until he lost a $5,000 ring.

Despite the attention, life on the road was a grind. Ride on the bus for 12 hours between cities, barely have time to shower and change, and then back on stage to perform. Between the McDonald's food, the blunts, and the constant travel, it was hard to know whether you were coming or going. The bus could break down, and an eight-hour drive could suddenly take 15.

Not that anyone was watching the clock. Wallace passed the time playing spades or Cee-Lo with Hawk Burns, Don Pooh, his onstage hype man Money L, DJ Enuff, or Lil' Cease and D-Roc, sometimes for as much as $1,000 at a time. Lil' Kim was either right next to the boys in the middle of the action, or sleeping.

Some of the shows on that first tour were busts. "I did five venues where there were like thirteen people in 'em," said Wallace. "My boys were telling me it was the promoters not doing their jobs, but I was slowly but surely thinking it was over. Then we came to Chicago, and my muthafuckin' ego was back on point."

Big enjoyed the bigger cities because, if he was there for a couple of days, he could relax. He could do laundry, shop, and he and the crew could always find a decent steakhouse and not have to subsist on McDonald's hamburgers.

When he wasn't actually performing, he kept busy with the Junior M.A.F.I.A. project. The record was released in 1995 and "Player's Anthem" and "Get Money" became instant hits. Even though they were not on Bad Boy, Cease and Lil' Kim, the stand-out stars from the crew, were treated like family, and Kim even turned up on Puffy productions. Wallace was proud of them, and happy he could look out for his peoples. "It's great, man," he said. "It feels great to know that when I was saying 'Junior M.A.F.I.A.' at the end of my records there was no Junior M.A.F.I.A. And I just felt that would be a tight name for the niggas to roll with. We wild, we young, and we tight like how a mafia would be trained. These niggas is actually getting $10,000 a show right now. They're getting paid. They're like fuckin' sex symbols. They're in magazines. Yo, this is great, man. I love it."

Another thing that made him proud was the success of Lil' Kim. Not only did people liked her style and her rhymes, but the 4'11" around-the-way girl now had a deal of her own through the label Wallace started with his heavyset homeboy Un.

To take Kim, this little raunchy broad from the 'hood, man..." Wallace said, shaking his head in disbelief. "Kim was crazy, man. She was a female Big, going all out for her ones, whether it be fucking a nigga to get some paper, whether it be robbing a nigga to get some paper, or whether it be anything she had to do to get some ones, she was doing it. To see her come up and be the fuckin' Queen Bitch of this game right now? It's dope." Whatever Kim meant to him, she clearly saw Big Poppa as much more than a boss.

Kimberly Jones remembered the day they met with crystal clarity. She was sitting on a trash can outside the Fulton Mall. "We were just there talking. He was not the kinda guy I was used to talking to," she said. "I would deal with niggas with money. But he had this confidence about him. This was around the time he did that Mary J. remix. He was the biggest manipulator in the world. Later he got me to rhyme for him. After I rhymed he said, 'I'm fucking with you, Ma. We gonna make some money.'" They also made time to get together, though Big kept their relationship on the low.

That was his life: shows, studio sessions and steering the careers of Junior M.A.F.I.A. The 2 Live Crew's Luther Campbell, one of the first rap artists to build his own successful company, was always impressed with Wallace's business acumen. "A lot of other people take a lot of credit for the business aspect of that whole crew," says Luke. "It may have been Un running the label, but Biggie was really the brains behind it all. Puffy takes credit for a lot of things with Faith and Kim, but a lot of that was Biggie. This cat did it without receiving the glory. Nobody talks about that."

Craig Kallman, now co-president of Atlantic records, said he could sense Wallace's genius in their first meeting. "Talking to Biggie you really could see how deep the well was for his own creativity," Kallman recalled. "Fortunately we got to him before Puffy identified his ability as a businessman and an entrepreneur as well as an artist. He really had an incredible mind. He was so musically creative and innovative. All credit to him for the concept of Junior M.A.F.I.A. And he gets the credit for the entire strategy behind Lil' Kim as well. They made such a powerful statement with her so immediately—both visually and musically. If he had lived, he really could have masterminded one of the great labels of the future."

Wallace felt more comfortable making his moves low-profile style. For one thing, it wasn't always easy clearing these side projects with Puffy and his boss, Clive Davis. Sometimes there was drama, but Wallace usually got his way in the end. He had to make that paper, and there was no time to waste worrying about who got the credit. Plus he had to make time for his fans.

"Big Poppa, Big Poppa," the women would scream before he got onstage. "Please, please, please, come over here so I can feel on you." One constant that never changed in his life were the girls. They were everywhere. In Raleigh, they waited in the hotel lobby at all hours. In Cleveland, right before the concert, they spotted Wallace backstage right before he went on to perform. Part of being "Big Poppa" meant showing love to all the ladies. Even the heavier ones or the ones who might not be considered so attractive—although he did not necessarily pursue them romantically, Poppa would be there a kind word for his fans. All these demands on his time meant that he had to be away from home a lot. Wallace never really had a chance to settle down with Faith, who had an album of her own to promote. The responsibilities of the road took a toll on their marriage

"Temptation is a muthafucka," Wallace said with a weary expression. "You're in the industry. Girls sucking your dick for nothing. Suck your man's dick just to get to suck your dick. That's the way it goes. It's crazy, but it's real."

"Now you got me. I'm going from state to state. It's possible for me to fuck ten bitches a day if I wanted to. It's crazy, but it's true. Now, if you're in a relationship for how long? Let's just say two or three years. And in that time I fuck four bitches, you gonna flip over that? I mean, shit, I could have fucked four thousand bitches. And you gonna scream on me like, *You cheating muthafucka!* You in Louisville, Kentucky, somewhere, and the shit come over you. Everybody makes mistakes. Shit happens, y'knowhatumsayin'? As long as it ain't no keeping in contact–type shit, like the girl from Louisville is trying to move to New York and be a part of your life and shit. Just take a fuck for what it is. A fuck. Y'knowhatumsayin'?"

"You're my only girl. You're the one that I love, the one that I'm with. If I happen to fuck up and make a mistake, I apologize, man. Just don't lose it. Cause it could have been a lot worse. Give me an E for effort, at least. Goddamn. I couldn't get an A, so I got a B-plus. Don't be mad at me. My feelings for you ain't changed."

Wallace shook his head. "I know that sounds crazy, and girls definitely don't want to hear that shit."

Faith certainly wasn't having it. She wasn't the Rita Marley or Jackie O type who would look the other way. If she sniffed anything, there was drama.

"Part of me wanted to be like, well, what did you expect? He is out there on the damn road," Faith said. "I mean you're not there. But then again, it's not at all like that's at all acceptable."

And she didn't take disrespect lightly.

"He called me one night from this phone in his hotel room after a show he had," Faith said, recalling a show that Wallace did in Virginia. "He's telling me, well, I'm letting such and such use my room tonight, 'cause one of the guys, he gotta share a room with Cease and he got a girl with him," Faith said.

"It just didn't sound right. First of all, you ain't giving up your room for nobody. I know you *way* better than that." She laughed. "Secondly, why would you call me and tell me that, when if you're going in their room, you could very well call me from their room anyway. So don't block me from calling you. I know he definitely didn't think that one out all the way."

So Faith called her best friend and had her come to the duplex in Brooklyn to watch her daughter, Chyna. She caught the earliest flight she could, and took a cab to the hotel, knowing that Wallace wasn't an early riser. When she got to the lobby, she saw Hawk Burns at the reception desk taking care of the bill, and sneaked past him so he wouldn't see her.

"I went straight to his door and knocked," Faith said. Nobody answered, but she kept knocking. She knocked to the point where it got annoying.

"Who is it," a female voice asked.

"Housekeeping," said Faith.

The girl on the other end opened the door just a crack, and Faith kicked her way in the room. "Faith beat the shit out of her," Big told Mimi Valdés in his first VIBE cover story. "Punched homegirl in the face like 30 times."

"I just grabbed the girl and went bananas," Faith said. "I looked over at him, and he was sitting in the bed, looking at me like 'Oh my God.'" Both Biggie and the girl were fully clothed, but it didn't matter to Faith.

"She was still in his room," Faith said heatedly. "I don't give a fuck! She don't got no damn business being in there. I was cursing him out and hitting her the entire time."

"I ain't fuck her! I ain't fuck her!" Wallace kept saying.

"If you didn't fuck her, you should have, stupid, cause she just got her ass beat!" replied Faith.

"He was over there looking at me all pitiful like, 'Why are you doing that to that girl, Faye?' I didn't care. I ain't say nothing else. I got right back in the cab and was back at the airport within a half hour. And I got on the next flight back to Brooklyn."

Her point was made. "That's the illest, right there," Wallace said. He and D-Roc caught the next plane back to New York.

"I was so nervous, I jetted to New York, 'cause I wasn't going to leave her buck-wildin' like that. The girl was mad cool, and I felt horrible, but fuck that," Wallace said. "I got on that plane."

"He was all over Brooklyn, asking, 'Have you seen my wife,'" Faith said, chuckling at the memory. "He finally caught up with me and wanted to plead his case and all, and I was like, you know, 'There's just really nothing you can say right now, buddy.' I was so mad."

Not that that lasted for long.

"That's the awkward thing about love," Faith explained. "He always knew the right things to say. Always. Always. That's probably how he got over so well. He always knew the right thing to say, no matter what."

Faith laughed again. Sometimes he could just look at her and make her melt.

"You mad at me, Ma? You know I love you." That's all he had to say, with the right look in his eye, and the right voice, and much was forgiven.

"I was definitely weak," said Faith, smiling. "Weak for him. Definitely so."

If things were tumultuous in Wallace's love life, there was plenty of drama in his professional life as well. It seemed that as soon as he escaped the streets, some street shit would happen, pulling Wallace back in.

A perfect example was what happened on May 6, 1995, after a show that was supposed to happen in Camden, New Jersey, at Club Xscape. Brook Herdell, the promoter of the show—and the second half of his $20,000 fee—were missing. Wallace reportedly demanded that the driver for the promoter, Nathaniel Banks Jr. take him to the promoter. Some patrons, also pissed for being out their money, followed the caravan.

When the promoter refused to come outside, Banks said the rap star got agitated. "If I don't get my money, I'm going to start punching muthafuckas…" is what Banks remembered Wallace saying. Before he knew it, Banks was on the ground getting stomped. He was also robbed of a necklace, bracelet, watch, cell phone, and $300 in cash

"I look up and see this three-hundred-pound mutha kicking me in the head, making grunting noises, and wobbling like a monster," Banks said. "People tell me he's really not that type of person. Maybe he had to do what he did because he might look like a punk if he didn't. Maybe he has to act out what he says on his records."

Wallace didn't deny being present, but he said he wasn't the one who beat Banks down. Without implicating the person who did do it, Don Pooh and Mark Pitts insisted that Wallace was not involved because they insisted that he stay in his car when the fracas took place. "Who knows who beat the shit out of duke?" Wallace said later. "That whole block was lined up with cars."

When Wallace and his people got in their cars to leave, they didn't realize that Camden police would soon issue a warrant for his arrest. The legal documents was sent to his mother's apartment as opposed to his new Fort Greene duplex.

Six weeks later, after finishing a show at Pulsations in Philly, a surprise was waiting for Wallace and his entourage. He noticed flares on the ground, and police giving directions.

"We were thinking it was a police escort, 'cause there were so many people outside that club," Wallace recalled. Police led their cars to a parking lot, where more office were positioned in front of and behind the car. Once the caravan stopped, the drama started.

"I swear on my mother, niggas rolled out on their stomachs and pointed rifles with infrared beams on my truck," Wallace said. "Meanwhile, I'm in the passenger seat, with a bottle of Dom Perignon, pissy drunk, like 'Oh my God, what the fuck is going on?'"

Next thing Wallace knew, he was lying face down on the ground with rocks and bugs in his face while a police officer pointed a shotgun with a flashlight mounted on it right at his head. "They took me to the precinct and niggas was giving each other mad high fives and doing belly slaps," Wallace recalled. But some of the police also asked him for autographs.

"They were like, 'My daughter Meghan loves ya,'" Wallace recalled with a grin. "So I'm talking to Meghan on the phone, and she telling me she want to go to my concert. I'm like, 'Yo, Meghan... talk to ya pops.' "

Since the law considered him a fugitive, Wallace spent three days in jail after the arrest, and no bail could be set. Ms. Wallace was so angry with him that they went through a period of not speaking, just as in his crack-selling days.

"That shit made my moms think of the old Christopher," Wallace said, "like I was still on the same bullshit. I'm telling her I ain't touch him, I didn't rob him, and she looking at me like 'Whatever.' That's my ol' M.O., y'knowhatumsayin'?"

"I'd rather be dead than in jail," said Wallace, reflecting on his short stint in the pokey. "I was shaking, throwing up cause that shit was mad dirty. Rats and mice all over. That shit was the worst."

Tupac Shakur could agree with Wallace on that point. And by the fall of 1995, he decided to do something about it.

During the summer of 1995, Suge Knight and his lawyer David Kenner flew by private jet from Los Angeles to Upstate New York to visit Shakur in prison and make him an attractive offer: sign with Death Row, and all his problems would be solved. No more jail, money in your pocket, and the security that comes from knowing that no one will mess with you anymore.

It sounded too good to be true (and it probably was), but what else was Shakur going to do? He wasn't in any position to hold out for a different solution. Control was important to him, and as a prisoner he had none. Serving the four years was not an option.

"I want a house for my moms," Shakur told Knight as the first order of business. They discussed money and a few other points, but not with the usual protocol for negotiating a deal with a major record label. David Kenner represented both sides—both the label and the artist—so he wasn't going to argue against himself. Normally the transfer of a contract from one company to another for an established artist could take months, even years. Shakur was signed to Interscope—but Death Row had its distribution deal through Interscope. Handshakes between Kenner and Knight and label co-owners Jimmy Iovine and Ted Field were all that was needed to transfer Shakur's contract from one company to the other.

All Shakur had to do was sign and it was a done deal.

Close relatives and friends urged Shakur not to sign with Knight, but they didn't have the money or the credit to get him out. Interscope had advanced all they were going to advance without any more money being guaranteed by Death Row.

Shakur's manager, Watani Tyehimba, a former Black Panther who had known Tupac since childhood, visited him in prison around that time. "I know I'm selling my sould to the devil," Tyehimba remembered Shakur telling him tearfully.

Shakur nonetheless signed Kenner's document. Kenner wired the $1.4 million. Within a week, the New York Court of Appeals granted bail.

And, just like that, Shakur was free on October 12, 1995. He got on a private plane and, within hours, he was in a Tarzana, California, recording studio. It didn't matter to him that Suge put up only $250,000 of the $1.4 million, with Interscope and MCA kicking in the rest. Suge made him a promise and kept his word. In the process, he won Tupac's enthusiastic loyalty. Suge said he would get him out, and he did. It was just as he had learned in his childhood: revolutionaries had rhetoric but gangsters made things happen. Good behavior, ironically, would have kept him in jail. Getting down with the Gs, however, would get him out, get his mama a house, and put him right back in the hot seat.

The Death Row crew that Shakur had joined was in disarray. Snoop was in court every day fighting a murder charge, and as far as Knight was concerned, Dr. Dre wasn't pulling his weight either—he was taking too long to perfect his beats. Death Row needed a superstar, someone who could step up immediately and start producing massive hits. Knight thought Shakur was that person.

From Knight's perspective, Dr. Dre was acting like Patrick Ewing. Sure, he was a great center—talented but temperamental. And he wasn't putting up the numbers like he used to. After a drunken night in 1994 where he raced the police down Wilshire Boulevard in his Ferrari, Dre was sentenced to 180 days in a Pasadena halfway house with work-release privileges during the day. Since then he'd been slowly fading away from the sound lab, spending more time in his Woodland Hills mansion than in the mix at Can-Am Studios where Suge made sure his team was pushing out hits 24 hours a day, seven days a week.

Knight hoped that bringing Shakur to Death Row would have the same impact on Death Row as getting Shaquille O'Neal from the Orlando Magic had on the Lakers. Like Shaq, Pac was a tireless competitor who would put up big numbers every night of the week. And from Shakur's standpoint, he was with a championship organization. He finally had the kind of backup that, in his mind, would help him through everything. "I'm gonna make Death Row the biggest company in the whole world," Shakur promised Knight. "I'm gonna make it bigger than Snoop ever made it."

"It's like a machine," Shakur said. "That's what Death Row is to me. The biggest, strongest superpower in the hip hop world. In order to do some of the things that I got to do, we gotta have that superpower."

In quick order, the machine he described went into overdrive. The first night after he got out of jail, Shakur recorded seven songs. In a matter of weeks, Shakur recorded enough material for a double album. Fueled by alcohol, weed, blistering talent, and raging emotions, Shakur poured out a musical avalanche.

Just when things were taking off for Biggie, he was arrested and charged with assaulting a New Jersey concert promoter.

Like Biggie, Pac was a studio prodigy. "I didn't realize a rapper could write the lyrics and deliver the vocals as fast as he could," marveled producer Johnny "J" Jackson, who had worked previously with Shakur on "Pour Out a Little Liquor," and later produced many of the best tracks on *All Eyez on Me*.

"After I'd been there laying down the tracks for an hour or two, he'd come in, sit right down, and write three verses in fifteen or twenty minutes," recalls Jackson. "Then he'd go into the booth and deliver the vocal—and it was on to the next track."

In Shakur, Knight had met his spiritual soul mate. Here was someone who worked even harder than Knight did, which was damn hard. Knight kept a bedroom at Can-Am Studios, and would often sleep there. Shakur treated the studio the way Knight once treated the football field—with focus and ferocity. Gone were the days of waiting week after week for Dr. Dre to finish a track. Shakur just banged the tunes out like clockwork. All that weed and Hennessy would slow most people down, and by the time they got to the booth, their vocals were mush. Shakur's words never slurred, and his mind never blurred.

And in Knight, Shakur had met someone who was even more hot-tempered than he was. As one of Shakur's friends put it, "That street shit had to be dealt with, and Suge had the power on the street."

"He rides like I ride," said Shakur. "With Suge as my manager, I have to do less. 'Cause before niggas wasn't scared of me. So I brought fear to them. Now I don't have to do that to do that. Muthafuckas is scared shitless of Suge."

Shakur's small jail cell had been replaced by a spacious suite at the Peninsula Hotel and an apartment on Wilshire Boulevard, among other places. Soon he had cars, all the luxury steel and rubber a black boy could dream of. Knight showered Shakur with more diamond-encrusted jewelry than he could wear, and gave him the keys to one of four Rolls-Royces to celebrate Snoop Dogg's February 20, 1996, acquittal in his murder case. There were trips to Mexico, Vegas, and Hawaii. And since Shakur had his marriage with longtime girlfriend Keisha Morris annulled within weeks of his release, life around Pac became the Motor Booty Affair, part two.

But it wasn't enough. It never was.

He still had the nightmares. He wore a bulletproof vest everywhere he went, and rolled with a team of bodyguards. He always made sure that wherever he sat he faced the door. Loud noises would trigger post-traumatic flashbacks. He told a writer who interviewed him soon after his release that, while driving to the recording studio, he heard a backfire that sounded like a gunshot, and tensed up while he was behind the wheel.

Death was not an abstract concept to Shakur. It was an everpresent reality— almost like a companion.

"Like Malcolm X knew he was going to die, I knew I was going to get shot," Shakur once said. "I know I'm not going to live forever. But I know I'm going to die in violence. All good niggas, all the niggas who change the world, die in violence. They don't die in regular ways. Muthafuckas come take their lives."

All through his 11 months with Death Row, it was work-play-work for Shakur. One minute it was the studio, the next it was an appearance at a late October *Soul Train* event, and the next he was in Westwood at Monty's Steakhouse, a popular U.C.L.A. hangout that became the unofficial Death Row Commissary. A few scant weeks ago he was on lockdown with "three hots and a cot." Now he had a luxury suite at the Westwood Marquis, keys to a luxury high-rise, and a plate full of lobster tails. He had come a long way in a very short time.

"I can't eat all this," Shakur said. "It's too much."

With Shakur's release, fears of an East Coast–West Coast confrontation rose considerably. In the minds of some people, Shakur coupling with Knight was the most dangerous collaboration since Meyer Lansky and Lucky Luciano.

Combs made himself scarce. He was supposed to make an appearance at Miami's "How Can I Be Down?" conference in Miami on October 21, 1995, but skipped it when he heard that Knight was bringing an "army" to Collins Avenue. On November 30, 1995—exactly a year to the day he and Shakur were assaulted at Quad Studios—27-year-old Randy "Stretch" Walker was murdered while driving near his brother's house on a residential street in Queens. His SUV was being followed by a black Acura that began shooting at him with a high-powered rifle. While trying escape, his SUV crashed and flipped over. Police said the killers fired shots into the wreckage before fleeing the scene. No suspects were ever arrested.

Wallace found out about Walker's death not by watching the news, but via his SkyPager's voicemail. He was friends with Walker too—Big and Pac had made a record with Stretch that was supposed to appear on the first Thug Life album. He had been expecting Walker to arrive at the video shoot for "Get Money" by Junior M.A.F.I.A. "I was busy all night," Wallace said. "I checked my messages, and the first one was from Stretch, saying, 'Yo, how do I get to the shoot, dog, where's it at?' By the time I got to the last message, it was Stretch's wife, screaming and crying, saying, 'Big, where the fuck are you? Somebody killed Stretch.' "

The date of the murder seemed like more than a coincidence. Word on the street speculated that Walker was murdered as revenge for the Quad Studios shooting of Shakur, even though he repeatedly denied being involved. Despite the fact that Walker and Shakur had been close since before the actor starred in *Juice* when they were both temporary label mates on Tommy Boy Records, they fell out after the shooting. Shakur was angry that Walker never came to visit him while he was being held at Riker's Island or at Dannemora prison. Walker felt wronged that Shakur had implicated him in the VIBE interview as being a part of the shooting. He was incensed that Shakur would question his manhood for doing as the armed bandits asked instead of rushing them. Walker felt that by standing up to them, Shakur had endangered all of their lives.

In his response to Shakur's comments, Walker stated that he remembered only one gunshot, not five, raising the question of whether Shakur was really shot in the head—as he claimed. Walker suggested that Shakur's head injuries could have come from being pistol-whipped, and that Shakur's gunshot wound in the groin might have been self-inflicted. "He tried to go for his gun and made a mistake," Walker told Fab 5 Freddy in response to Shakur's VIBE interview.

"But I'll let him tell the world that. I ain't even going to get into it all like that."

"Why would he go and do an interview like that?" Walker said. "He's supposed to be a street nigga, he should have kept it in the street... I want him to get a reality check. Recognize what the fuck he's doing. Niggas on the street live by rules. And that rule right there, that's a rule never to be broken."

Whoever had broken the code of silence, Walker was the one who ended up dead. And after his death, the conflict between Wallace and Shakur only escalated.

"I think he would have been the only one that could bring Big and Pac together," Cease reflected years later. "Cause he knew the real on both ends. He used to be trying to tell Pac, 'Yo, nigga you tripping. You know Big ain't have nothing to do with that shit.' And Pac would tell Stretch, 'I ain't trippin. What are you on the other side?' But I think at the end of the day Stretch woulda brought Big and Pac together. Just by being here, he woulda said, Someone put an end to this shit."

When asked by the British author William Shaw what he felt when he heard about Walker's murder, Shakur's response was uncharacteristically cold.

"I didn't feel," Shakur said. "I felt for his mother and his wife. I didn't feel anything for him. Honestly."

A statement he later made to *The Source* mirrored that sentiment (or lack thereof). "He didn't do what your dog is supposed to do when you get shot up," Shakur said. "When I was in jail, nigga never wrote me, never got at me. And he

"He rides like I ride," said Shakur after signing with Death Row. In Shakur, Knight found someone who worked as hard as he did.

started hanging around Biggie right after this. I'm in jail, shot up, his main dog, and he hanging out, going to shows with Biggie. Both these niggas never came to see me. Ain't no words. The rules of the game are so self-explanatory."

Life on Death Row seemed to be changing Pac, much as life on the corner had changed young Chris Wallace. Though he was known for his harsh statements against his perceived enemies, Shakur was like Muhammad Ali—there was always an implied wink. Ali could call Frazier a gorilla or an Uncle Tom up and down the street, but no one (other than, perhaps, Frazier) thought he really meant it.

"I always called Pac the George Jefferson of the music business," said Luther Campbell, who knew Wallace and Shakur and tried to encourage them to iron out their differences. "He's a little guy running around, you know, he just be talkin'. He don't mean nothing. He ain't gonna hurt nobody. He just be talkin' talkin' talkin'. You know, little guy disease."

Former Tommy Boy publicist Laura Hines, who set up some of Shakur's first interviews when he was a member of Digital Underground, noted his "profound sense of victimhood." If he got it into his head that someone was his enemy, she said he would often brood over it to the point of obsession. "More than anything," she said, "he never wanted to feel vulnerable."

After moving to Death Row, Shakur's public pronouncements became more menacing, as if the shooting and the jail time had transformed him into something even he wouldn't recognize. Tupac the "Ridah"—West Coast slang for a gangsta at war, derived from drive-by shootings—was even more dangerous than Tupac the thug. And the "real" Tupac was no longer visible.

"Pac was a like a chameleon," said Big Syke, a rapper who collaborated with Shakur. "Whatever he was around he turned into. And when he got around Death Row he tried to be that."

Never was this more apparent than at a 1995 Death Row Christmas party held at the opulent Chateau Le Blanc mansion in the Hollywood Hills. Mark Anthony Bell, a high school friend of Combs's, was reportedly escorted to an upstairs room where he was interrogated about the shooting of Knight's friend Jake Robles, and asked to provide the home addresses of Combs and his mother. Bell told police that when he refused he was beaten. The questions kept coming, and Bell said Shakur was whispering instructions in Knight's ear. Knight then allegedly forced Bell to drink a champagne flute of his urine. He told police that he attempted to jump off a second-floor balcony to escape. Bell said Shakur was punching his hands, making him let go of the railing. Bell said he was pulled back into the room, and that Suge then offered him money for the information.

The next day, at a Valley hospital, Bell was treated for numerous bruises, a hemorrhaging left eye, and a deep laceration on his left elbow. Four days later he filed a robbery and assault claim against Knight, Shakur, and the other men he recognized there. The district attorney refused to press charges because Bell didn't report the assault at the time the policed showed up—despite the fact that Knight was standing right there at the time.

Bell filed a civil suit against Knight and Death Row, settled out of court, then took his $600,000 and moved out of the country. But that wasn't an option for Biggie and Puff, who were still trying to conduct business as usual.

But it was at a party at the House of Blues, when Shakur ran into a familiar face, that the war between East and West truly got personal.

The familiar face belonged to his wife.

When Faith Evans and Christopher Wallace's marriage began to fall apart, it wasn't a huge blow-up but a gradual fade-out. Both were on the road constantly, and Evans never stopped wondering about whether or not Wallace was faithful.

There wasn't much to wonder about—he wasn't. On one hand, he was involved with his protégée Lil' Kim, who seemed to enjoy taking public digs at Evans. Wallace had also begun seeing Tiffany Lane, a tall beauty from Philadelphia who appeared as the Faith look-alike in Junior M.A.F.I.A.'s "Get Money" video. Lane would soon became known by her rap alias, Charli Baltimore.

Though Wallace told her of his plans to make her part of "The Commission" —a rap super group that would also include B.I.G. and Jay-Z—Lane understood that she was not the only woman in Wallace's life. Even so, things sometimes got a bit out of hand.

"There were so many girls," she said. "They didn't care who was standing next to him. If they wanted to flash their tits or pull up their skirts while wearing no underwear, that's exactly what happened. Sometimes he looked more scared of those girls than I was. It's impossible for any man to be around that much shit and not test the waters."

Faith still cared for him, even when their marriage was deteriorating. "I tried and tried, acting like this or that didn't happen," she said. "It's like I gave up hope. But I never stopped doing for Big. He was my husband."

Big might not have admitted it to Faith, but the marital tension bothered him too. DJ Enuff remembered him playing her album—the one with sad songs like "I remember the way you used to love me"—over and over while riding on the tour bus. "When he was depressed, we were all depressed," Enuff said. "He would play all the slow jams. He didn't want to be talked to. No one could bother him. All he wanted to do was hear that damn Faith record. I love Faith, but, you know, Can you put something else on? But he was going through it. Then he would be, like, This is my baby. I love her. Faith did something to him that no other woman did to him. I don't know what it was, but he really did love his Faith."

Evans figured that Wallace must be enjoying the life of a gigolo. But she didn't enjoy being married to one. "I knew that wasn't what I wanted for my marriage. I didn't want my husband to be doing that at all. And we just kind of separated." Aside from her personal life, Faith did not feel respected professionally. She had an almost platinum album with her solo debut *Faith*. But she thought people weren't really checking for her. Too many people were caught up in the fact that she was Wallace's wife, not that she had an incredible voice, or could write songs, which she was doing long before she met her husband. She felt the need to prove that she could make a go on her own.

She came out to Los Angeles, stayed with a friend, and started working with a group called Tha Truth. She went out with friends one night, and ran into Treach from Naughty By Nature. Treach told her that Tupac wanted to say hi. "So I met him," she said. "And pretty much that was it. We took a couple of pictures in the club, and he told me, 'Yo, I want to work with you. I like your song. I heard your stuff when I was locked up.' I was basically like 'Cool, maybe we'll work together.' "

That she would be so friendly with a sworn enemy of her husband might seem dubious to outside observers, but Evans insisted that the rivalry never crossed her mind. As far as she knew, Wallace didn't consider Shakur an enemy.

"Big still totally liked him," Evans said. "He never gave me the impression that he was not feeling [Shakur]. He always said that was his boy. Of course, once [Shakur] started dogging him out, [Wallace] said, 'Duke is wild,' like, 'I don't know what the fuck is going on,' but he always had good things to say about Pac. Biggie really wanted to understand why this guy was saying he had set him up when he knew he didn't. I wanted to be able to ask him myself."

She didn't try to hide the fact that she'd run into Shakur the next time she talked with her husband.

"I met Pac," she told him.

"Word? What did he say?" she remembered him asking. "I know for a fact that he still had hope that they would figure it all out," she said. She could tell that Wallace just wanted to talk to his old friend and ask him, "How could you even think I would do some shit like that?"

Then Faith ran into Shakur again, this time at the release party for the *Waiting to Exhale* soundtrack. They talked about the song he wanted her to sing on. That night, they went out to Can-Am Studios to record some rough vocals.

"I was definitely naive and hasty going to the studio without it being something that was officially cleared," Evans admitted after the fact. "I didn't know until I got to the studio and saw all these Death Row cats that this is where I am. You don't even know what I was feeling inside. I was petrified."

As she left, Shakur said that he would talk to Bad Boy about getting a song clearance. And as far as she was concerned, that was that. Evans didn't realize that anything was amiss until she started getting calls from Wallace.

"You don't be seeing Misa out there?" Wallace asked. Misa Hylton-Brim, Combs's former girlfriend and the mother of his eldest son, Justin, was alleged to be dating Suge Knight at the time. She later denied this. But the rumors served their purpose, ratcheting up the tension. There was a persistent story that Knight had posed for a photo holding Combs's son in his lap, and that he planned to turn the shot into a magazine ad with the caption: "Bad Boy Can't Take Care of Their Own." The ad never appeared, but the atmosphere of stress was getting thicker.

Evans assured Wallace that she hadn't seen Misa. She was hardly in touch with anybody from New York, and hadn't even met Suge. Evans wasn't worrying about any deeper implications. She hadn't done anything wrong. She had told Wallace the truth. But she had neglected to mention the song she recorded.

It wasn't until the January 14, 1996, issue of *The New York Times Magazine* hit the stands that all hell truly broke loose.

The cover photograph featured Knight in a red suit flanked by Snoop and Tupac, who was holding a few thousand dollars in cash. The accompanying article was written by Lynn Hirschberg, who had spent months around Knight, getting deep inside the Death Row camp. She went with them to a prizefight in Las Vegas and hung with Knight at his custom-car shop hours before he flew to New York with David Kenner to bail Shakur out of prison. But none of these details caused as much furor as a single exchange on page 50:

"The wife of a top rapper bought this for him," Knight said of Tupac's outfit.

"Who's that?" asked Hirschberg.

"Notorious B.I.G.'s wife Faith Evans. She bought him this and a suit and some other stuff," Knight said, turning to Shakur. "And how did you thank her, Tupac?"

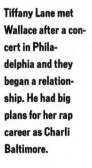

Tiffany Lane met Wallace after a concert in Philadelphia and they began a relationship. He had big plans for her rap career as Charli Baltimore.

"I did enough," Shakur replied, his eyes gleaming with mischief.

In a subsequent VIBE interview, Powell asked Shakur directly about the rumors of his relationship with Faith. "You mean the rumor that I fucked her?" The rapper began laughing hysterically. "I ain't gonna answer that shit, man. You know I don't kiss and tell." Shakur's response never ran in the magazine, but it didn't matter. The damage was already done.

This time it was Faith Evans who received a loud knock on her hotel room door early one morning. She was back from Los Angeles, but had moved out of the Fort Greene duplex and was staying in a midtown Manhattan hotel.

"Biggie was banging on the door so loud that I wanted to call the cops," Evans recalled. "I couldn't do that. I had to finally let him in."

Wallace wasn't just upset; he was wrathful.

"He went bananas," said Evans. "He was screaming. He was cursing. He was grabbing me like this," she said, mimicking with both of her hands the way that Wallace grabbed her arms and shook her.

"I was crying, like 'No, no, no. You know that didn't happen. It's not like that.' I couldn't say anything but the same thing over and over again."

Wallace started tearing up the room. He pushed her against the wall.

"But I was so busy crying and upset and scared, none of that mattered," she said. "I was just waiting for the whole argument to be over or for him to leave, or for him to do whatever he was gonna do. Just do it."

She fled to the bathroom and Wallace left the hotel room.

Moments later she heard a quieter knock. It was D-Roc.

"You all right?" he asked.

"No," Evans said, still bawling. "You know that shit ain't true."

"I know, I know," D-Roc said. His deep, gravelly voice was calm. "Chris don't believe that. He don't believe that. The nigga is just mad. You know? He mad."

For the first time, Evans chuckled through her tears.

"I can see that."

A few weeks later, it was Faith's turn to be angry again. She and Wallace were picking up the pieces of what happened to them and how things went wrong. He had been questioning her about Shakur and she decided that she wanted to get in a question of her own: was he messing around with Lil' Kim?

"Yes," he replied, quietly.

"Her too?" she said, incredulous.

"You caught me," he said, sounding almost relieved. "I pulled it off all this time, but yeah, I've been fucking her."

"The way they played it, I would have never known," Evans said. "Never, ever, in a million years. I was totally shocked."

It made sense when Evans thought back on all the clues. The skit on *Ready to Die,* where Kim did the voice of the girl having sex with Biggie. The fact that Kim was the one who went on the radio reporting

Faith told Biggie that she only laid down some vocals on a song with 2Pac. Shakur said there was more to it than that.

that Evans and Wallace were having problems—even before the whole Tupac debacle.

"It was just strange to me, like, 'Why is this little girl talking to my man like that?' " Evans said. "*She's* making the announcement that me and Biggie broke up?"

Faith made a subtle but lasting statement when she had the B.I.G. tattoo on her right breast altered to read "B.I.G. FAY." That got his attention. Wallace made one last attempt to patch things up by inviting Evans down to New Orleans for a show that he was doing with Junior M.A.F.I.A.

"You should come with me," he said. She knew by then he was seeing Tiffany Lane as well as Kim, so as far as she was concerned, their relationship was over. But she still loved him. She couldn't help it. And she wanted to see Kim. For real.

"I was determined to get her," Evans said with a laugh. "I knew she was going to be there. I remember being backstage. I was telling all of the guys, 'Don't let her come on this side, 'cause I'ma punch her out.'

"I don't like to fight," she said, in retrospect. "I ain't no troublemaker. But when somebody does something to me and it makes me feel like I gotta get them, God, I won't rest."

Back at the hotel, Wallace worked his charm. After all, they were still married.

"That's the awkward thing about love," Evans said. "When it ain't right, you just can't walk away. You can't just leave it alone. You just gotta be like, oh, come back for one more time."

She got her revenge on Kim a few weeks later. In March, Faith found out she was pregnant. By the time Wallace found out that he had another child on the way, there were other issues that had to be dealt with.

As the year came to a close, East-West tensions were at an all-time high, and it wasn't just Wallace and Shakur's problem anymore. On December 16, 1995, after Wallace mentioned playfully on the radio how Snoop and the Dogg Pound were in town to film their video for "New York, New York," someone shot up the group's trailer on location in Red Hook, Brooklyn.

The video depicted Snoop, Daz, and Kurupt as Godzilla-like creatures, stomping through Manhattan, knocking over monuments. Snoop kicked over one of the World Trade Center towers. Although the lyrics to the song had nothing to do with dissing New York, people got offended by the video.

Capone and Noreaga responded in kind with "L.A., L.A." The song, which also featured Queensbridge all-stars Mobb Deep and Tragedy, specifically took Daz and Kurupt to task. In the video, the L.A. duo are thrown off the 59th Street bridge, bound in rope from head to toe. Within a month, Ice Cube, Mack-10, and W.C. would jump into the fray, calling themselves the Westside Connection.

"It's getting to the point where people from the East Coast won't be safe out here," Dr. Dre observed. "And vice versa."

"It was horrible," said Audrey LeCatis, a fomer employee at Arista, Bad Boy's parent label. "Everybody was on edge. And you couldn't do what you needed to do. You couldn't get shows. You couldn't do your job. The whole industry was sick with that bullshit. And it was bullshit."

Despite all that happened, including the embarrassment of the Faith and Tupac controversy, Wallace never said anything publicly about what was happening. He didn't drop any response records, didn't make a call to radio gossip jock Wendy Williams, or indulge in any of the usual knee-jerk responses that so often result when rappers are embroiled in a public feud.

Instead, Wallace was calm about the whole thing. Methodical even. His few comments were conciliatory, never emotional. "If the muthafucka really did fuck Fay, that's foul how he just blowin' her like that," Wallace told VIBE in one of his few interviews during that time. "If honey was to give you the pussy, why would you disrespect her like that? If you had beef with me and you're like, 'Boom, I'ma fuck his wife.' Would you be so harsh on her? Like you got beef with *her*? That shit doesn't make sense. That's why I don't believe it."

Whatever he may or may not have believed, Wallace, Evans, Combs, and the rest of the Bad Boy Family flew to Los Angeles for the Soul Train Music Awards in March 1996. Faith's was nominated for Best New Artist and Female Artist of the Year. Wallace's "One More Chance (Remix)" was nominated for Song of the Year (pitting the Brooklyn rap don against pop stars like TLC and Whitney Houston). Bad Boy artists Total and Craig Mack also made appearances.

From the time they landed at LAX, there was static in the air. A *Details* writer working on a profile about Combs described one incident that occurred just days before the awards ceremony. Riding in the back of a rented Mercedes, Combs happened to pull up next to Knight and Shakur, who were waiting at a stoplight. The reporter witnessed Combs's driver pass a gun back to one of the bodyguards. Afterwards, Combs emphasized to the writer that this was not an offensive gesture, but more like a "just in case any shit goes down get ready" gesture. While their cars idled at the light, Knight and Combs looked each other in the eye and exchanged nods. Shakur seemed to have missed the whole thing.

"We made eye contact, acknowledged each other, the car left," Combs told the writer immediately afterward. "I don't want you to be saying, 'We were driving by, the gats started coming from everywhere, they started taking aim, but the cops were there, so they can't do what they intended.' It don't be that type of vibe. Everybody around may want it to be—want the two powers against each other, almost like spiders in a jar. But Death Row are doing good, they paving the way for us to good." Combs took great care to put a positive spin on things. "He ain't my friend, but everything's cool."

Nothing much was cool that night at the Shrine Auditorium, the site of the Soul Train Awards. A stylist didn't have Wallace's size 14EEE shoes. He almost pulled out of his performance out of frustration.

In their dressing room, Combs convinced Wallace to go on with the show. ,He borrowed shoes from a bodyguard, then took to the stage performing "One More Chance" with Combs and Faith Evans. But that was as close at he and Faith would get all night. Although she was three months pregnant with his son, their brief reconciliation was over. During the ceremony, they sat on opposite ends of the auditorium and left separately—which may have been for the best.

Death Row was very much in the house. Tupac's *Me Against the World* won the award for Best Rap Album. Biggie's remix of "One More Chance" won R&B/ Soul or Rap Song of the Year, beating out Whitney Houston, but Wallace heard boos when, during his acceptance speech, he gave his obligatory shout out to Brooklyn. While Big stood on stage dressed in a white suit, Tupac was running around the aisles wearing camouflage from head to toe. The real drama didn't happen until after the Bad Boy contingent got ready to go back to their hotel.

"After Big won his award, we was leaving," Cease recalls. "Suge, Tupac, and two other niggas rolled up in a Hummer. Pac got stuck in the window trying to hop out and shit. I guess he was trying to surprise a nigga. He got stuck in the window, hat falling off, he's all dressed up in fatigues, looking real crazy. And he's just yelling, *Westside nigga! Da da da da.*"

"That was the first time I really looked in his face," Wallace said later. "I looked into his eyes and was like, Yo, this nigga is really bugging the fuck out."

Big didn't say nothing. Big just looked at him like, What's wrong with you Pac? You tripping."

That's when Knight approached Wallace. "He was like, 'Yo, I wanna talk to him,'" Cease said. "'I just wanna talk to the man. Nobody wasn't really holding a nigga back. Security wasn't doing nothing. So my boys took the guns off they waist. It was like, Man you better back up. Back up.'"

According to Cease, Knight started calling for police. "Suge was trying to send a nigga to jail," Cease said. "He was like, 'He has a strap officer. He has a strap.'"

"His niggas start formulating and my niggas start formulating," said Wallace. "Muthafucka starts screaming, 'He's got a gun! He got a gun!' But we're in L.A.

What the fuck are we supposed to do, shoot out? That's when I knew it was on."

Big's boys back him up into the limo and told him to get us the fuck out of there. They had niggas on both sides of the Shrine—all Death Row. They had that shit surrounded. They had they little plan set up. Fuck that. Pac was doin' what he do best. He put on a show."

"He was on some tough shit," Wallace told VIBE's Larry "Blackspot" Hester. "I can't knock them dudes for the way they go about their biz. They made everything seem so dramatic. I felt the darkness when he rolled up that night. Duke came out the window fatigued out, screaming, 'Westside! Outlaws!'"

The moment was so cinematic it reminded Wallace of Shakur's haunting screen debut, when he portrayed Bishop, an rebellious teenager who becomes a homicidal maniac in Ernest Dickerson's 1992 film *Juice*.

"I was like, that's Bishop!" Wallace said. "Whatever he's doing right now, that's the role he's playing. He played that shit to a tee."

And with an audience of industry heads and reporters on hand, the incident set off a frenzy of nervous gossip. The next day's *Hollywood Reporter* said Tupac was the one with the pistol, an assertion Wallace denied. The article also said that someone in Wallace's crew was handcuffed by police, but that no arrests were made.

It was the last time Wallace and Shakur would ever lay eyes on each other. Cease said neither of them even tried to sit down with the other and talk. "It was too serious," Cease said. "Cause everybody was scared of Suge. And then they tripping on some tantrum shit. We're more like, we don't wanna indulge it and make it worse than what it is. But they was trying to destroy Big's career, like really investing a lot of time into trying to destroy my man's shit."

Shakur moved the war to wax, presenting his case through rhyme. Plugging into the power of rap, which Public Enemy's Chuck D famously likened to a black CNN, Shakur took the beef straight to Wallace with a track that rocked both coasts. "Hit 'Em Up" was perhaps the most scathing battle rhyme ever committed to tape. Set to the melody of JM's "Players Anthem" (the song Big and company were working on the night Pac was robbed at Quad Studios), the lyrics made Ice Cube's virulent "No Vaseline" sound like a ballad.

Seething with anger, Shakur's voice could only be described as manic as he openly declared war on Wallace, Combs, and all their friends and affiliations. Tupac had something for everybody—Junior M.A.F.I.A., Combs, the entire Bad Boy Records staff, Wallace of course, and Faith too. "You claim to be a player but I fucked your wife," Shakur boasted. He even dissed Mobb Deep, one of New York's most highly regarded rap duos, presumably because they said "thug life we still living it" on their record "Survival of the Fittest." The man who declared thug life (a "movement" that he started) to be dead did not appreciate anybody else reviving it. "Don't one of you niggas got sickle cell or something?" Shakur taunted. (In fact, Mobb Deep's Prodigy was born with the blood disorder.) "You gonna fuck around and have a seizure or a heart attack. You better back the fuck up before you get smacked the fuck up."

The first time Wallace heard the song, which was leaked to mixtape DJs in the summer of '96—and would later be accompanied by a music video—his eyes glazed over in disbelief. A powerful battle rhymer in his own right, Wallace could have come back with a classic response. But he chose to hold his tongue.

"The whole reason I was being cool from day one was because of that nigga Puff," he later explained. "'Cause Puff don't get down like that." As BDP had observed on their song "Stop The Violence" back in 1988: "real bad boys move in silence." And so it was with Combs.

Not that Junior M.A.F.I.A. didn't consider a response. "We heard that shit," Cease said. "I was mad. I was like, Damn he put *my* name in this one." But he was even more stunned by his friend's reaction. "Big was just sitting there laughing. Shit was like a joke to him. 'Hush,' he said. 'Silence is golden. I'm not trying to start no battle. I'm trying to get a check. Let people buy the album when it come out and find out what I have to stay.'"

"We was about to go write about them niggas," said JM's Larceny, who considered himself a 2Pac fan before "Hit Em Up" dropped. "But Big was like, 'Leave that shit alone. You gotta learn how to be the bigger person in a situation.'"

But Shakur just continued as many public insults against Wallace as possible, hoping to get some sort of response.

"Biggie is a Brooklyn nigga's dream of being a West Coast nigga," said Shakur in yet another incendiary interview. "None of my lyrics do you hear about me putting a gun to a pregnant woman's belly." (He was referring to a line on "Gimme the Loot" that puff deleted before the album's release.) "You can't be a player killing babies, nigga. Robbing pregnant women ain't no player shit."

Shakur assumed that Biggie's song "Who Shot Ya"—and LL Cool J's response, "I Shot Ya"—were meant as a comment on the Quad Studios robbery. In fact, Wallace's song was recorded long before Shakur was robbed, and its lyrics reportedly addressed a minor disagreement between Wallace and LL Cool J, who was in the studio the night "Who Shot Ya" was recorded. Not that it mattered anymore. Shakur was stuck in warrior mode. Even though he would eventually acknowledge—on the song "Against All Odds," released posthumously under the pseudonym Makavelli—that he believed others were responsible for setting him up, he kept coming after Wallace, spurning all calls for public reconciliation.

"That's corny," Shakur said when VIBE's Kevin Powell proposed a meeting. "That's just for everybody else to be calm. For everybody else to understand what's going on. They just want to hear what the conversation is about."

Yet Shakur seemed more than willing to air his side of the grievances in public: "How can I be peaceful and leave my door open and be calm and be relaxed when I know the niggas that broke in my house are right across the street? I'll forgive, but never forget. I would rather been shot straight up in cold blood. To be set up? By people who you trusted? That's bad. They know in their hearts—that's why they're in hell now. They can't sleep. They can't go nowhere. They can't look at themselves, 'cause they know the prodigal son has returned."

Predictably, Tupac's fans were beginning to take up the cause. Luther Campbell recalled a concert in St. Louis that included himself, Biggie, and Busta Rhymes. As the top-billed artist, Biggie was supposed to close the show, but because of the controversy, the promoters changed their minds. "They asked *me* to close the show at the last minute," Campbell said. "I was like, what the fuck? He's the fuckin' hot cat." But when Campbell watched Biggie's performance, he understood why the promoters had changed their plan. "I ain't never seen no shit like that in my life," he said. "You had one side of the crowd for Biggie and one side Tupac. The Tupac fans were singing that Tupac song, the dis song, and then you had Biggie fans screaming *'Biggie, Biggie.'* I was like, yo, this shit is *fucked* up.' It was a sold-out crowd and them people was out there saying 'TU-PAC!' "

Through it all, Luke marveled at the fact that Biggie never retaliated to Pac's recorded attacks. "If I'da went onstage, and public opinion woulda been screaming obscenities about me? I'da went in that motherfucker and I'da made some kinda record," Luke said. "They coulda checked me into the nearest studio right next to the fucking arena. It woulda came out right then, Jack. I know he was hurt by that, 'cause he jetted right afterwards. We ain't even talk, but I saw the look on his face."

Whenever the subject of his old friend came up, Wallace shook his head. "There's shit that muthafuckas don't know," Wallace would say. "I saw the situations and how shit was going, and I tried to school the nigga. I was there when he bought his first Rolex, but I wasn't in a position to be rolling like that. I think that Tupac felt more comfortable with the dudes that he was hanging with because they had just as much money as him." Biggie always seemed to come up with a reason to believe that Shakur might become a friend again.

"He can't front on me," Wallace said. "As much as he may come off as some Biggie hater, he knows. He knows when all that shit was going down, a nigga was schooling him to certain things. Me and Stretch—God bless the grave. But he chose to do the things he wanted to do. There was nothing I could do, but it wasn't like he wasn't my man."

Combs's response in the pages of VIBE was more aggressive.

"I never knew of my life being in danger," he said calmly. "I'm not saying that I'm ignorant to the rumors But if you got a problem and somebody wants to get your ass, they don't talk about it. What it's been right now is a lot of mov-iemaking and a lot of entertainment drama. Bad boys move in silence. If some-body wants to get your ass, you're going to wake up in heaven. There ain't gonna be no record made about it. It ain't gonna be no interviews. It's gonna be straight up, 'Oh shit, where am I? What are these wings on my back? Your name is Jesus Christ?' When you're involved in some real shit, it's going to be some real shit."

Just because Wallace didn't directly respond to "Hit 'Em Up," didn't mean that he was above addressing his personal issues in song. Once word got out that Faith was pregnant, people began wondering out loud whether it might be Shakur's baby. In 1996 Biggie hooked up with a rising Brooklyn rapper named Jay-Z and recorded a duet on the rapper's debut album, *Reasonable Doubt*. The song was "Brooklyn's Finest," and it sought to neutralize all the specula-tion with a single line: "If Faith has twins, she'll probably have two Pacs. Get it? Tu... Pac's." Instead of lashing out in anger, Wallace chose to defuse his pain with humor. Those who caught the joke understood that Wallace knew he was the father of Faith's baby. How else could he be so comfortable acknowledging the absurdity of the whole situation?

Faith wasn't exactly amused when she heard the song. "I was like, You know where you were that night," she said. "Why don't you count back? How are you gonna explain to your son, who looks just like you, that you made a record that's gonna be around forever saying I was having someone else's baby?' "

But humor was Wallace's way of dealing with hardship since he was in elemen-tary school. His wit had brought him this far and he knew it would never desert him. "I got to make jokes about the shit," Wallace said. "I can't be the nigga running around all serious. The shit is so funny to me because no one will ever know the truth. They'll always believe what they want to believe. Pac says he fucked her. I asked Faith, 'You fucked him?' She said no. So am I gonna hate her for the rest of her life thinking she did something, or am I gonna be a man about the situation? I can't hate nobody. That's not my nature."

Fifty percent of business partnerships, like marriages, end badly. It's just the way things happen in the entertainment business. The creative guy wants to go in one direction; the money guy wants to go in the other. It's happened to all of the truly great record companies founded by two different people.

Jerry Wexler decided to leave Atlantic, the label he co-founded with Ahmet Ertegun, because he wanted to produce R&B and Ertegun wanted to pursue '70s arena rock. Their parting was bittersweet but respectful. Wexler got a nice settlement, credit and royalties on all the records he produced.

When Rick Rubin decided to leave Def Jam, the label he founded in his NYU dorm room, he and Russell Simmons had a heart-to-heart in a Greenwich Village diner and settled the majority of their issues with a handshake.

But when Dr. Dre decided to leave Death Row records in March of 1996, he left with only the clothes on his back, and his name as an artist. That's it. The masters and publishing rights to all his hits with Snoop, even his own songs, were all left behind. This split was more akin to Tina Turner's divorce from Ike Turner than it was the proper dissolution of a friendship.

It took some time in jail for Dr. Dre to realize that Death Row Records was run much the same way. "I got wrapped up in all that old Hollywood bullshit," Dr. Dre told Ronin Ro in a VIBE cover story. "You know what I'm saying: the clothes, the jewelry, the fly cars with the big sound systems pulling up in front of the clubs. But incarceration bought me down to earth and actually turned Dr. Dre back into Andre Young."

Things had been going sour for a while. With all the guns and the hangers-on in the studio, the atmosphere at Can-Am was more akin to a prison than to a creative environment where free experimentation could take place. The straw that broke the camel's back was the night Dre witnessed a studio engineer catch a beat down for rewinding a tape too far. After that, it was hard for him to stomach the work.

Death Row wasn't really his label anymore—if it ever was. In an early interview, Dre described his relationship with Knight in terms of a family: "Me and Suge, we like brothers and shit," he said. But as time passed, Dre realized he had no control over who was signed to the label anymore.

"It got to the point in the studio where brothers were sticking their hands out like, 'Yo, what's up? We just signed with the label,'" Dre recalled. "And I was like 'I don't even know you."

"You Can't See Me" and "California Love"—songs recorded for the *Helter Skelter* project with Ice Cube and for Dre's own follow-up to *The Chronic*—had the original vocals erased so Tupac could rap over them. Suge wanted Dre to do all the production on Hammer's comeback album—which was like asking Francis Ford Coppola to cast Jean Claude Van Damme instead of Al Pacino to play Michael Corleone in a sequel to *The Godfather*.

Dre had seen his oldest friend, Eazy-E, die of AIDS, and yet, because of their business disagreements, he never got a chance to say a proper good-bye. As

Danny Glover put it in *Lethal Weapon,* Dre was "getting too old for this shit." He had done his share of partying, bedded his share of girls, smoked his share of chronic, and was coming to realize what all mature adults realize after a while—there's more to life than the party.

As Dre faded himself out, Pac was moving up. "Suge is the boss of Death Row," Shakur said, "and I'm the capo. That's my job to do what's best for all of Death Row." Shakur criticized Dre for not being present at Snoop's trial. "He was owning the company and he chillin' in his house; I'm out here in the streets, whoopin' niggas' asses, startin' wars and shit, droppin' albums, doin' my shit, and this nigga takin' three years to do one song! I couldn't have that. But it was not my decision. Suge was coming to me."

Knight eventually came by Dr. Dre's house to pick up the master tapes of his Death Row recordings. Suge claimed he came alone and Dre called the cops. Dre claimed that Suge rolled deep, with "eight or nine muthafuckas," and that he gave Knight everything he wanted after making copies for himself.

But quiet as it was kept, Dre was not the only one growing weary of life on Death Row. For the six months he spent there, Shakur seemed to be the label's staunchest supporter. "I'm a soldier," he said. "I don't give a fuck if I don't get along with anybody else on the label. This is for Death Row. When it comes to the point where I feel it can stand on its own, I will move on. But me and Suge will always do business together, forever."

In the opinion of one Harvard Law School professor, Tupac would have made a "damn fine lawyer." He'd clearly mastered the barrister's art of double-speak. On the surface, he had clearly stated his lifelong allegiance to Suge Knight and Death Row. But check the fine print: "When it comes to the point where I feel it can stand on its own," Shakur said, "*I will move on.*"

According to court documents filed on behalf of the Shakur estate as part of their civil suit against the label, Shakur was preparing to leave Death Row. As a $300 million company, Death Row should have been able to stand on its own, with or without him. In the original contract Shakur signed in jail, all of his master recordings would belong to Knight and Death Row. Since he could finish at least one complete song every day, there were between 40 and 60 unreleased tracks just lying around. Even if he never recorded another song, Death Row would still have five albums worth of material ready to go.

Tupac was playing a lawyer's game, hustling both sides against the middle. Even as he was loudly claiming lifelong allegiance to Knight, he was quietly pulling away on the sneak tip. He would have to step away gingerly, allowing Knight to save face, but on the other hand, separate his business interests from Knight's.

The problem came, when he opened a production company called Euphanasia. While Combs might not have been thrilled about Biggie's side projects—the cameos, the Untertainment venture, the Junior M.A.F.I.A. and Lil' Kim albums—he never tried to shut it down. But Shakur had to struggle to branch out under Suge's iron-fisted rule.

"We weren't getting copies of the financial accountings," said Shakur's family friend Yasmyn Fula. "We'd ask for them, and they'd send a present—like a car."

That's why Shakur wouldn't let his cousin Katari's group the Outlaws sign with the label—even though they appeared on "Hit 'Em Up" with him. "He didn't want them to live in bondage," said his mother Afeni Shakur.

Shakur was represented by David Kenner on the West Coast and by Charles Ogletree for non-entertainment issues. When Ogletree attempted to settle some of the various lawsuits Shakur was facing, he'd reach a figure with the disgruntled parties, and then ask Kenner for money to close the deal. It never came.

"It was as if he had no life except that given to him by Death Row," Ogletree said. When the accounting finally did come in from Death Row, he learned that he owed the label $4.9 million. Although his quadruple-platinum album had earned the company $60 million was of no consequence, Everything from his cars to his bail to his jewelry had been billed back to him as recoupable assets. But when Shakur fired his lawyer David Kenner, even the most hardened gangsters on the Row were shocked. "Tupac was brilliant, but he wasn't smart," one insider told *The New Yorker*. "He didn't realize, or refused to accept, what anyone from the street would have known—that you can't fire David Kenner, that you can't leave Death Row."

After a tense appearance at the 1996 MTV Music Awards (during which host Chris Rock greeted Suge Knight in the crowd, then added, "Don't kill me") Shakur decided he was ready to come home. On the morning of September 7, he told his girlfriend Kidada Jones that he was going to the Tyson fight in Las Vegas that night with Suge. He appeared listless and said that he didn't want to go, but he couldn't break his word. There was talk of him flying out to see his mother in Atlanta, but instead, they packed and drove to the Luxor hotel.

"It looks so evil," Kidada said, looking at the black pyramid with the white cap. The security detail, normally so heavy, was in disarray. No one had proper the weapons permits, so no one could carry guns. Normally there would be two bodyguards assigned to Shakur—but on that night there was just one: Frank Alexander, and his attention was divided.

Shakur and Knight were late to the fight, as was customary, but their homeboy Tyson was still in his prime—it wasn't worth sitting down for anyway. In less than two minutes, Tyson disposed of Bruce Seldon. Shakur was ecstatic. "Did you see Tyson do it to him?" he told a camera crew. "Fifty punches! I counted. Fifty punches! I knew he was gonna take him out. We bad like that. Come out of prison and now we running shit."

Shakur made his way through the lobby of the MGM Grand, high on post-fight adrenaline, when he was stopped by a member of the Death Row entourage, the Mob Piru Blood Travon "Tray" Lane. Tray saw a face that he didn't like—it was Orlando "Baby Lane" Anderson, a Southside Crip who, Tray said had jumped him with eight or nine other Southside guys at the Lakewood Mall and stolen his diamond-encrusted Death Row pendant.

Shakur walked up to Anderson, and asked him a question.

"You from the South?"

Suddenly, Shakur and the Death Row crew were on top of him, punching and kicking. The fight was quickly broken up, Shakur and Knight left the Grand, as did Anderson, who declined to file a complaint against them.

Shakur went back to the hotel, pumped up from the second fight of the night. He was ready to go to Knight's club 662 (the name spells M.O.B. on a phone keypad), for the after-party benefit. He refused to wear his bulletproof vest, saying it was too hot. Instead of taking his Humvee, he decided to ride with Suge Knight in his black BMW 750.

The caravan rode first to Knight's house just off the Las Vegas Strip, then back onto the Strip toward the Flamingo Hotel. Normally there would be a car behind them filled with armed guards—but tonight it was the Outlaws and a bodyguard, none of them armed. As they were waiting at a traffic light, a white Cadillac pulled up to the right of Knight's BMW. The driver's left hand came out, holding a .40-caliber semiautomatic pistol. Fourteen shots were fired into the passenger side door and then the Cadillac slipped off into the night.

Tupac was hit four times as he attempted to climb into the back seat.

When the police arrived Knight—with his hands the air—tried to explain that he and Shakur were the victims. Shakur was rushed to University Medical Center's intensive care unit. He lost a lot of blood, and then, two days later, his right lung. Four days later, doctors induced paralysis, so that Shakur wouldn't hurt himself by tossing and turning.

His eyes opened briefly when Kidada Jones played Don McClean's "Vincent" on the stereo next to his bed. The song was a favorite of Tupac's, one from his lean days with his mother and sister in Baltimore when it was the only record they owned. At the time another of his prized possessions was a book of paintings by Vincent van Gogh, given to him by a neighbor.

"Do you know I love you?" Kidada asked. Shakur responded to questions by moving his feet and squeezing her hand. "Do you know we all love you?"

Shakur slipped into a coma.

"I feel close to Vincent Van Gogh," Shakur once told Kevin Powell on Riker's Island. "Nobody appreciated his work until he was dead. Now it's worth millions. I feel close to him, how tormented he was. Marvin [Gaye] too. That's how I was out there. I'm in jail now, but I'm free. My mind is free. The only times I have problems is when I sleep."

Tupac Amaru Shakur drifted into permanent sleep on Friday, September 13, 1996, just after 4 P.M. He was 25 years old.

Christopher Wallace was shocked to hear the news that Shakur had been shot. But then he also remembered how resilient his former friend was.

"I know so many niggas like him," Wallace said. "So many rough, tough, muthafuckas. When I heard he got shot, I was like, 'He'll be out in the morning, smoking some weed, drinking Hennessy or whatever.' You ain't thinking he going to die." But after six days of fighting for his life, Shakur surrendered. "When he died, that shit fucked me up."

Faith's phone rang that night. It was Biggie, and he was crying. "He was in shock," Faith recalled later. "And I believe it's fair to say he was probably afraid."

"When you're around muthafuckas," Biggie said, "you just keep thinking a nigga making so much money, their lifestyle should be more protected. You know what I'm saying? Their lives should be more protected where things like a drive-by shooting ain't supposed to happen. You know what I'm saying? I was thinking that that shouldn't have happened, man. He's supposed to have lots of security. He ain't even supposed to be sitting by no window."

Wallace had little time to mourn his friend. He was having problems of his own. Because of the records that Shakur had made, Wallace and other New York rappers like Mobb Deep and Capone and Noreaga suddenly found themselves on the suspect list. Every time *MTV News* mentioned Tupac's death, they flashed pictures of Wallace and of Randy "Stretch" Walker, amid sound bites about the East Coast–West Coast rap war.

Wallace felt horrible about Shakur's death—and he was upset about how his name had gotten tangled up in the mix. The Saturday after Shakur died, his old friend dream hampton asked Wallace if he was going to the funeral.

"Naw, man," he told her. "This nigga—he made my life miserable. Ever since he came home. He told lies, fucked with my marriage, turned fans against me. For what?" Even if he's wanted to attend, he knew that his presence would be a distraction for the family. Wallace would do his grieving in private.

Meanwhile, back in Los Angeles, war broke out among Crip and Blood sets immediately following Shakur's shooting in Las Vegas. Mob Piru, Leuders Park, and Elm Lane Piru Bloods were on one end of the battle, and Southside, Kelly Park, Atlantic Drive, and Neighborhood Crips on the other.

Bobby Ray Finch of the Southside Crips was murdered on September 11, 1996, in a drive-by shooting. Timothy Flanagan and Marcus Childs of the Mob Pirus were killed soon after. And so it went, back and forth, until 10 other shootings were reported, some 13 in total. Meanwhile, the Las Vegas Police Department reported that Knight was being "less than candid" with them about details surrounding Shakur's shooting.

About a week after Shakur's death, the well-known rap photographer Ernie Paniciolli had a heart-to-heart conversation with Wallace. Paniciolli had been photographing hip hop culture since its inception, and Wallace, who used to see Ernie's work in magazines like *Word Up!* and *Fresh* when he was just a fan, respected him. The two men were at the same video shoot on a chilly September night and Paniciolli hopped in Biggie's Pathfinder SUV to keep warm.

"What's up?" said Ernie, slamming the door.

"You ain't come here to talk to me," Wallace said, smiling. "You just came to get in out of the cold."

"Yeah, whatever."

They sat in silence for a minute. Wallace was listening to a Tupac album on his CD player.

"Yo, man, what's the deal with all this?" Paniciolli asked. He didn't have to spell it out for Wallace. He was curious about all the talk of an East versus West rivalry. As an elder who had seen hip hop grow from the days of park jams to a multi-million-dollar business, it never made sense to him. "I'm not a writer or a reporter. I'm a photographer, man. I tell my story with pictures," Paniciolli said. "Talk to me."

Wallace paused, listening to the song for a minute.

"Let me tell you something," Wallace said in a low voice. "In five years me and Duke would have been doing things together. We would have been recording together and we would be taking all the money 'cause individually, nobody can touch us, and together you *know* nobody can touch us."

He shook his head, thinking of all the good times they had shared together, and imagining all the lost opportunities. First Stretch got killed, and now Tupac. And to think they had all given up the street life to get into the music industry because it was supposed to be safer.

If two of his homeboys weren't dead, he might even have laughed about it.

Faith Evans's phone rang. "Kim's here," said the voice on the other line, "at the studio." It didn't matter that she was seven months pregnant. Evans had a bone to pick—and the little boy growing inside her would have to understand.

"Naturally I caught a cab to the studio," Evans said. She brought her cousin along with her.

"Here's what we're gonna do," Evans told her when they got to Daddy's House, the midtown Manhattan recording studio that had been built to Puff's exact specifications. "I want you to look in every room."

Shakur and Knight's last ride together down the Las Vegas strip, September 7, 1996.

She waited for a few minutes, and her cousin came back.

"I ain't see her," her cousin reported. "Stevie J is in there and Puffy, and some light-skinned girl."

Evans walked up to the room in question. Sure enough, the "light-skinned" girl sitting at the table writing rhymes was Kim. Puffy and Stevie J were busy at the mixing board. Evans looked at her for a long time. This was her chance for a heart-to-heart conversation. They could talk about Christopher sister-to-sister. But instead she decided to kick her ass.

"I ran in there so fast and I just jumped on her," Evans said. "I might have gotten in two good hits. It was over like that, because by the time Puffy and Stevie saw me they turned around and got me off of her.

"I was so happy to be on her like that," Evans says with a cackle of delight. "I would never, ever do that again. But I was so mad. She must really be out of her mind to think that she could just be going around talking on the radio about me and my husband. Oh *no*. I was mad, mad, mad. And I felt like that was really all I could do."

Wallace didn't have to worry about Faith beating Tiffany down next. The New Jersey Turnpike would take care of that.

Biggie hadn't had a good week. Tupac was dead, and everyone thought he had something to do with it. The Nathaniel Banks assault case in Camden, New Jersey, was nearly resolved, but then, like a dummy, Wallace caught some more cases: On March 23, 1996, soon after coming back from L.A., Wallace and D-Roc were arrested outside the Palladium at 4:30 in the morning. They were coming out of a Faith concert when two fans started talking shit. When they jumped into a cab, Wallace and D-Roc followed them for two blocks. At the corner of Union Square and 16th Street, they smashed out all the cab's windows with a baseball bat. Police arrested them and charged them with assault.

Days later Wallace and Cease were busted again, this time for smoking weed on the street outside of Fulton Mall in Brooklyn.

Then, in July, police officers came to Wallace's crib in Teaneck after Mase dropped by and illegally parked his car in a fire zone outside Wallace's home. The cops came to the door, smelled weed burning inside, and returned with a search warrant. Inside the house they found a big bag of marijuana and four semiautomatic weapons with infrared sights, enlarged bullet clips, and filed-off serial numbers. Lil' Cease was arrested along with Wallace and other members of Junior M.A.F.I.A. went in with him on charges of disorderly conduct.

On September 17, Wallace, Cease, and Tiffany went to the Lexus service department to pick up their car. It wasn't ready, so the dealership loaned them a Dodge Astrovan that they could drive home.

Cease was rolling too fast and the brakes weren't right. It was raining, and the road was slippery.

"I had just paid the toll, and we were on the turnpike going north," Cease said. "So I'm hitting this turn, and the shit just starts sliding on the water. We went over the curb on the over side. I'm lucky no car was coming the other way." My face was fucked up on the steering wheel. B.I.G. couldn't get out..." Tiffany flew up and hit the windshield. She woke up feeling something wet on her head and hearing Wallace's voice.

"Wake up, Ma!" he said. "Wake up!"

"I'm thinking it was rain," Tiffany recalled. "It was actually blood."

Her ankle was fractured. She would need a neck brace and numerous stitches for the gash on her forehead. Lil' Cease lost his top row of teeth on the steering wheel. Wallace, meanwhile, couldn't move. He was trapped between the seat and the dashboard, and had to be cut him out of the van. As the saw blade sliced through the metal-and-fiberglass van, Biggie lay in the rain unable to move. It would be a while before he could move around again.

No, it had not been a good week. But the worst was yet to come.

ONE MORE
CHANCE
(THE REMIX)

CHAPTER 7

" I'm the rapper with clout everybody yap about
Check it out—guns I bust 'em
Problems with my wife don't discuss 'em... **"**

There he was, flat on his back in his room at the Kessler Institute for Rehabilitation, with the answer to all of his problems ringing in his ears.

Slow down, B.I.G.!

Slow down. That's what he should have told Lil' Cease as they drove home through the rain. Slow down. What he should have told himself before he and D-Roc ran after that cab and smashed out the back windows on account of those dudes talking trash. Slow down. What he should have thought before he, Cease, and Money L got popped for smoking blunts at the Fulton Mall—stupid. Smoking in public when he already had fresh possession and gun charges from that embarrassing arrest in Teaneck.

And now here he was in West Orange, New Jersey, in the same room Christopher Reeve had occupied after he was paralyzed in a horseback riding accident. Damn. If something like that could happen to Superman, what about the Black Frank White, Mayor of Bed-Stuy, and King of New York? Was Reeve thinking about the same sort of thing when he was there trapped in this room, unable to move without assistance?

If Wallace turned his head to one side, he could look at the wheelchair, waiting there for him. He could look down at his shattered femur—the thick bone running through his thigh—and think about all the work that lay ahead of him. Those damn parallel bars! Because of his weight, he'd be lucky to get out of the wheelchair on his own. He'd probably have to use a cane for the rest of his life. But at least he was alive.

Slow down.

It wasn't as though he had much of a choice. He couldn't do much with a shattered leg. No parties. No studio sessions. No shows. No planes to catch. Nothing. But all that seemed less important now.

He was supposed to be working on his next album. He could still work on lyrics. "I'll make your mouthpiece obese like Della Reese. When I release, you'll lose teeth like Lil' Cease. I used to be strong as Ripple be, until Lil' Cease crippled me."

It didn't matter what he went through in his life, he could always find something funny to say about it. That was the way he dealt with uncomfortable situations—he made fun of himself. "Black and ugly as ever . . . The chicken gristle eatin'; Slim-Fast blending fat greasy mother fucker." Being a rap star made it easier to laugh at self-deprecating jokes.

He didn't even need to read the papers or listen to Wendy Williams to know what people were saying about the accident. *Big felt so guilty and sad about Tupac's death, the nigga flipped out, got pissy drunk, and rolled his car.* That was what folks on the street were whispering. Anyone who knew him knew he didn't know how to drive, but that didn't matter. The rap rumor mill was more interested in drama than in the truth.

"That just goes to show you how people just be running their fucking mouths. They don't know shit." People were gonna say what they wanted to say. Myth and innuendo had a power far beyond his control—hadn't all this East Coast-West Coast mess and the rumors about Biggie, Tupac, and Faith proved that? Why waste energy trying to right the wrongs of the past—he had enough things to think about in the present.

The here and now.

Wallace reflected on a conversation that he'd had a few days ago with his therapist, the guy they sent in to help patients deal with the latent mental and emotional effects that result from having a crippling accident. An older white man, soft-spoken, who on the surface had absolutely nothing in common with a young black thug from Brooklyn. And yet this man sat and talked with him, not at all intimidated by him or who he was supposed to be.

"You're probably the only person in here who doesn't have too much to say," the man said to him.

Wallace nodded, grunted, and kept listening.

"When you're on your feet," the man continued, "you're always looking straight ahead. But when you're crippled, and you're on your back, you're looking at the sky. You're looking at God. Why don't you talk to him?"

Wallace laughed. This guy was buggin'. Biggie, the 'Hail Mary full of grace, smack the bitch in the face' nigga talking to God? He wouldn't know where to begin.

But as he lay there, alone in the dark, completely sober for the first time since he stopped being Christopher Wallace and became the Biggie Smalls, he stopped laughing. And before long, he did find himself talking to God. What surprised him even more was how quickly God responded.

So he started talking to Him. About where he was. And where he was going.

"God was like, you moving too fast, BAM! Slow down. Lay in this bed for the next two months and think about what you're going to do," Wallace said to himself. "Think, Big. Focus your mind."

It was the first time in nearly three years that he'd had the chance to think about anything. He was a creature of impulse—and his life was driven by passionate bursts of activity. As soon as he got money he spent it. Sometimes on himself, but mostly on his family and friends, just as he did when he was in the game. Back then he never thought about the future. Like when he met Faith and married her without really thinking about it. The women who threw themselves at him at the studio, backstage, the hotel lobby, whatever. Most of them got a chance. But now he had what those girls in the video used to beg for, "one more chance."

Faith Evans with Christopher Jordan "C.J." Wallace, born October 30, 1996.

The party was about to stop. Friends had become enemies, some had even ended up dead. There was much to regret and lots of time to think about it: the weed charges. The gun charges. The assault charges. The lawsuits that could have easily been avoided. Losing Faith, both figuratively and literally. Tupac's accusations, musical threats, and now his murder.

On top of everything else, his fan base was beginning to shift. The same people who once called him the savior of East Coast hip hop were now calling him the cause of its ills. All the Gucci, glam, and gun talk was now beginning to lose its luster. People were saying that a nigga had gone Hollywood. That success had made him soft. His head was swelling.

And in the midst of all this turmoil, another Wallace was about to make his debut. The little boy he always wanted. On October 30, a new Christopher Wallace made his debut: Christopher Jordan Wallace. His father wasn't able to be there for the delivery, but he'd made up his mind: From now on, it was all about building a foundation. A future. Time to get his priorities straight and, as his mom would say, get a life. The situation was still tense between him and Faith, but they both agreed that it was important for their child to have two parents, and that they'd work things out for him. They couldn't always agree with each other, but they both agreed that they adored their new son.

Holding another little life in his hands reminded him of something that he hadn't really thought about since T'Yanna was born—here was someone who didn't care about the Notorious B.I.G.—only Christopher Wallace.

He would sit in his wheelchair, holding the boy, so vulnerable, so innocent, in his hands. Looking at the new life, and playing with his daughter, who would come visit him at Kessler, gave him new perspective on his own life, and what he had to do. Seeing his daughter and son gave him a reason to work hard at healing himself so he could get on with life.

When he first had T'Yanna, he was young, dumb, and didn't really give a fuck whether he lived or died. When she woke up and said, "I want my daddy," and he wasn't around, it wouldn't faze him. But now, staring down at Christopher Jordan Wallace Jr., it was different. He had the maturity to know that he was needed. "When I'm looking at my daughter or my son," Wallace said, "it's something to live for. When I finally realized it, at least it wasn't too late."

"Your life is not a stage," his mother would often remind him during their frequent phone conversations. "You don't have to be a performer."

Yet that was precisely what he was—a performer. And he had to get back on his feet. And back in the studio. Not just because he was losing his fan base. Not just for the sake of his ego. He needed a hit record to secure his future. A tour to keep money coming in so he could realize his other dreams, like a house for his mother, a new life for himself away from the hustle and bustle of New Jersey and New York. The means and location to establish a legacy for his children, a financial seed that could flourish long after his departure from earth.

He had talked to God from his bed, and God answered him back, clear as day.

Wallace needed a plan. A life after death.

Sean "Puffy" Combs, meanwhile, had never stopped planning. He had a master plan for his company that went into effect way before Wallace suffered his car accident. Combs knew the only thing that would guarantee Bad Boy's survival in the rap game was hits.

In the lobby of his office, on a white placard with blown-up black block letters, was a reminder of Combs's credo. These were the principles that people who wanted to stay in his presence needed to share: LIFE IS NOT A GAME. ONLY THE FITTEST AND MOST AGGRESSIVE WILL SURVIVE. SLEEPING IS FORBIDDEN. A SECOND CANNOT BE WASTED. ONCE SECONDS ARE LOST YOU LOSE. AND LOSING IS FOR LOSERS.

As B.I.G. had grown larger over the years, so had the infrastructure of Bad Boy Records. The fledgling days of the company, being run from Combs childhood Mount Vernon home, were long gone: they had Manhattan offices now, bright, shiny, and futuristic, a vision of glass and steel. And a custom-designed recording studio, Daddy's House, nestled in Times Square, his very own Cape Canaveral from which countless rap rockets would blast off into the uppermost reaches of the pop atmosphere. The success of B.I.G, Craig Mack, Faith Evans, and the Bad Boy vocal group Total and 112 had not only outshone Uptown Records, it established Combs as a true pioneer, a force to be reckoned with, and a person who hated to be second-guessed. It didn't matter what record he wanted to sample, what clothes he wanted to design, or even pursuing the seemingly absurd notion that he could one day become a rap artist himself, Puff wanted to do it his way—no questions asked. You doubted him at your own risk.

"We call him the Lord—that's the joke," said Evans to a reporter. "The Lord said. And if it's not like the Lord said, then it has to be changed."

When Puff wasn't in the studio, he was in a dance club, watching the floor, observing firsthand what was getting the crowd pumping. When he wasn't in a club, there were frequent stops at Hot 97, which had transformed from a Latin dance-music station to the nation's first genuine 24-hour hip hop station, pumping Bad Boy releases from day one.

It wasn't just about being the best rap label in the world for Combs, it was about being the most exciting company in the world, breaking all the rules, selling Harlem to the Hamptons and vice versa. While his old mentor Andre Harrell was taking over Motown Records in a bid to recapture the magic of Berry Gordy, Puffy looked to the future. He wanted Bad Boy to be the hip-hop Bill Gates, with Bad Boy as the genre's dominant operating system. Every magazine, music video channel, and radio station would feature one of his artists. The best way to win the so-called East vs. West musical argument was to flood the market with sheer volume. He said as much on a song with Lil' Kim: "I got no time for fake niggas / Just sip some Cristal with these real niggas / From East to West Coast spread love niggas / And while you niggas talk shit we count bank figures."

As usual it was all there in the lyrics. "Thought I told you that we won't stop" was more than a cute slogan sprinkled all over 112's first smash hit, "Only You." For Combs it was a way of life, and summarized his 24-7-365 lifestyle. Nothing ever got in the way of progress. Not City College, not getting dropped by Uptown, not the war of words and threats between his camp and Death Row, nothing. But all the stress of the threats, the bad press, the eyes of the street began to weigh heavily on Combs. It was no longer fun to be at Bad Boy. One constantly had to look over one's shoulder. And business was beginning to suffer.

"We needed focus," recalls Ron Lawrence. "Puffy knew that we couldn't do it in New York because of all of the bullshit that was going down. We needed to just get away from all that stuff."

So after the Soul Train Awards incident and the showdown between Big and Tupac on March 29, 1996, Puff decided it was time to get out of town—in characteristically dramatic fashion. Within days after the event, Puffy escaped to the relative quiet of Maraval, Trinidad, with his core group of record producers, Stevie J, Deric "D-Dot" Angelettie, Nashiem Myrick, and Ron "Amen-Ra" Lawrence, engineers Axel Niehaus and Tony Maserati, a slew of drum machines and samplers, discs and DATs, several crates of records, and a mission.

"Puffy had a master plan," remembered Lawrence. The producer recalled a meeting at Daddy's House between the Bad Boy heads and the stable of "Hitmen" just prior to their departure.

"For the next two years, I wanna have radio on lock," Puffy said. "Call the girlfriend, wifey, or whatever, and let 'em know that you're not gonna be around for a few weeks. We're gonna get away from all this drama, put our heads together, and when we come back, we're coming back with hits."

Teddy Riley had been one of the first hip hop producers to discover the Caribbean Sound Basin on the island of Trinidad. It offered the best of both worlds—an island paradise with pristine beaches, sunshine, and sand, coupled with a recording studio modern enough to handle the demanding sonic needs of a major rap producer spoiled by the 48-track behemoth studios scattered around Los Angeles, Atlanta, and New York City. Combs hoped that the waters of Trinidad would do for his sound what the waters of Miami Beach did for young Cassius Clay.

"If I'm trying to be the heavyweight champ in 1996," Puff told a reporter who followed him there, "I gotta go away for a little training camp."

T'Yanna Wallace, age four. "When I'm looking at my daughter or son," said Christopher Wallace, "it's something to live for."

Combs wasn't kidding. With his Hitmen production squad in full effect, he took over the entire studio. As long as an engineer was at the board someone was at work 24 hours a day. The first week alone was responsible for 35 complete tracks—some of them destined to be multiplatinum hits for Wallace, other for Combs's own forthcoming solo album *Hell Up in Harlem*.

"It was like a training camp," said Lawrence, agreeing with Combs's analogy. "We woke up and we went straight to the studio. We got on the drum machines and, um, till late, till early in the morning. It was just, just a working cycle. Got up, ate breakfast, you know, at times we played some ball or jumped in the pool, but it was just constant work."

Every day produced potent songs. They were bank-

able hits that would more than finance the expense of putting up so many people in an island paradise for a month.

Before they flew down to Trinidad, Angelettie brought a "whole bunch of records" by Lawrence's apartment and started throwing them on the Technics 1200 turntables in his home studio. He put on Herb Alpert's "Rise." The second Lawrence heard the break, he liked it: Not the trumpet part of the popular '80s instrumental jam record—a staple of roller rinks from coast to coast—but the bass break in the beginning. "I was like, yo, this is what we got to do when we get down there."

And that was how they did it. Someone would come up with the beat, someone else, like Stevie J or Chucky Thompson, who could play numerous instruments, would come in and sweeten the track. To "Hypnotize," J added a bass line, played on a keyboard. On another track, it might be live drums. Almost all of the Hitmen produced records that were collaborations. Invariably, Stevie J or Lawrence or Angelettie would end up with a credit on a record produced by Nashiem Myrick or Carlos "Six July" Broady, or vice versa.

"That's why there's so many names on the records," said Angelettie.

"We would have an assembly line," explained Lawrence. "Somebody would

Puffy and his hand-picked production squad, the Hitmen, poured all their energies into making B.I.G.'s album Life After Death a classic.

bring a sample, and then somebody else would put drums to it. And then some-one else would add some additional production to it. And at the end of the day, once the sample goes down the line, it's created into a masterpiece. So everybody played a different role."

"No one got an ego or wanted to get a big head about 'Man, I don't want...' said Stevie J about a collaborative spirit that was reminiscent of what the Funk Brothers did for Motown, or what the MGs did for Stax. "Whatever its gonna take to make this a number one classic, not a hit, but a classic, let's do it. We want to be remembered as a group of people who make classic material, not just hot beats for today."

Nashiem Myrick took the opening strains of the Dramatics's "In the Rain," and expanded it into the dramatic "Somebody's Gotta Die." What started off as a simple piano loop and some atmospheric echo effects from the old record became a full-blown symphonic blockbuster by the time the crew was finished.

Even before Wallace had the chance to add his vocals, the track exuded ambiance. Dark alleyways, gunshots, and mystery. The sound was cavernous bounced over 48 full tracks, the same amount that film composers use for major motion picture soundtracks.

"Every song is a movie" said Angelettie, co-producer of such hits as "Been Around the World," "It's All About the Benjamins," and "Mo Money, Mo Problems." "If we don't have a story, we don't do it."

The visual element was one of the most important elements of the new sound Puffy was urging his Hitmen to go for. The idea was to provide drama—to expand the realm of the sound, to provided backing tracks that would make the sonic movie that was *Ready to Die* feel like a low-budget film.

If a Dr. Dre–produced gangsta rap album evoked the gritty, visceral feel of an early Martin Scorsese flick à la *Taxi Driver,* Combs was going for epics of Michael Bay proportions—think *Armageddon*. Strings, sound effects such as gunshots, slamming doors, footsteps, voices murmuring in the background.

Another thing Puffy was known for was his blatantly pop records. They were homages to the point of being remakes. The unspoken rule among producers was that if you could recognize it, it wasn't a good sample. To the Pete Rocks and RZAs of the world—guys who would paste together sonic collages one drum hit at a time—songs like MC Hammer's "U Can't Touch This" were sacrilege. Not just because of the wack rhyme—but because the Rick James "Superfreak" loop was so obvious and unimaginative. Puffy didn't care.

"Yes, I'm a beat jacker," he told Jeannine Amber. "That's my shit! But you can't say you ain't gonna dance to my shit. When that muthafucka comes on, your ass is jigglin'."

If it was a hit in his ear, it was a hit. Old or new. His approach was to take records from the late '70s and early '80s that people would easily recognize—and sample them anyway. Not only did he want his records to sound orchestral and huge—he wanted to capture the pop sound of the '80s, and use that as his sonic base to rock a party and move major units. No one else had the balls to do it.

"People never really gave us the credit for that," Lawrence said. "They look at it as, well, you know, you just took David Bowie's 'Let's Dance.' But they never really understand or gave us the credit for the artistry that actually went into it."

Puffy reasoned that if the white-bread radio programmers in their early forties who still controlled the airwaves could identify the sample, they'd be more prone to play a given record. In order to pass muster with "The Lord," every record needed to have a *big* sound. And if it was already based on a hit song, it made it even easier to be a hit song. It could be a bad investment to write new songs. Why take the chance?

Wallace had worked his way back to normalcy, and by the time he was ready to begin recording *Life After Death* in earnest during the fall of 1996, he was itching to go. Recording was not only an escape from his condition, it was an escape from the Kessler Institute of Rehabilitation.

At first he thought the people there, like most white folks, were going to be afraid of him. That they would look at his appearance, the fact that he had guys like D-Roc and Cease around him, and give him problems. "I was, really, was thinking they was gonna give us bullshit 'cause I'm like a young rapper," he said. "I got a thug nigga sleeping in there making sure nobody don't come in there fucking with me. Every morning these niggas is wheeling me to mutha-fucking therapy. I got two big-ass niggas. Junk jewelry, diamonds, you know what I'm saying? I'm rolling up in therapy and nothing but old people. And I'm running in there with some real Brooklyn shit. They was feeling me, though. They gave me my love. When they asked they kids who I was, they were like, 'You got *who* up there!?' Then they start saying, 'My daughter likes your new video.' "

He would sit there in his wheelchair, or in bed, thinking of rhymes, ready to get back to work. Combs would come by to visit him, bringing tracks, some of them from the Trinidad sessions, others hot off the boards of an outside producer. A fellow patient alerted Wallace to the fact that, with a doctor's promissory note, he could get a weekend pass to go to the recording studio.

"I was locked up, thinking of escape," Wallace joked. "I got into the studio and started knocking out joints."

And the joints started piling up. Fast. Wallace recorded at a breakneck pace, his idle time making his brain work overtime. The records poured out of him.

"He was a late afternoon, evening dude," remembered Deric Angelettie. Part of his responsibility as the A&R executive responsible for the record was to organize all of Wallace's recording sessions, help clear samples, hire and organize the producers of the various tracks, and keep Wallace in the recording booth, happy, on the job.

After his accident, Wallace recorded at a breakneck pace, all that idle time making his brain work overtime. He'd get wheeled into Daddy's House and sit around, smoking and listening to tracks real loud.

"I'd usually tell Big, 'Be at the studio around six.' Which meant eight, eight-thirty," said Angelettie with a laugh. "And he'd be there until two or three or five, depending. And we'd just in there writing and bullshitting."

Wallace would show up with either D-Roc, Lil' Cease, G, or another member of Junior M.A.F.I.A. driving him, either get wheeled in his wheelchair, or, as he got a little more mobility, walk in with a cane, sit around and listen to tracks. Everything would be laid out for him to make the environment as conducive to his creativity as possible.

"Every day, the same shit," Angelettie said, chuckling. "You walked into Studio A or B, there's ice and glasses, and cups, liquors, and chasers. Alize, Moët, Cristal, whatever he was feeling like. Bacardi. They was really on Bacardi Limon for a minute, 'cause that's when it first came out. Plenty of Dutchmasters and Backwoods. Lil' Cease had the weed out, rolling L after L for Big and the rest of the crew. A little bit of chocolate thai. Might be one or two chicks sitting on the couch, or in the lounge. There'd be empty bags of food, or they just ordered food. His cronies making phone calls." Angelettie said with a laugh, lost in the memory. "Bitches, phone calls, and the beat real loud."

Because it was 100 percent dedicated to Bad Boy projects, Daddy's House offered a level of comfort and flexibility that wasn't possible anywhere else. Located just off of Times Square, it had a club-like atmosphere. There was a private lounge. Huge color monitors with Playstations and VCRs connected for movie and video-game binges. All the latest samplers and effects, a mixing board to die for, and speakers powerful enough to rival Madison Square Garden's.

"It was home," said Angelettie. "You can take your shoes off, you can work as many amount of hours you want. You could keep going even if the engineer is tired. You know what I mean? We can stop the session if we need to continue something else. We could do whatever we wanted to do in there. And it was family in there so like, you know, whatever we did in there stayed in there. Bitches coming there to freak out, y'knowhatumsayin'? If somebody was in there doing something a little extra besides weed, then that's what happened."

D-Dot Angelettie's job was to keep the volume high, the atmosphere chill, but to make sure that, no matter what, records were getting made. On the surface, it may have looked as if Wallace was wasting time and money. But when he finally recorded his vocals, he was as regular as clockwork. Twenty to 45 minutes and you had a hit song, like a "Mo Money, Mo' Problems." A complex album cut like "Niggas Bleed" might take an hour or so. If things got too relaxed, Angelettie was always the one who cracked the whip.

"When it got beyond regular bullshit, and we starting to like toss money away," Angelettie said. "Then I'd step in and be like, 'Come on Son, clear the room. Give Big an hour.' "

Wallace would sit there just like he was in his old bedroom on St. James Place, listening and murmuring lyrics to himself, over and over.

"A lot of times we be sitting on the floor a half an hour, just me and him," Angelettie recalled. "And I'd be like, 'What you got?' When he did 'Hypnotize,' he just leaned over to me and whispered 'Biggie Biggie Biggie, can't you see? Sometimes your words just hypnotize me.' He just hummed it to me. Went back to nodding. Passed me the L, and he'd just keep nodding."

Once the rhyme reached critical mass in Wallace's head, it was important to track the vocal immediately and try to get it right the first time. "Once he's ready to lay, he want to lay it and go," remembered Angelettie. "He don't want to lay it and sit around for an hour. That's his final task. He'll lay it, put it on cassette, give us a pound, and they cleaning up they shit and they out. He ain't sitting around chilling after that."

There was only one other condition that was crucial to Wallace's process: Puffy couldn't be there when he laid his vocals. They would spend hours talking about the albums, line for line, but if he could help it, he recorded alone.

"He would try not to go into the vocal booth if Puffy was around," recording engineer Lynn Montrose confirmed. Montrose, one of the few female engineers in the industry, recorded numerous vocals for Wallace's album, and always found the rapper charming and polite. "You don't want to go into the vocal booth and as soon as you go in Puffy is like , 'No, I don't like your tone,' or whatever. That would be a large part of his waiting; waiting for Puffy to leave."

Most songs could be recorded in a day. Others took longer. It depended on his general mood, and what was happening in his life. "He might have been too busy, or he might have gotten too high, he might have had a stressful day," remembered Angelettie. "The Faith shit, still got the Tupac shit, still got baby-

Celebration time at
Daddy's House after
the completion of
Life After Death.
Puffy's sweatshirt
is by Brooklyn
Mint, the clothing
company Wallace
was trying to start
before he died.

mother drama, and you still got to pay bills. Your normal life still goes on, so he's dealing with a lot of shit. Every day is not happy and peppy and bursting with love."

But time wasn't the biggest factor. Quality was.

"Big is the true MC—he doesn't have a certain style, per se. He fits every song," said Myrick. "He writes like a songwriter would write. He writes in melody. That's why he has these different styles on each track and it fits so perfectly, it fits like a glove. A lot of MCs are just lazy, you know, they just have they set rhythm and how they rap, and they go at that in every song. Big comes different in every song. Every flow is different."

At times he called himself "the black rhinoceros of rap" or "the praying mantis," but the animal Wallace resembled most was a chameleon. For a song like "Warning" or "Gimme the Loot," Biggie was a master narrator, switching perspective, voices, and flows two or three times in one song. And then there were the free-style showcases, the songs that would take him back to his basement days of rhyming over breakbeats while 50 Grand worked the decks, way before he ever dreamed of becoming a superstar. Those were the kinds of tracks that DJ Premier specialized in producing.

Both Premier tracks on *Life After Death*, like "Unbelievable," before them, were instant classics—stripped down, intricate lyrical workouts tailor-made for a tenth-degree black belt MC like Wallace. Nothing cute to hide behind, just naked, raw rhythms, the kind of stuff that Puffy, with his pop sensibilities, hated.

"Puff didn't like 'Kick in the Door," Premier recalled. The song was more avant garde than anything Premier had ever done. The beat was a loop of a horn line from a classic Screaming Jay Hawkins song, "I Put a Spell on You," matched to a funky drum pattern that was deliberately offbeat. It was a sink-or-swim track that had the potential to be either the dopest thing ever or something locked away and forgotten about. Everything depended on the vocalist.

"We were arguing in the elevator," remembers Premier, who made a special tri up to Daddy's House to preview the track for Combs.

"This joint ain't hot," Combs told Premier. "Pre, you ain't giving me that Tunnel banger," Puff said, referring to the N.Y.C. nightclub that Funkmaster Flex turned into the compulsory testing ground for rap hotness. "You ain't hitting like you did last time with 'Unbelievable.' I need something hotter."

"Has Big heard it?" asked Premier, unfazed.

"Nah. He ain't heard it yet."

"Why don't you give it to him? If he don't like it, I'll change it," Premier replied.

"But I ain't feeling this," Puff said.

Hours later, Wallace heard the track at Daddy's House. "Man, are you crazy!?" he said, dialing Premier on his cell phone. "Yo, come back tonight. Let's track it tonight."

Premier came to the studio to upload the sample and tune up the track. "There was a lot of Bacardi Limon in the house," Premier remembered. The beat was playing loud, and Wallace, as usual, sat there nodding to the beat. There were people all over the place, and, like clockwork, a few cops showed up, and the Lysol scramble was on.

"This joint ain't hot," Combs told DJ Premier after listening to the "Kick in the Door" demo. "Has Big heard it?" Premier asked, unfazed. "Nah," Puff said. "Why don't you give it to him?" said Primo. "If he don't like it, I'll change it."

I was like, damn, what the hell is going on, remembers Premier, and everyone else was like, 'The police is here again,' "They said it happened all the time. So we put our trees out, waited. I told [Big], "Damn, you just in here working, doing your thing. Why they giving you a hard time?' "

But nothing stopped the lyrical bum rush. After the cops cleared out, Big got back to work. Premier was surprised by how upbeat Wallace was despite hobbling everywhere he went.

"It was two, three in the morning, and you're sitting there, tired of waiting. And them boom, he's finally like, 'Yo, I'm ready,' " Premier recalls of the session for "Kick in the Door." In typical fashion, Wallace finished the first two verses in less than half an hour. "Your reign on the top was short like leprechauns / As I crush so-called thugs, fake willies and rapper dons," is how he began, one of the hottest rap records ever. He spent a few days thinking about the third verse, then finished it later. Premier was surprised how upbeat Wallace was despite hobbling with a cane everywhere he went.

Between the studio, his court dates, and physical therapy, Wallace was too busy to be depressed about breaking his leg. He was making progress. He knew that the record was good, he was having fun, and once the Camden case was settled for $40,000, one of his biggest legal hassles was out of his head. With his healthier diet, he was even losing weight now that he could move around a little more. His sleep apnea was getting better too, giving him more restful nights.

"He lost about thirty pounds," remembered his mother. "He said, 'Ma, I'm gonna be out there wearing my Calvins,'" suggesting that he intended to follow in Mark Wahlberg's footsteps as an underwear model. 'You watch.'

That was the ultimate goal of *Life After Death:* to cut through all the distractions and get all eyes on B.I.G. Wallace wanted his fans to know that—despite his riches and stardom—all was not gravy. He'd been through the murder of Tupac, people being jealous of his success, the love triangles, all of it was weighing on him. The album was a fictional outlet for Wallace to deal with all of it, and make some great music in the process.

"I call this album *Life After Death,* because when I was writing stuff like 'Fuck the world, fuck my mom, and my girl,' I was dead, man," Wallace said. "There was nothing but anger coming out about everything: about having to go out to sell crack, to hustle for a living. Nothing but anger. But now I can't do that anymore."

"People know that Biggie ain't on the corner selling drugs no more. Why would anyone want to hear about that? I got other problems now, like people in Brooklyn. It's these goddamn haters, man. It just isn't good enough for them to say, 'Damn, he's from Brooklyn, he was selling drugs and robbin' muthafuckas and he took a talent that he had and he built it into something so strong that we're proud of him.' Instead, they're like, 'Fuck Biggie.'"

The album was a way for Wallace to get things off his chest, yet at the same time keep all his different audiences on their toes. A song like "Somebody's Gotta Die," "Niggas Bleed," or "I Got a Story to Tell" would remind people that hip hop has never had a better storyteller. A rhyme like his verse on "Kick in the Door" or "What's Beef" would demonstrate that he was a rapper's rapper whose skills went way beyond dropping designer brand names. On "Notorious Thugs" and "Playa Hatas," he would prove that nobody could freak as many different styles as B.I.G. And with "Hypnotize" and "Mo' Money, Mo' Problems," he proved that even his more mainstream joints could rock a hardcore crowd. And just in case you forgot, he could still smack you with a grimy classic like "Ten Crack Commandments."

The goal with *Life After Death* was to make an album that wouldn't as much improve upon its predecessor as dwarf it. *Ready to Die* was a slice of Brooklyn life, a street record that aspired for higher things, *The Terminator* of rap records. But *Life After Death* was supposed to be *T2:* twice as long, three times the budget, more special effects, but losing none of the character and personality.

As his friend and BK heir apparent Jay-Z observed, B.I.G.'s first album was "told from the outside looking in" whereas *Life After Death* was "told from the inside looking out." Or, put another way: "*Ready to Die* wanted to achieve that success and then in *Life After Death* it was coping with that success and dealing with that success."

Yet despite his newfound maturity, as a lyricist and as a person, Wallace still wanted to be the acknowledged for what he was: the baddest rapper alive.

"Who's your favorite MC?" Wallace asked Chairman Mao during one of the *Life After Death* sessions. When the esteemed rap scribe didn't answer quickly enough, Wallace jumped in—"See I want you to say 'Big.' Without hesitation. He's the best.

"I mean some MCs that I see I kinda assumed in the beginning had genuine love for me, they look at me now like, 'Oh, that's that nigga right there, he crossed over. He used to be hard.' 'Nigga, I'm the hardest nigga in hip hop. My shit comes off so strong and my hardness is sincere because I lived all that shit.

"I used to do a whole lot of fucked-up shit," he said. "And it was really expressed on *Ready to Die* and you couldn't really expect me to still be doing fucked-up shit on *Life After Death* because it would be kinda phony. [This time] I was just more focused on making records. Certain feelings, certain emotions I just wanted to express in my music. I got a newborn son. My peoples just had kids. I'm just trying to blossom more into being a father and a man. More than just that buck-wild teenage nigga that was just out there wildin'. I don't want muthafuckas to just look at Big and say, 'Oh shit, there go Big the dope MC.' I want people to look at Big like, 'Look at Big. He grew. He's a businessman now. He's a father now. He's taking control of his destiny. He's movin' up.' "

The sound of *Ready to Die* was largely shaped by one producer, Easy Mo Bee. This time around, with a real staff of Bad Boy hit makers on retainer, the process was more of team effort. Even outside producers like Mo Bee, RZA, Havoc, Buck Wild, Kay Gee, and Clark Kent would have their records altered by Puff and the Hitmen so that, as a cohesive whole, every track on the album would fit into the story being woven through Wallace's lyrics.

Easy Mo Bee, for one, felt frozen out by the new process. For many of the producers, besides the beat itself, there was less interaction on the content of the song. Bee was at the "I Love the Dough" sessions while Jay-Z and Wallace were pacing around the room, mumbling to themselves as they both wrote their verses in their heads, but they both left before they recorded their verses. He wasn't around when they actually laid them, despite leaving word to call him when they got back. "Goin' Back to Cali," another Mo Bee beat, had no title when he left the demo behind—it was a chopped up variation of Zapp's "Mo Bounce to the Ounce," no vocoder effects or nothing.

"I wanted L.A.'s attention," Mo Bee told *XXL*. "That was always the L.A. anthem. You got this East Coast/West Coast bullshit, and I felt that maybe through music or a beat, anything that gets everybody in harmony."

But there was a controversy over the song's title. "If I was there, that song wouldn't have been titled no 'Going Back to Cali,' " Mo Bee said adamantly. "I would have disapproved the title because once again, the climate at that time. I was traveling back and forth in California. And every time I got off the plane, it was like my eyes were looking left and right like, yo, yo, yo. I'm set up to go somewhere just looking left and right, checking everybody out, trying to make sure I say the right thing to everybody.

"I know for a fact, even if Big wasn't thinking nothing like that, Puff knew that I was uncomfortable with that and he knew that I probably would have tried to argue against it. I loved it though. Beautiful song. But the title? 'Going Back To Cali'? Oh, I was not cool with that.

When the song got made and it was final I couldn't even get a copy. When I found out the title my heart dropped, man. I was like, Yo, why'd they name that shit that, man?"

The simple answer was because they could. Not that it was necessarily a good idea. But *Life After Death* was being assembled the way a movie is. Mo Bee got a taste of the Hollywood pecking order firsthand: : Actor (Big), Director (Hitmen), Producer (Puff), and then somewhere way down at the end of the line, the screenwriter.

"The producers are like the screenwriters," Angelettie explained. "They come with the ideas. And we take that screenplay. And we're producing that. And we're directing that. And you get your credits, like you supposed to. Producers would give us tracks that were eight tracks and we may finish them with thirty-eight tracks. 'Cause we added strings, vocals, extra choruses, people singing in the background. We were known for sound effects."

But there was no question about which track mattered the most: whichever one contained B.I.G.'s vocal. When he was sizing up the premier track that became "Ten Crack Commandments," Wallace remembered a sidebar to Khary Kimani Turner's article in the July 1994 issue of *The Source*, "The House That Crack Built" about drug dealing in Detroit. The sidebar offered practical insights on the finer points of drug dealing. And Big decided that the Primo track offered the perfect way to adapt it as a song. The result was a masterpiece that everybody was feeling. (Well, almost everybody: Public Enemy's Chuck D, whose voice was sampled for the song's opening countdown, was offended by the song's drug theme and filed suit for the unauthorized usage.)

The double album was all but complete when Big and Primo got down to work. "I didn't know it was going to be called 'Ten Crack Commandments,' remembered Premier. "He just told me, 'I want it exactly the way you laid it out on the promo, don't change anything.' And I was like, no problem."

Someone wheeled Wallace into the booth, and he sat there, head up, ready to rip shit. Primo's track began to play, and Big burned through the whole song in a few short takes from his wheel chair, as he did most of that second record. It still hurt too much to stand without a cane or a walker. But Big didn't seem to mind. Like everything else life handed him, he found a way to make it fun,

He told Premier, "When I do my first video, I'm gonna dance in my video." Premier said. I was like, "Word, Big? You think you gonna be able to dance? And he said, 'Watch'." Then Wallace raised himself slowly out of wheelchair, almost able to support himself without assistance. He did a little wiggle and bounce with his shoulders, then plopped back into the chair with a smile.

"Ten Crack Commandments" was the last song recorded for *Life After Death*. As soon as he finished the verse, Wallace was elated. He knew, right off the bat, that the song was something special: Biggie talking about the crack game like an old grandfather schooling the youth who are still caught up in the grind. He didn't tell them not to do it, but his advice was so real, he might have prompted a few to have second thoughts.

"As soon as we finished that record, Biggie yelled on the mike and said, 'Preme, it's over! It's over! I'm the greatest. I did it!' "

That memory has stayed with the veteran rap producer ever since. "Those are exactly the last words I ever heard that man say."

While Big concerned himself with being the greatest MC ever, Combs was focused on making the biggest rap record ever. Clocking in at over twenty songs, *Life After Death* was a double-barreled blast calculated to slay the competition and scare the mainstream into submission without compromising Wallace's artistic vision.

On songs like "My Downfall" and "You're Nobody Till Somebody Kills You," Wallace was already playing with macabre imagery, much the way he had done with *Ready to Die*. There were no direct references to Tupac on the album death (except the ones deeply embedded in the lyrics to "Long Kiss Goodnight.") . Nor were there any tearful tributes. But death and enemies were lurking behind every other track. If you listened carefully to songs like "Long Kiss Goodnight" you could convince yourself that he was speaking about Shakur's murder. It was as if Wallace and Puffy were throwing it in the face of the whole morbidly fascinated audience. Like, you thought they were gonna kill me? *What?* I'm still here.

Puffy decided to do the photo shoot in a graveyard. After rejecting the idea of posing amid clouds with angel wings. The album cover, with Biggie posing by the hearse, was almost a taunt, the kind of bodacious move that Muhammad Ali would make, like daring people to doubt him and then proving them wrong. Wallace wasn't as much taunting death as much as he was asserting that I'm here to stay. Even if my album cover and title appear morbid my career is nowhere near death. *Life After Death* was meant to be a resurrection of sorts.

"I never did nothing wrong to nobody," Wallace told Chairman Mao while recording the album. "I ain't never did anything wrong to Tupac. I ain't never do anything wrong to Faith, nothing wrong to Kim, nothing wrong to nobody. And I kept quiet. I kept my mouth shut. I figure if I had been sitting here riffin' it'd seem like I had a point to prove. I know I ain't do nothin', so it don't make sense for me to say nothin'. I just let everybody do they thing. On March twenty-fifth, all answers gonna come out. You gonna hear what Big got to say. And on top of hearing what I got to say, you gonna spend thirty dollar to hear it. Fuck it."

The album was finished in late January of 1997 to meet a March 25 release date. The hype machine was in full gear; Wallace had cover stories lined up with all the rap magazines and a major feature in *Spin*. There was a national radio promotional tour lined up, along with television interviews, and plenty of concert spots. There were plans to do two big video shoots. It would be the largest promotion ever for a Bad Boy artist. Puffy was drawing on all of Arista's clout to ensure a number-one slot when the album debuted.

But in order to make the plan work certain things had to happen. First of all, Wallace had to go back to Cali.

YOU'RE NOBODY TILL SOMEBODY KILLS YOU

CHAPTER 8

> **66** Yea though I walk through the valley
> of the shadow of death
> I will fear no evil—for You are with me
> Your rod and your staff, they comfort me
> You prepare a table for me
> in the presence of my enemies. **99**

Christopher Wallace couldn't stop smiling.

Wallace was in high spirits as he sat by the pool at the Four Seasons Hotel on Valentine's Day. The sun was bright, there were women by the pool, and he was just sitting back, loving his life. And who could blame him? It was Valentine's Day, February 14, and here he was, posted up by the pool at the Four Seasons Hotel with a Frosty glass in his left hand and a blunt in his right. A Brooklyn thug basking in the sun like a sea lion. It was a scene worthy of his first single, "Juicy," in which he fantasized of "Living life without fear. / Putting five carats in my baby girls' ear. / Lunches. Brunches. Interviews by the pool. / Considered a fool cause I dropped out of high school."

He had accomplished everything he had ever set out to accomplish. It was a beautiful thing. But was also kinda scary.

I couldn't think of a single rapper who didn't lose a step after they blew up. Big Daddy Kane. Ice Cube. Chuck D. Even at times, the God of all Gods, Rakim. More than anything, I was wondering how someone who as successful as he was could avoid falling off.

"What keeps you motivated?"

Wallace smiled.

"Knowing that I got a three month old son that has to survive," he said. "And making sure my daughter's straight. I still ain't there,. I still got a lot more things to do."

Like what?

"I wanna master this rapping shit, so I can kind of be confident in what I put out. You know what I'm saying? Like if TLC or Boyz II Men drops an album, they know they're gonna sell five million. I wanna kind of be comfortable in my status as an MC. And at the same time, I wanna open up a few businesses. Name it Big Poppa's Chicken And Waffles. Everything in the restaurant is real big. Like, the tables are big, the chairs are big, it's a big clock, a big jukebox, the forks is extra big. Food, the chicken is big, the waffles are big, everything is just real big. You know, I'm trying to get with Heavy D today, and I want to talk to him about opening up a "Big and Heavy" big man's clothing store. You know, try to get me some of these labels that I mention ever so much in my raps, that their sales is boosted up so much in the urban areas, you know, saying all these kids wanting to get $300 glasses, and $700 sweaters..."

The more Puffy was talking about being a rapper, it seemed that the Notorious B.I.G had his sights set on being a full time C.E.O.

"I'm around of a nigger like Puffy who's learned from niggas like Russell and Andre and Clive, you know? Even when he on the phone. I'm in his conversations. I'm not supposed to be. I hear that money, I hear that money talking and I'm like, Okay, What you going to do? How much you gave for this? I'm always asking questions. And he's not that nigga that's gonna lie. He tells me."

Wallace definitely wasn't the mad rapper anymore. But his old fears weren't unfounded. The sharp change in his surroundings, the way his music changed after the success of "Players Anthem," the fact that he never once responded to Tupac Shakur's disrespectful antics—or anyone else's for that matter,—all could lead one to believe, that the thrill was gone, and the champ had gotten punchy. The disses weren't just coming from the West Coast anymore, but from the East. Groups like the Roots, whose video "What They Do" was a parody of champagne-popping clichés—many of which started with Biggie. The digs were subtle, but obvious if you knew what you were looking at. Raekwon's *Only Built 4 Cuban Linx* album contained a scathing skit that attempted to draw Nas into Rae's conflict with Biggie.

On Nas's 2002 song "Last Real Nigga Alive," he traces the roots of the competitive friction among the three brilliant young MCs. "Big told me Rae was stealing my slang," he raps. "And Rae told me out in Shaolin Big would do the same thing." Nas kept his cool, even when Biggie subtly dissed him on "Kick in the Door." Six years later, he's still big enough to admit that "I borrowed from both them niggas." Brooklyn's own OGC took things even further, with a video featuring one of the rappers in the group, at a New York concert, knocking an overweight rapper with a leather jacket, Coogi sweater, and Kangol off the stage.

Wallace shrugged the whole thing off. He didn't care if the audience wanted "Ready to Die Again." His life had changed and so had his music. The important thing was for him to be happy.

"I remember when I was in high school" he recalled, "and an English teacher once went around the class asking, 'What would you hate to lose more than anything in the world?' Everyone else was like 'my moms,' or 'my gold chain.'

The teacher finally got around to me. I said, 'My temper." It was a funny story, but he was very serious. If I lose my temper, something's gonna go down, he said. "My temper be fuckin' up sometimes. I say grow from your mistakes and hopefully you can stand the repercussions."

"I often have to say to myself, watch what you're doing, Big, 'cause you're not on Fulton Street anymore. If a nigga say, 'Fuck you,' you can't shoot at him. You just can't do it, Big."

Wallace's eyes glimmered as his hearty chuckle filled the air. "Okay, fine, I'll be the cool dude. I have security, and they can handle that. I'm just the cool dude. Write the raps, do the shows, all that. It's not like I'm biting my fingers, like, *Damn, I wanna shoot somebody,*" he said, bugging his eyes and munching on his fingertips for comic emphasis, mocking the image of a trigger-happy psycho.

The beef between coasts didn't make any sense, either socially or financially. Never did. Imagine if, during the heyday of the '60s soul movement, there was friction between Motown and Stax, with all of Detroit pitted against Memphis, with the Four Tops and Sam and Dave coming to blows, and Marvin Gaye bragging that he slept with Wilson Pickett's wife. Sure, Motown competed with Stax for radio play, market share, and record sales, but it was understood that each label broke new ground for the other. People who grew up on Stevie Wonder eventually discovered Isaac Hayes. Everybody made money—and the music that resulted was unforgettable. With hip hop, egos seem so fragile and success seems so fleeting that both must be carefully guarded and jealously defended.

"This shit is beautiful, man," Wallace said. "It feels like a few million miles from Brooklyn."

Well, only three thousand. But it wasn't just the California sunshine that had Big feeling that he was on another plane of existence. The King of New York had left his troubles back home. The only sounds now were the steady buzz of his vibrating pager, the splash of children playing in the pool, and the waiter asking him if his lemonade needed to be refilled.

"Being out in Cali was a major vacation for him," said DJ Enuff, who declined an invitation to join Big and crew on that trip. "I think he escaped so far that he forgot about reality. You're in the wolf's den, you're in California, you're in the home of Tupac who was just killed a half a year earlier? What are you doing out there? So who's to say, when you go out to Cali, you know, Pac's peoples or Suge's peoples or whoever's peoples won't say, Yo, let's get this nigger Big. You know. Pac's dead, why he ain't dead?"

But Biggie was not thinking those negative thoughts. He was sitting on top of an album that he knew was going to put him back on top, silence all the nay sayers, and slaughter whatever competition remained. There was confidence in his voice, ease in his demeanor, and a sense of purpose in his eyes. This wasn't the same kid I met three years ago on St. James standing on his stoop, wondering whether or not his album was going to go gold, and fearing that if he did blow up, plush surroundings would deaden his ability to make compelling music.

The move to Los Angeles was a way for Bad Boy Records to test the waters, to see how much resistance they would face breaking the very expensive *Life After Death* album to the second-largest radio market in the country.

A full year before the California trip, Sean "Puffy" Combs revealed one of the promotional secrets behind Wallace's and Craig Mack's initial success: "[We] donated three months outta their life to go on a major tour," he said. "That's the way you bug radio, believe me. Be nice to everybody, work overtime, do two shows a day, make everyone like you. Give up three months, then your records will last two years."

Those two years were up. Now Combs had to figure out a way to get people to fall in love with Wallace all over again, this time with at least some of the audience potentially hostile.

The grass roots were on Combs's mind when he came out to Los Angeles with Wallace. It was easier for people on the West Coast to resent Combs, and to hate Biggie when they were figures on MTV, always lounging in expensive cars, sipping champagne, living the high life. The best way to break through that was for people to see them out in the clubs—hanging out, partying, making stops at the mix shows, being seen out and about. The more they were seen, the more approachable they were, the more Los Angelenos would realize that they had love for the West Coast—and love for them.

"Big thought, 'While I'm out here, maybe I can try to clear some of this shit up," Lil Cease explained. "He used to call Puff, like 'Yo Puff, call somebody at the radio station. Tell em I wanna come up and talk about some shit. Like fuck it, I'm out here. I might as well get something done. Instead of just me sitting around waiting for this nigga to make a move. I could be out here doing something."

Cease said that Puff was happy to help. "He was like, 'Oh you wanna work while you out here? I'll set you up an itinerary.' That's when Puff starting setting up shit for Big to do. Interviews. Record stores. All the magazines. Big was doing it. He was like fuck it. I got some shit coming out. Let me get my shit together. He out there hustling. Scrambling. Like end of the day, nigga ain't thinking about none of that East-West shit. It's time to work it's time to work. You can't stop him from his business."

Not even a federal investigation was enough to slow his roll. Biggie was aware that his movements were being monitored while he was in Los Angeles. They were out to prove that rap labels like Bad Boy and Death Row were just fronts for criminal activity. And the undercover agents weren't very subtle about it. Who else could these white men taking pictures be? Rap photographers always introduced themselves.

"One time Big was in front of the hotel," Cease recalled. "I came downstairs, and he was waiting for the limo to pull up. So the nigga's just sitting out there with the cane in front of the hotel, and I'm like, Hold up. I see a man in front of him taking a picture. Then the dude jumped in his car, made a U-turn and drove away. I said, 'Did you do a photo shoot?' He's like, 'Nah, it's the feds.' He said it real nonchalant. And I'm like *Word*? Big said, 'Yeah, I'll pose for a picture. At least I got some protection.' "

"There was some nervousness about them being out there," remembered Wallace's manager and close friend Mark Pitts. "But once he got out there, Big had a way of putting people at ease." Pitts recalled how Wallace and his entourage went out to a club and met some resistance from people there—some of them bitter about Tupac's recent murder and suspicious that Wallace must have had something to do with the shooting, as revenge for Tupac's "Hit 'Em Up" and the whole Faith debacle.

Wallace, unfazed, stared them straight in the eyes and smiled. "You know you love me, stop playing." From that moment on, tensions at the club were eased and a good time was had by all.

There wasn't any overt tension coming from Death Row. Since Tupac's murder, the company was in a tailspin. Despite having recently renamed itself the "New and Untouchable," Death Row Records was anything but impregnable.

Dr. Dre, the musical heart and soul of the label, the most powerful producer in the industry, let alone the West Coast, had left. Snoop Doggy Dogg was quietly preparing to break out. Creditors from limo companies to American Express were filing suits. There were reports that the FBI, ATF, and DEA were investigating everything from drugs to money laundering and the label's alleged ties to the Mob Piru Bloods and jailed drug dealer Michael "Harry-O" Harris, who supposedly supplied the seed money to get the thing started in the first place.

Steve Cantrock, the Coopers & Lybrand accountant who did the label's book was in hiding and was supposedly blabbing to the FBI (and the *Los Angeles Times*) about being beaten and coerced into signing a $4 million IOU for overdrafts on the Death Row Records expense accounts. And now Suge, because of his role in the fight at the MGM Grand scant hours before Tupac's fatal shooting, was facing a parole violation. A surveillance camera captured Knight, Shakur, and several associates kicking Orlando Anderson as he lay on the floor. The arrest violated his probation stemming from a 1992 incident in which he reportedly pistol-whipped two aspiring rap producers for using a phone that was specifically reserved for him.

Despite numerous character witnesses, a bizarre recantation of the assault charges from Orlando Anderson, and a rambling but heartfelt plea by Knight himself, Knight was sentenced by Judge Stephen Czuleger to nine years in state prison on February 28, 1997.

"You really had everything going for you," said Judge Czuleger. "You blew it,"

With Tupac dead and Suge Knight off the streets, Bad Boy was making its presence known—in Los Angeles recording studios, in the clubs on Sunset Boulevard, and on local radio stations. The message was being sent wasn't subtle—while our enemies fall, we stand tall.

Snoop Dogg and Puffy Combs made a joint appearance on the *Steve Harvey Show* a few weeks before Knight was sentenced, both publicly declaring an end to the East Coast–West Coast beef.

The feeling was that, with Suge behind bars, the streets were open again. When the cat's away, the mice will play. Puffy showed up at the House of Blues one night for a concert that featured Warren G. and Nas. Heads turned as he laughed it up with fellow rap industry notables, enjoying the show from the V.I.P. balcony.

The locals didn't take this open presence kindly. The feeling around town was that Bad Boy was getting a little too comfortable.

One security guard who worked the door at many of the hot nightclubs that Combs and Wallace frequented warned that the Bad Boy Family was being much too visible in Los Angeles. The streets were watching. It was all well and good to ball out, and have your fun, but better to do it privately.

"You need to tell your boys to get the fuck out of here," the guard said one night. "This is still Suge's fuckin' town."

Combs didn't show any signs of slowing down, and neither did Wallace.

"L.A. fucked Big's head up," said Klept of Junior M.A.F.I.A. "Just by being out there, and seeing how much love you getting and all the gazillion bitches on some extra, extra shit. So that's why he got relaxed, not being on point."

While Wallace enjoyed his time by the pool, he was up bright and early the next morning, Saturday, February 15. There was plenty of work to be done. His primary reason for coming out west two weeks before the Soul Train Music Awards was to shoot a video for his album's first single, "Hypnotize." The clip, which would take three days and $700,000 to shoot, was more than just a promotional spot to help sell records. It was a loud, expensive statement that let the world know, "I'm back and bigger than ever."

In 1996, Death Row had upped the ante for hip hop videos with Hype Williams's breathtaking "California Love," a post-apocalyptic vision of Dr. Dre, Tupac, and a band of freakazoids roaring through a desert wasteland as hip hop road warriors. The clip pushed hip hop visuals even further than Hype had taken things with his earlier videos like Wu-Tang Clan's "Can It Be All So Simple" and Biggie's "Big Poppa." It was more than just using wide lenses, slow dissolves, dramatic lighting, and an expensive wardrobe. Hype realized that rap videos could aspire to the level of Michael Jackson's groundbreaking "Thriller" video. They could be mini-movies in their own right with their own narratives and moods. His video for R. Kelly's "Down Low," based on Tony Scott's *Revenge,* was a massive hit on MTV. Rappers were already making audio movies—having visual narratives that were as compelling as their songs was the next logical step.

Though he wasn't as famous as Williams, Paul Hunter was moving music videos in a similarly cinematic direction. Hunter was a young video director who had just started making a name for himself. His clip for Aaliyah's "One in a Million" caught Combs's attention and he hired Hunter to direct "Can't Nobody Hold Me Down." With its underwater photography, unique lighting, and dazzling group performance shots, the video helped the audience get used to a concept that, at first, seemed rather far-fetched: Combs as a credible rapper.

With "Hypnotize," Hunter had twice the budget and an even bigger agenda: to make one of the most exciting rap videos of all time. The idea hit him as he was walking through JFK Airport's '60s-style TWA terminal. His cell phone rang.

"Sup, Paul. It's Puff. You got any ideas, 'cause we ready to go."

Hunter paused. He didn't have a clue. But he had to come up with something quick. He looked around the terminal and saw people walking through a tunnel.

"Yeah," Hunter said. "I see you and Big driving down a tunnel. Backwards."

"Sounds hot," said Combs. "What else?"

"Hypnotize," as Hunter and Combs conceived it, was to be a mini adventure movie, full of intrigue and high-speed pursuits worthy of James Bond. Biggie and Puffy dodging bad guys on foot, being followed by cars with tinted windows, black helicopters chasing their speedboat. The two would elude danger until they finally reached a players' hideout, featuring beautiful women of all shapes and shades—even a few mermaids swimming in a fish tank behind the couch. Throw in some dancers, a live panther, and Biggie doing the shake and shimmy—somehow it would all make sense.

One month and three quarters of a million dollars after that cell-phone call, Hunter, with a Steadicam on his shoulder, filmed Puff, Big, and some women on a speedboat just off Santa Monica. The opening scene of the video called for Wallace and Combs to be lamping Big Willie–style with a couple of beautiful females, sharing a champagne toast, the last quiet moment in the video before black helicopters thunder down from above and ruin the mood. Everything had to be perfect, from the currents of the waves and the cloud cover, to the timing of the shots, or else hundreds of thousands of dollars in rentals and personnel would go to waste.

There was trouble from the start.

Earlier that afternoon, when Wallace had shown up at the set with D-Roc and the rest of his peoples, they scared the shit out of the boat's captain. He took one look at the tall and (in his mind) ominous black men smoking weed and exchanging profanities, and suddenly he didn't want to rent out the boat anymore.

"He changed his mind," recalled Hunter. "He saw a lot of rappers, it was loud, and it wasn't as organized as he wanted it to be. He started talking about safety rules and stuff like that."

A tall, lanky presence with long dreadlocks and a calm demeanor, Hunter handled the situation with the captain the best he could.

"We just kind of Bogarted him," Hunter said. "We said, 'We're not going to let you out of this deal,' and we got on the boat."

Soon the boat was on the open water. Moving fast, skipping across the waves like a flat stone. Slapping the bottom of the boat against the water so hard, Hunter could barely keep the camera focused while Biggie rapped along to the playback. Biggie was driving the boat, just after finishing off a huge blunt. "I was praying to God that we didn't run into a rock or another boat."

But at least a trained sailor was onboard. Sort of. Despite his misgivings about the whole adventure, the captain stood next to Wallace and Combs, protecting his boss's investment. But Combs didn't want to see him in the shot. "Puff put his hand on top of the guy's head, and he literally started strong-arming him to his knees," Hunter said. "He was down on his knees, driving the boat. You could see him pop his head over the steering wheel to see if we were gonna crash into somebody."

There was no crash. On Sunday, the production moved to dry land, but it was no less nerve-wracking. One shot involved Wallace and Combs in a convertible being pursued by men on black motorcycles who were shooting at them. While Wallace rapped, Puffy drove the car into the Spring Street tunnel in reverse. Hunter was excited by the fact that the same tunnel was one of the locations used by Ridley Scott in *Blade Runner.*

"I said we're gonna make this look like a movie," Hunter said. "We approached it like the big boys, but we had to do it in a lot less time."

Time was money, and Hunter ran a tight, highly organized production. Combs micromanaged everything from the clothing to the action. Meanwhile Wallace mostly chilled with his homeboys in his trailer, smoked weed, and looked for food to eat. Hunter remembers him as being very cooperative, questioning nothing about where the camera was or what was expected of him. "He just seemed like a funny guy," Hunter said. "The most intimidating presence was the people around him. One-on-one he was like a soft teddy bear. All he wanted was a bowl of cereal and some fruit and he was happy."

Production on "Hypnotize" wrapped early Tuesday, February 18, but not before filming all Monday evening on a Culver City soundstage teeming with female extras, sexy dancers, an animal trainer, and attractive swimmers wearing huge rubber fish tails.

Around 8:40 P.M., between camera setups, Hunter and his assistant directors kept things moving as quickly as they could on a rap video set. After all, call time had been four hours ago, and things were only just getting started.

The chicken-head extras stood on the sidelines trying their best to look pert and pretty, some of them complaining about standing around all day and how it wasn't fair that they weren't getting fed. The professional dancers worked on their routines. Choreographer Fatima Robinson gracefully put the girls through their paces, a seductive routine that fell somewhere between the Dance Theater of Harlem and Atlanta's famous strip club, Magic City. Cameramen, boom operators, gaffers, makeup artists, and other assorted crew members lined up to get some catered soul food (downwind from the extras who stood on the cold soundstage in cocktail dresses, looking hungrily at the spread). Combs huddled with Hunter, talking about the rest of the setups for the night, and asking for slight adjustments.

While all of this was happening, the real star of the show was wheeled onto the set.

"ALL RIGHT!" said a beefy white trainer, flanked by two assistants and carrying a walkie-talkie. "Nobody approach the cat!"

The cat in question was a huge black leopard that went by the name of Crystal. Hunter couldn't get the panther that Combs had requested, but any large jungle cat would suffice in a pinch. Crystal stared with confusion as everyone on the set looked toward her cage with shock, backing up. She sauntered around the cage, reacting subtly to the beat of "Hypnotize" as the song played in the background.

D-Roc stood next to G and Lil' Cease, watching the cat being wheeled on the set. D-Roc chuckled, turning toward Cease.

"Whose idea was it for this shit?"

"Puff's," said a nonchalant voice behind them.

The three of them turned around and saw Wallace, sitting in a director's chair near the monitors where Hunter and Combs were looking at some footage. The tiny monitor showed Wallace, leaning on his cane, rhyming, and an identically dressed Combs, making rhythmic hand gestures, dancing in front of the Panaflex camera moving up and down on a SuperTechnocrane with a telescopic lens.

Wallace soaked in the scene, his chair parked directly in front of the cage. The two baddest black cats in the room stared at each other.

"The cat just adds ambiance, that's all," Wallace said.

"That's some ill shit," said Lil' Cease, his reddened, heavy-lidded eyes widening slightly with admiration.

Wallace turned toward Cease with a smile on his face. "You got to show the cat who's boss. That's all. He made eye contact with crystal, still sauntering in her cage. "Lookit. This is my shit! They better let that cat know who's running this video."

Everyone within earshot laughed.

"I'm about to call my barber and have him cut my initials into his fur," said Wallace. "I'm trying to sell five million albums this time out, nigga. If I need to, I'll ride that cat like a horse."

One of the animal trainers nailed an O-ring into the ground and attached a long, heavy cable to it, pulling, making sure that the connection wouldn't give. The main trainer began talking to Hunter, who was trying to take it all in.

"You've got to keep the music playing," the trainer said. "Let her get used to it so she doesn't jump when you turn the sound up. I want to let her walk around a little bit, to settle down, to get comfortable.

Each assistant held one door to the cage open as the trainer walked in and attached the chain to Crystal's collar, leading her out.

"Quiet," he barked. "No sudden movements."

Wallace looked directly at the cat. He started twitching, making nothing but sudden movements, bugging his eyes to look crazy. He barked at the cat, taunting her. D-Roc and Lil' Cease laughed.

Once the trainer connected the cat to the O-ring, Combs and Wallace stood about five feet away. The dancers began moving in the background, and Hunter conferred with his cinematographer, getting their camera angles together. The trainer walked up to Wallace, handing him the chain that controlled the cat.

"The cable is actually holding on to the cat," the trainer explained. "She's stronger than you or I could imagine."

"I'm telling you, I can handle that," Wallace replied with schoolyard bravado. "That chain is for the safety of the cat. 'Cause I'm a wild nigga."

"What if it breaks loose?" the trainer asked.

"I ain't gonna run," Wallace replied. "I'm in no condition to run." He pointed to his leg and the cane for emphasis. "If you see me and the cat in the jungle and I run into the cat, help the cat."

While Wallace talked shit, the trainer threw the cat her favorite teddy bear. Quick as a flash, the cat snatched the bear in her powerful jaws, wagging her head from side to side.

"That's Puff," Wallace said, grinning and nodding toward D-Roc and Cease, who were cracking up. "That's how it's gonna snatch up Puff if he gets too close."

Combs, who was standing closer to the cat than Wallace, had a slightly different expression.

"Playback!" yelled Hunter.

The music kicked in, and Wallace started rapping. He delivered his lines with even more ferocity and energy than he'd shown before the cat's arrival, as if inspired by the big jungle creature. While Puff, who had been dancing in his charismatic camera-hogging fashion before, became noticeably more subdued in the cat's presence. He danced behind Wallace, close to him, but was careful not to step on the cat's tail.

As soon as the take was over, and Combs moved away from the cat, laughter erupted on the sidelines from both friends and crew.

"Puff's shook," Wallace said, laughing. "I told you the cat ain't like you!"

With the video in the can, there wasn't much for Wallace to do out west but hang out, make a few radio appearances, both in Los Angeles and up north in the San Francisco Bay area, and make promotional plans for the next few months.

When they came back to Los Angeles, Wallace and D-Roc went by the tattoo parlor on Sunset Boulevard, near the House of Blues, where they got tattoos of the Twenty-third Psalm etched into their forearms. It was Big's first and only tattoo, and "a whole lotta work" for the tattoo artist Mark Mahoney, who had just finished with Shaquille O'Neal. Big had recorded a song with Shaq for the ball player's album. O'Neal invited Wallace to his record release party. They talked briefly about B.I.G even being in Los Angeles, and the tension in the air.

"Yo, man," O'Neal said, "be careful."

Don Pooh could have used that advice himself. On Friday March 7, the night of the 11th Annual Soul Train Awards, Don Pooh, who now worked for Violator

Management, overseeing the career of the female rapper Foxy Brown, had his mind on a million other things besides watching the L.A. traffic.

While he talked on his cell phone leaving the Fatburger on La Cienega across from his hotel, the Nikko (now Le Meridien), Pooh ran past one car without seeing another one coming from the opposite direction. His body crashed against the windshield and he rolled over the hood of the car onto the concrete, a broken bone sticking out of his leg.

"I swear to God, there was this lady all in white, staring down on me while I was flat on my back, holding my hand, telling me that it's gonna be all right. It's gonna be all right. I turned and she was gone," remembered Pooh.

Pooh was admitted to Cedars Sinai Hospital, located within walking distance of the hotel. Violator management head Chris Lighty paid for Pooh's admission by putting the bill on his platinum corporate American Express Card, and Pooh was rushed into surgery, where pins were inserted into his shattered leg. Hours later, while he lay in his hospital bed, the phone rang in Pooh's room. It was Wallace.

"What the fuck? You trying to break yourself up, man?" Wallace joked over the phone. "I just broke my legs too, man. What, you want to have a cane just like I do?"

The two friends reminisced about good times and caught up with each other's recent movements. Wallace told Pooh how excited he was about the new album.

"I'm trying to focus this time around," Wallace told him. "I'm really trying to do it. World tour, the whole nine. I'm just trying to be real humble, man, and just give it my all." He told Pooh to get better, and promised him, "we're gonna get out there and we're gonna do this, y'knowhatumsayin'?"

Wallace started his reelection campaign as the "playa president" of hip hop that night, using his *Soul Train* appearance the way a politician does a convention. Wallace was there to present an award to Toni Braxton for Best R&B/Soul Album. With no Tupac and no Suge, no one anticipated anything like the drama that had happened the previous year.

Wallace's name was called and he strolled onto the stage, flanked by Combs and the Bad Boy R&B quartet 112. They were greeted with a loud unpleasant sound. Through the magic of television, the murmur sounded like applause to the home audience. But inside the Shrine Auditorium, there was no doubt— those were boos coming from the cheap seats. That's where the general public sits, the people who had to pay to come to the show. Some of them threw up hand signs, their fingers intertwined to form a *W*, representing "Westside."

"What up, Cali?" Wallace said.

He was showered with more boos, but ignored them. He smiled at the audience, not looking at all as if he anticipated anything bad. His eyes glimmered with that same confident, sarcastic expression that was his trademark, especially when he was in situations like that, outnumbered by playa haters. It was the same face that all politicians, from Richard Nixon to Bill Clinton, have used in front of hostile crowds, never letting them know that their disapproval bothered the candidate in any way whatsoever.

Stop playing, Wallace's expression said. *You know you love me.*

A few hours later, in his suite at the Westwood Marquis, Wallace was still in a playful mood. He sat with his driver Gregory "G" Young, who ordered food for both of them. D-Roc popped his head in for a minute, but G was hanging the tightest tonight. He and Wallace watched the time-delayed telecast, waiting to see how the tense appearance looked on TV.

Wallace strolled onto the stage, flanked by Combs and the Bad Boy quartet 112. They were greeted with a loud unpleasant sound— boos coming from the cheap seats. "What up Cali?" Wallace said, smiling.

As usual Big had jokes. About himself. The other presenters. Everybody.

"Maxwell is such a smooth muthafucka, boy, you know he got to be from Brooklyn," Wallace said as G laughed. "I bet you he be getting' all them exotic bitches, too."

Wallace looked beat, but of course their work was not finished. Room service had delivered a sausage pizza, which was resting on top of his bowling ball paunch as he leaned back in an easy chair.

"I'm supposed to be in the studio at ten tonight," he said. "But I'm kinda tired and want to relax and shit."

Wallace was to go record his vocals for the Bad Boy CEO's forthcoming album *Hell Up in Harlem.* One song, set to a sample of the theme from *Rocky,* was called "Victory." The other, built around a Barry White break, was an ode to hundred-dollar bills titled "All About the Benjamins." Wallace was supposed to write both his and Puff's verses for "Victory," putting down a reference vocal for Puff to record over later. Then he would lay his verse for Benjamins and be out. The plan was for him to come back to the hotel, grab a quick nap, then go to the airport in time for an 11 A.M. flight to London to kick off the international press tour. That was the plan anyway. None of the bigwigs from Arista who had set the whole thing up, knew that he wasn't going.

"I canceled that shit," Wallace said. "I just ain't fucking with it," he offered as an explanation. "I don't want to go to Europe right now. The food is horrible. I know I'm supposed to be mature and want to try different things and sample different lifestyles, but I just ain't in the mood for that shit right now. I just finished my album. It's about to drop in two weeks. I'm loving Cali and I've been out here a month, and I don't want to go nowhere."

Even if he wanted to, some of his road dogs didn't have passports with them. There was no way he was going out there without his full team. He smiled, took a bite from his pizza and a swig of Sprite. His eyes remained locked on the television screen.

"The weather is positive, the women is positive, and the weed is positive." G and some of the other guys in the room chuckled. "That's why I came out here, to kick back and relax. Too much snow at home."

Keith Sweat came on the television screen, and Wallace smiled. "That nigga is dope," he says. "I love that nigga Keith Sweat. Wendy Williams on Hot 97 said that nigga is forty-one years old. For real, Keith is the smoothest forty-one-year-old nigga I ever seen in my life."

Wallace was getting older himself. He was now the father of two children.

"What's being a father like?" I asked.

"Cool," he said, "but I can't really do it the way I want to do it, 'cause I'm mad busy and shit. But I want to wake up with my kids, get 'em ready for school and take 'em to school. I want to participate in all that shit."

He sat back, munched on his pizza and cracked a few more jokes, waiting to see himself on the screen. Did he ever get sick of seeing himself on TV?

"Hell no!" Wallace said. "I'm like damn, am I big enough on screen? I need more shine. I want to do a little sitcom or something. I got a little personality. I think I could do something like that." He'd already appeared on a couple of TV shows and read for a film, but he was sure there would be time for that later.

"What's the biggest misconception you think people have of you?" I asked.

"Probably thinking I had anything to do with that Tupac shit," Wallace said. "Fuck it. If the muthafuckas want to hate me because they think I did something, they probably ain't the right people to be fucking with anyway. You know what I'm saying?"

"Could you have imagined, a year ago, that Tupac would be dead and Suge would be in jail?"

"I wouldn't, but I wouldn't have been surprised," Wallace said.

There's certain ways you supposed to go about shit, you know what I'm saying? When you start making a whole bunch of money, you kind of got to, like, slow down. When your lifestyle is moving too fast, it's got to be on you to slow that shit down. You know what I'm saying?

"You just can't keep being pissy drunk, drinking liters of Hennessey and smoking two, three ounces of weed. You partyin', you fuckin'. And as soon as niggas say something slick, you beatin' they ass. Something's bound to happen, you know? You got to be big enough to say, fuck it."

"See I was kind of flowing down that river, too, for a second," he explained. "But when I had that car accident I was in the hospital for, like, two, three months. And it kind of made me able to sit down and be, like, 'Big, you're moving too fast. When you get on your feet, it's time for shit to change.' "

A few moments later, Wallace saw himself on the screen. He was expecting the boos, but the television broadcast polite applause. Anyway, the people in the room were more focused on the gold-plated diamond-encrusted likeness of Jesus hanging around Biggie's neck. It glimmered in the stage lights. "The Jesus piece is banging," Wallace said happily.

G laughed. "It's crazy, son!" he yelled. "It's off the hook!

I asked Wallace if the piece was meaningful to him or just a cool accessory.

"I think that if there were more people that were into the Lord, there would be a lot less shit going on in the world," he said.

"I think people need to realize that these are tests and obstacles that everyone has to go through. A lot of niggas want to give up and do wrong, but they don't even think God is in their corner. What I respect about God is that he always steers you in the right direction."

He rolled up his sleeve to show me the fresh tattoo on his inside right forearm, in the form of a weathered parchment, were the verses of Psalm 23:

The Lord is my light and my salvation, whom shall I fear?
The Lord is the truth of my Life, of whom shall I be afraid?
When the wicked, even my enemies and foes, came upon me to bite my flesh
They stumbled and fell."

"This is how I feel sometimes," he said. "I want to feel like this all the time. That's why I went and got it, to reassure myself that no matter what goes wrong, no matter how bad shit is looking, God is right here. He's not behind you, He's right here. As long as you believe in Him and in His strength, all these jealous people, all these sharks, all these bitches that's out here to get niggas, and expect you to fuck them and get on some real ghetto grimy shit and these haters—He'll stop all of that. He's gonna find you the road to take to avoid them.

Pushing his sleeve back down, Wallace continued. "What I'm doing right now is right. I'm taking care of my mother, my kids, and my peers. It's legal and I'm using a talent that I have to express myself and get paid; so it's only right that I follow the road without having to be involved in all of that extra shit."

It wasn't that Wallace was born again, or that he was about to join his mother at the Kingdom Hall Temple any time soon. But he had matured. Now he didn't need anyone else's approval for the way he decided to live his life: not his record labels, not his boys—nobody's approval but God's. He had taken the time to evaluate his relationships and decide who was in his corner and who wasn't. Wallace felt that Puff was one of the people who had joined his true circle of trust.

"You know, I used to think Puff was just one of them happy-go-lucky niggas, man. I knew so many niggas like that in the drug game, get-rich bitch niggas. Mostly that's what I always thought he was. Like, one of them, niggas in the hustling game that just knew a bunch of people, was mad cool, and that used to happen to be in a neighborhood where there were a lot of crack heads. He had a little bit of money put it into the drug game, and quickly he made a whole bunch of money. But he never went to war with no niggas. He never had problems with no niggas trying to take money from him, because he just was a cool nigga. That's how I always looked at Puff, like there's a cool nigga who just happened to be in the right position at the right time. Not really a fake nigga, but I knew he wasn't no street nigga. And at that time, when I first met him, street niggas meant everything to me.

Wallace paused for a moment as if he was reminiscing "But after getting to know him, and know his views and his feelings about certain things, I know he was a real nigga. "He's just an all-around cool dude, you know. He ain't no problem nigga. He just want to have fun. He was telling me today that he didn't even get to enjoy the success of Bad Boy, because when he first got everything, he was more on some, 'People ain't think I could do it because I got fired from Uptown shit,' and he worked hard to prove himself. And then when we started blowing up, that's when the East Coast–West Coast stuff started jumping off. And now after all that shit is over with, he has to deal with all these rumors about him," Wallace said, making an allusion to the "Puff Daddy is gay" rumor that Wendy Williams spread on Hot 97 (a rumor that eventually cost her that job).

"It's too much," said Wallace, shaking his head in disbelief. Then he switched into manager mode. When Combs became an artist. Wallace agreed to steer his career. This role reversal was the ultimate expression of trust. It's just an obstacle, that's what I told him. If you were to fold now, it would be a waste of time. Just hurdle over that shit."

Lil' Kim?

"Let Kim do her thing," he said. "She's cool when she wants to be, but she moves too fast, and she don't understand shit," he said. "I would hate for her career to be so hot in the beginning, but she hurt so many people and got so many people mad with her ways and actions on her way to the top that when it's time for her to do something else, everybody turn they back on her. She don't understand humbleness. I never had to deal with that with niggas. I tell niggas what to do and they do it. I made the records, sold the records, listen to me. Kim's always like 'Why can't I do it this way?' So many headaches. I'm not asking your opinion, I'm telling you to do shit. 'Well I don't want to do it that way,' and we argue and we bitch and she does it the way I want it, and the shit's a hit. And now she's on some new kick and I'm through with it. The album is out, let's move on."

Wallace exhaled. "I just wish I could be with someone like Cease. Not 'cause Cease does whatever a nigga tell him to do, but he respects my judgment. I would never tell you to do something that would have you fucked up. I only do it the right way, cause that's the only way I know how to do it. My track record is looking pretty good. She make it seem like I want to sabotage her shit."

Faith?

Wallace laughed. "We still ain't speaking, but it's all good. I can't chase her. She wants certain things that I can't do. But she brought a beautiful son into this world, so I'm happy about that. I can treasure that forever, even if your relationship doesn't work out. I always wanted a son and I got one, and that's all that matters to me."

Are you satisfied yet?

"Nah, I ain't have that yet," Wallace said. "I feel there are a few more dues to be paid on my part. I think there are a lot more lessons I need to learn, a lot more things I need to experience, a lot more places I need to go before I can finally say, okay, I've had my days. "Wallace's voice grew more forceful." A lot more shit has to go down. 'Cause I want a lot more.

"Niggas ain't the same young buck, 40-drinkin' niggas that don't give a fuck if they live or die. I want to see my kids get old. I want to go to my daughter's wedding. I want to go to their son's wedding. And you ain't gonna be able to see it wildin'."

The last full day of Wallace's life, Saturday, March 8, was not unlike any other Saturday in his life. He called his mom and both his baby's mamas to ask about his kids, listened to the music he made in the studio the night before, and asked his peoples, "Where the party at?"

Voletta Wallace was surprised to learn that her son was still in Los Angeles, that he hadn't left for London yet. She told him that she was helping her sister Melva with her wedding rehearsal. They had to go buy champagne for the wedding. She inquired about his safety in the way mothers do, but Wallace assured her that he was fine, that they had plenty of security, both off-duty police officers as well as some guards they hired from a private firm. She would only later learn about the phone calls from New York warning her son that he wasn't safe.

One person who was pissed at Wallace for missing the London flight was his manager, Mark Pitts. Pitts and "D-Dot" Angelettie went by Wallace's room to pay him a visit.

"Big argument," Pitts recalled with a laugh. "Big, big argument. My argument was dog, we gotta do this, man. We got to do this, dog. You're messing up. We gotta do this. And his thing was just, like, 'Yo, I'm tired. I need a break. I just finished my album. I don't really feel like getting on no plane right now to go overseas.' "

All wasn't lost. Wallace played them the rough mixes of the vocals he recorded the night before to "Victory" and "All About the Benjamins." Angelettie was completely blown away by Wallace's verse on "Victory," not just the way he slayed the intricate rhythm, but his lyrics as well. They were blazing from the opening line: "Hey yo, the sun don't shine forever / But as long as it's here baby girl then we can shine together."

"Oh my God," Angelettie said.

Later on, when Wallace talked with Lance "Un" Rivera, who was in New York, it was about how excited he was for March 25, the day that his album would come out, shock the world, unite the coasts, and make the radio stations play all Biggie, all the time.

When he was alone, he called Jan to ask about T'Yanna. They laughed and joked for a long time.

"I was looking sexy up there, right?" Wallace said of his appearance at the Soul Train Awards the night before.

"You know you looked good," said Jan. "You know you were looking sexy." Out of all the women in his life, she had never lost her love for Christopher. Never let herself become poisoned by the jealousy of competing with other women.

"He was telling me that he really missed T'yanna a lot," Jan remembered. "He really wanted to see her. And that was kind of the first time I ever heard in his voice that he really missed her like that. I told him to call me when he touched down someplace steady where we could make arrangements. Someone could bring her out to see him."

When he talked with Faith, the conversation quickly deteriorated and they hung up on each other. Wallace finished his pizza, got dressed, and got ready to go out to party instead of going to the studio to lay more vocals.

"Biggie was supposed to go to the studio that day. He didn't want to go to the studio. He was like, "I finished my album. I just want to celebrate with you," Combs remembered. 'I just want to have a good time. Let's go to this VIBE joint. Hopefully I can meet some people, let them know I want to do some acting.' That made me proud; he was thinking like a businessman."

G rounded up the troops and they hopped in the Suburban and drove to Andre Harrell's house, where Puff was staying. They didn't even get out of the car. They just sat there for a long time, blasting "Life After Death" at high volume, ready to go. It was about to be on.

The party, sponsored by VIBE magazine and Qwest Records, was at the Petersen Automotive Museum, located on the corner of Fairfax and Wilshire, a huge post-modern building with a car protruding from its side. It was billed as an official after-party for the Soul Train Awards—a post-awards weekend celebration. Because of the number of New York–based record industry heads in town and the fact that Bad Boy was out in force, it was also seen as an informal record release party for *Life After Death*. Every major celebrity, music executive, baller, and attractive female in town, it seemed, had an invitation.

VIBE's fashion editor (and eventual editor in chief) Emil Wilbekin had a bad feeling the moment he walked into the party. The son of Cincinnati's Commissioner of Buildings and Inspections, Wilbekin had been trained, from the time he was a kid, to always look for exits, to assess the safety of any building he entered. There were too many people inside this spot, and too many crowded out front.

"Escalators, up and down, glass railings, and no elevators" Wilbekin said, "The place was basically a death trap. I felt weird from the moment I walked in there."

Wilbekin peeped the room, nodded his head a few times, and decided to leave.

"I said, I'm not having this, and my friends were like, 'You can't leave, you work for the magazine, it's their party,' but I was like, 'I'm leaving,' " Wilbekin said. "I don't know why, but when my mind told me to leave, I left."

He missed a hell of a party.

Music was blowing, gin was flowing, ladies were dancing and the fellas were just sitting on the sidelines saying wow. From the accounts of many who were there, it was one of the best parties they had ever seen.

"That party was sick," remembered Angelettie. "We must have popped eight hundred bottles of Cristal. Smoked about fifteen pounds of chronic. It was crazy. Women all over the place."

It was an especially sweet occasion for Angelettie, not only because he was hanging out college buddies like Combs and Pitts at the pinnacle of their success, but also because of the way people were reacting to the songs that he produced. "The Theme" by Tracey Lee had the crowd moving. Then the DJ mixed in Big's new single "Hypnotize" and the place went bananas. The song played no less than eight times in a row. It was the first time Big had ever heard it in a club. He smiled brightly, his eyes hidden behind dark glasses.

Combs sucked in the atmosphere with a smile on his face. It was his kind of scene: model chicks and wall-to-wall celebrities from Wesley Snipes and Chris Tucker to Whitney Houston and Bobby Brown. It was the sort of party he dreamed about throwing when he and Angelettie were promoting at Howard, and now he was a guest of honor, the man profiting from every fifth record the DJ threw on the turntables. Combs was a good dancer, and normally he would have been out there on the floor showing off some moves, but he stayed next to Wallace the whole night by request.

"Big was like, 'Yo Puff, tonight could you just sit here with me all night?' Combs recalled later. And I thought, cool, we're gonna sit here and kick it. We was drinking and listening to records, sitting at the table the whole night." Cane in hand, Wallace surveyed the room, his mood chipper. "He's proud of himself," Combs recalled as if reliving the moment. "talking about how stuff's gonna be better when his record comes out."

"I'm gonna make them love me," Wallace told Combs. "I can't wait till they hear that track 'Goin' Back to Cali' so they know I got nothing but love for them."

Faith Evans was in the party too. She and Wallace made eye contact and barely nodded toward each other. Neither one said a word.

Def Jam founder Russell Simmons sat near Combs and Wallace.

"I was throwing paper at him, telling him how much I liked his record," remembered Simmons. "These girls were dancing for him, and he was just sittin' there, not even moving his cane. I wanted to be like him. He was so cool, so funny and calm."

As with many Los Angeles music industry parties, there were gang members from both the Crips and the Bloods in attendance. Among the guests were Dwayne "Keefee D" Davis and his nephew Orlando Anderson. The two men, reputed members of the Southside Crips, had been implicated in Tupac Shakur's shooting. DJ Quik was also there with a posse of Mob Piru Bloods from his Compton stomping grounds. Because no one was throwing up signs, who-riding, or otherwise attracting attention, few people thought anything strange was going on. The party was blazing, but from all accounts, drama-free.

But like all good things, the party came to an end. With almost 2,000 people overcrowding the place, and 200 more clamoring to get in downstairs, fire marshals shut it down at 12:35 A.M. The word was already out: those in the know were supposed to head over to the house that Interscope executive Steve Stoute had rented in the Hollywood Hills. This would be a "real" party, a low-key event where everyone could chill without all the hangers-on and autograph seekers.

As people filed out by escalator and elevator, Combs and Wallace hung back

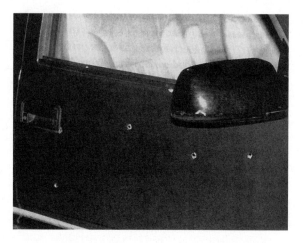

momentarily, slowed by Wallace's bum leg. They posed for a few quick photos, and, five minutes later, made it down stairs to the GMC Chevy Suburbans that they had been renting all month from Budget Rent-A-Car of Beverly Hills. A few weeks earlier he had stopped by Beverly Hills Motoring to check out their customized bullet-proof car armor, but did not buy it.

Seven nine-millimeter slugs ripped through the GMC Suburban's door and window, striking Wallace in the chest and abdomen.

Puffy climbed into a white Suburban with three of his bodyguards at the head of the motorcade. Behind him was a forest-green Suburban with G driving, Wallace riding shotgun, and D-Roc and Cease sitting in the back. Puffy's other bodyguard and close associate, Paul Offord, drove behind Wallace's vehicle in a black Chevy Blazer, flanked by an off-duty LAPD officer.

A few cars back, Deric "D-Dot" Angelettie, Mark Pitts, and rapper Tracey Lee shared a white limousine.

"It just happened that the limo that me and Mark were in was facing the opposite direction of where the Suburbans was, and we couldn't make a U-turn," Angelettie remembered. "We had to go out the driveway of the museum, and the police had the blocks blocked off, so we had to drive the long way around and catch up with them and meet the cars going this way."

Inside Wallace's car, G turned on the CD player as they pulled out. "Goin' Back to Cali" started booming, and everyone in the Suburban smiled. The song sounded good. "Y'all niggas is a mess thinkin' I'm gon' stop / Giving L.A. props," Biggie rhymed. "All I got is beef with those that violate me / I shall annihilate thee."

Puffy's Suburban, still in the lead as the group made their way to Fairfax, crossed Wilshire Boulevard to make a left, passing through the yellow light just in the nick of time. Wallace's car, heading north on Fairfax, was stopped at the light in the left turn lane.

Soon after Wallace's green Suburban stopped at the light, a black Impala pulled up to the right side of the dark green Suburban Wallace was sitting in

Wallace turned his head, expecting to see some fans or somebody he knew, asking where he was rolling to; better yet, it could be some fly females wanting to join the caravan.

From his vantage point behind Wallace in the backseat Lil' Cease could see the man who was driving the car a black man with a receding hairline wearing a bow tie and crisp shirt. Cease focused on the man's hands. His left hand on the steering wheel, and, his right hand holding something else. He couldn't quite tell what it was until he stuck it out the window.

It was a .40-caliber automatic.

BOOM!

People standing outside the Petersen Automotive Museum, many of them black and Latino, knew the drill the second the first shot rang out. Anyone who'd ever gone to a few hip hop parties knew the drill. It wasn't the Fourth of July, so no one had firecrackers. Only one thing could make that crisp, sharp sound. Everyone ducked down.

BOOM!

Lil' Cease and D-Roc ducked in the backseat, seeing the muzzle flash, trying to pull Wallace down in his seat.

BOOM!

Combs's white Suburban screeched to a halt and everyone inside ducked down. "Oh shit!" someone said, looking backwards. "They hit Biggie's car! THEY HIT BIGGIE'S CAR!"

BOOM!

Mark Pitts, D-Dot Angelettie, and Tracey Lee were chilling in the back of their limo as it took the long way around Wilshire behind the museum to the back of Fairfax. They ducked down instinctively when they heard the shots.

BOOM!

Offord and the off-duty cop, blocked by the white Toyota Land Cruiser, could hear the shots but couldn't exactly see what happened. Offord slammed on the brakes.

BOOM!

The dark Impala moved north, toward Wilshire, making a right on Ogden.

BOOM!

Cease and G scrambled out of the car and started pointing in different directions. "I was right behind Big," said Cease. "I jumped out of the car, searching myself to see if I'm shot. But the only one they hit was Big."

D-Roc remained in the car. Frozen. Looking into Christopher Wallace's eyes.

His friend looked back at him without saying a word. He couldn't. He was breathing hard. Trembling like a leaf. His tongue sticking out as he fought for air. Slumping toward the steering wheel.

"Biggie was just looking at me with this real shocked expression," D-Roc said, "like he couldn't believe it."

D-Roc looked up. Puffy had made it back across the intersection and was at the passenger side door, which was now riddled with bullet holes.

"Big!" he said frantically, pulling open the door. "BIG!"

"Where's the hospital!" Combs screamed. "WHERE'S THE HOSPITAL!" It was impossible to tell how badly Wallace was hurt, but they knew not to wait for an ambulance.

Puffy's driver Kenneth Story replaced G in the driver's seat, Puff hopped in the back, and the car roared off toward Cedars-Sinai Medical Center, which was less than five minutes away. They ran lights and honked horns, turning the Suburban into an ambulance.

By the time D-Dot and Mark Pitts's limo made it around the block, car horns were honking. D-Dot rolled down the window.

"Someone shot your man, Puff. And Big too," Angelettie remembered somebody saying. Already the misinformation was spreading.

The limo peeled out as Pitts and Angelettie made an educated guess that their friends must have gone to Cedars-Sinai.

Their limo reached the hospital a few minutes later, and pandemonium had broken out. People from the party stood out in front of the ER entrance crying.

Stevie J asked everyone in the room to hold hands with him and get down on their knees and pray.

Combs was on his knees praying. Faith was there. A doctor in a white coat walked toward them, slowly.

Pitts went inside, while D-Dot stood off to the side, comforting a female friend.

"NOOOOOOOOOOOOO!"

D-Dot rushed through the doors of the ER. It was Lil' Cease, rolling around on the floor. Screaming. Holding his head in anguish.

Seven nine-millimeter slugs had ripped into his chest and abdomen, causing massive injuries and internal bleeding. Doctors tried to resuscitate him for twenty minutes, but he never regained consciousness.

Christopher George Letore Wallace was dead. It was 1:15 A.M. He was 24 years old.

Outside the hospital, the police had cordoned off the green Suburban. The

Los Angeles Times

MONDAY, MARCH 10, 1997
COPYRIGHT 1997, THE TIMES MIRROR COMPANY/ CCI / 86 PAGES

Notorious B.I.G., left, leaves a party with producer Sean Combs shortly before being shot to death.

Gangsta Rap Performer Notorious B.I.G. Slain

■ **Crime:** Star is shot to death in vehicle after leaving music industry party in the Mid-Wilshire district.

By ERIC LICHTBLAU,
CHUCK PHILIPS,
and CHEO HODARI COKER
TIMES STAFF WRITERS

**Clinton
of China
Plan, A**

■ **Campaign finance:**
possible funneling of ille
U.S. lawmakers. Feinstei

By DAVID G. SAVAGE and R

press was already there, with television cameras. Flashbulbs were going off.

The cops on the scene, aware that the Bad Boy entourage included off-duty officers, started asking questions. Why didn't anyone call an ambulance? Why didn't anyone get, at the very least, a partial license plate number? Why didn't anyone pursue either the shooter or the white Land Cruiser? Were the moonlighting officers trying to avoid embarrassing revelations about their after-hours gig?

Combs, Pitts, and D-Roc sat there, passing around a cell phone. Which one of them was going to make the call, the hardest phone call that any one of them ever had to make? Mark Pitts passed the

Coming just six months after Shakur's death, Wallace's murder was front-page news on both coasts.

phone to D-Roc.

"How am I gonna call this man's mom? "he asked in despair." I grew up with this kid."

But D-Roc knew he had no choice.

The phone rang, reverberating loudly through 226 St. James. Voletta Wallace reached up, clicked on the lamp by the nightstand next to her bed, and looked at the clock. It was 5:21 A.M.

Something was wrong.

"Hello?" she said.

"Ms. Wallace?" It was Damien. She heard screams and cries in the background. "Ms. Wallace?" She knew Damien was a hard rock. The kind of Brooklyn-bred ruffian her son looked up to because he was hard and loyal. The silent type who wasn't prone to outbursts of emotion. And she could hear him on the other line. Sobbing.

"Ms. Wallace?"

Voletta Wallace dropped the phone. She didn't need to hear anything else. Her baby was gone.

THE LONG KISS GOODNIGHT

CHAPTER 9

> 66 Laugh now cry later,
> I rhyme greater than the average playa hater,
> and spectators buy my CD twice
> They be like, Damn he's nice... 99

Don Pooh never got that early morning phone call on March 9.

Though he was in the same Los Angeles hospital as Wallace, his friends didn't want him to hear such startling news from just anyone, especially given his delicate condition. They wanted to break it to him gently, for him to hear the news from "family." So while Pooh slept, someone called downstairs and requested that they suspend phone service to Pooh's room for the night, thinking that they were doing him a favor.

They forgot about the television in his room.

"I wake up, and the television news is on," remembered Pooh, "and I hear this voice say 'Brooklyn rapper slain. Details after we come back.' I'm figuring it's an up-and-coming rapper that lived in L.A., who moved from New York, and got in a fight with someone at a club and got killed. The last thing I'm thinking is that it's a big star."

But when the news came back, he saw a picture of Christopher Wallace. Then they flashed the roped-off crime scene at the Petersen Automotive Museum, then the bullet-ridden green Suburban, then images of people crying outside of the emergency room of Cedars-Sinai Medical Center.

"Nurse! NURSE!"

Pooh picked up the receiver. The line was dead. He threw the phone at the wall. Then the bottle of water on the table near his bed. Then the utensils. He had a full-blown temper tantrum.

"Come here! Come here!"

The nurse walked in.

"They just killed my friend! Turn on my fucking phone! They killed my friend!"

The nurse looked at him with a mournful expression. Tears rolled down his cheeks. It didn't really matter who he called. It wasn't going to change what had happened.

"I was supposed to meet up with him that night," recalls Luke. "Me and Snoop was in the studio in L.A. doing a song. That was the first time we ever really linked up after our little controversy. So we're in the studio doing our song and Biggie was at the party and we kept in contact with each other. I was gonna take Snoop and them over there with me after we finished recording." They expected it to be a quick session, but they never did complete the song.

"That was a little nervous time for Snoop because he had just broke off his relationship with Death Row," Luke recalls. "He was a little on the edge at that time. He was being a little careful of himself as well as his family and his friends. So we sitting up in there talking about a guy being careful. And Snoop had a police guy as his security, and that's who told us what happened. The police guy heard over his radio that Big had gotten shot at this party. And we was like, Naw man. And that's when the phones started ringing. Everybody's phone started ringing at the same time: the studio phone, Snoop's phone, my phone, every damn phone in the place. All I remember is a bunch of goddamn phones ringing. And people saying, "Big got shot." It shut that whole session down. We was all in shock."

By the time Voletta Wallace and Jan's plane landed at LAX, the rest of the country had been talking about Wallace's death all morning and afternoon. The mood that carried the day was numb, mournful shock.

Los Angeles's Power 106 and New York City's Hot 97, America's two biggest urban radio stations, both owned by Emmis Communications, did a live, nationwide simulcast. It was both a tribute to the Notorious B.I.G. and a discussion of the previous night's events. The radio stations were inundated with phone calls—everyone from artists to local fans. Some crying, some talking about the good times, all of them decrying the violence and senseless nature of it all.

"We need to talk intelligently and tell people there is no rivalry," said Dr. Dre, calling in from L.A.

"I'm sick of this shit," said a mournful Q-Tip from New York. "We need to wake up. If we say we're ready to die, we're going to die."

By the next morning, candles and flowers marked the spot where Wallace was shot in front of the automotive museum. People in his Brooklyn neighborhood, were holding vigils on Fulton and St. James. A graffiti artist in the Bronx was already working on a mural in Wallace's honor. Some record stores started moving copies of *Ready to Die* to the front of their record stores, and called BMG record distributors to order additional copies of *Life After Death,* anticipating even higher sales of what was already supposed to be the hottest album of the quarter. Tempo Records, located across the street from USC on Hoover Street, planned to double its initial order of the album.

"We did the same thing when Miles Davis and Tupac died," said the store's manager, Raymond Comeaux. "Whenever an artist dies, we have to pack the shelves."

At the downtown offices of the *Los Angeles Times,* where I was working as a staff writer, the Metro and Calendar sections had an early morning meeting, dividing up the coverage. As quickly as the various stories came together for Monday's paper, the more people we talked to, the more we realized how little we actually knew. There were conflicting stories on everything from the number of shots fired, to the make, color, and type of vehicle reported fleeing the scene, to the direction they traveled in. The code of the streets was in effect: those who knew wouldn't tell, and those who told didn't know.

Despite the attendance of over two thousand guests, hundreds of whom were standing outside of the venue networking, macking, or waiting for their cars at the time of shooting, no one saw "anything." As LAPD Detective Raymond Futami told the *L.A. Times,* "I think that there's a lot of people who are not coming forward. I'm sure there's a little bit of an intimidation factor . . . because of the reputation of some of the people who are involved in this case." The same thing that happened with the Tupac Shakur case was about to happen with Wallace's murder investigation, lots of speculation but little cooperation.

As we got off the phones with our various sources, the different water-cooler theories abounded: It was a drive by performed by a crazed fan who blamed Big for Tupac's murder in Las Vegas. It was a professional hit, orchestrated by Suge Knight, the telltale sign being that it came six months to the day after Tupac was shot—surely that couldn't be a coincidence. Then there were reports of Combs hiring gang members as part of his security detail, most likely Crips, since many Bloods were already aligned with Suge Knight. The theory—which Puff vehemently denied—was that these members killed Wallace over money that either he or Combs owed to the gang. The hit was actually meant for Combs, who had enemies on both coasts who, as he would later rap famously on "Mo Money, Mo Problems," would "rather see me die than to see me fly."

The problem was that none of the theories, however plausible or implausible, could be proven. The only thing that was certain was that two of the best and most popular rappers in history were dead, and both of them, Geminis born within weeks of each other, were murdered in nearly identical fashion. There have been other tragic moments in music, like the 1959 plane crash that claimed the lives of the Big Bopper, Buddy Holly, and Richie Valens; or 1970 when Janis Joplin, Jim Morrison, and Jimi Hendrix died within months of each other; and, more recently, John Lennon's 1980 assassination in front of the Dakota in Manhattan. Even the 1994 suicide of Kurt Cobain, who Biggie once called "that crackhead who killed himself." But this was different. These guys were from the street. They had been shot at before, and in Tupac's case, shot numerous times. And even though both swore that they had mellowed out and were heading for new frontiers—Tupac, with his engagement to Kidada Jones and his quiet moves toward leaving Death Row, and Wallace with his children, new album, and new mature perspective—they were now both dead.

Who was responsible? And why? Were the motives as nakedly obvious as revenge? Or was something much more sinister afoot? Both of these rappers were franchise players, big moneymakers for their respective labels—both of which were under investigation by Federal agents. Who would possibly benefit from two such deaths?

The scuttlebutt in the street was that Death Row must have been involved somehow, no matter how tangentially. There were whispers about how Suge Knight and others affiliated with the Pirus blamed Combs for Jake Robles's death in Atlanta in 1995. People said the Bad Boy family was living it up too publicly in Los Angeles, almost reveling in the fact that Tupac was gone and that Suge was incarcerated. No one had any proof, but anyone with a chair in a barbershop had an opinion on the matter.

Busta Rhymes arrives at Wallace's memorial service on March 18, 1997.

Norris Anderson, who was running Death Row, while Suge Knight began serving his sentence, quickly deflected blame for the situation when questioned over the phone by Philips and Williams. His statement appeared in the initial *L.A. Times* coverage of the event on March 10.

"It's ludicrous for anyone out there to blame Death Row," claimed Anderson. "Snoop and Biggie and Puffy have been in the press recently trying to squash all the media madness. This is a terrible tragedy. Death Row knows how bad something like this can feel. It happened in our own backyard with Tupac just a few months ago. My condolences go out to Biggie's family. I feel horrible for them. This killing has got to stop."

Ms. Wallace, flanked by Jan and Faith, stood in the Los Angeles county morgue and officially identified the body of Christopher Wallace, signing off on the death certificate. None of them had gotten any sleep. Jan was in such shock that by the time she unpacked her bag, she realized that everything she packed was useless—she had been on automatic pilot. Faith cried silent, bitter tears, realizing how frivolous their last arguments were, and guilty about the fact that they saw each other at the party but didn't even speak to each other.

Ms. Wallace was staring at her little boy. His mouth was slightly open. That mouth would never smile again, never tell another joke, never say, "Come on, Ma." She wanted to cry but she couldn't. She was too angry.

Who did this to Christopher? And why?

She had lots of questions but there was much work to be done. There was a funeral to arrange. There were grandchildren who would need to have the concept of death explained. She had to get out of Los Angeles. She had to go home.

Mary J. Blige and Lil' Kim, gave each other support in their grief at Wallace's funeral service.

First, Wallace's body had to be transferred from Los Angeles back home to New York. Clive Davis selected the prestigious Frank E. Campbell funeral home on the Upper East Side of Manhattan to handle the arrangements (which were paid for by Arista Records). As the place where last rites were held for Rudolph Valentino, Judy Garland, John Lennon, and Jacqueline Kennedy Onassis, Campbell's knew how to offer privacy for very public people.

Ms. Wallace kept up a strong, stoic face through the whole ordeal, even as everyone else around her began to crumble with grief.

Journalist, filmmaker, and friend dream hampton was with D-Roc and Cease within hours of Wallace's passing. They sat in Wallace's hotel room, surrounded by reminders of a man who had planned on living, his custom-made Versace shirts and pants strewn around the room. D-Roc sat in shock talking to himself. Cease was inconsolable. The three of them had seen so much over the last four years, from the corner of Fulton, when all they could do was dream about living the high life, to flying first class and living that dream. And now the biggest dreamer of all was gone.

"This nigga who ain't never hurt nobody..." D-Roc said, the words tapering off in silence. "I could see if it was one of us... I been shot mad times, niggas get shot...' He kept reasoning out loud, stoically trying to make sense out of nonsense, then slowly melting into tears.

Within hours of Wallace's death, many of the New York–based music industry people who had planned to take the Sunday night red-eye, pushed up their flights, trying to get home on the first thing smoking.

"I just wanted to get out of there," said Emil Wilbekin. "I felt scared." He ran into some of his colleagues at the airport, all of them with listless expressions. "I remember that no one would even talk to each other. Everyone just wanted to get home and feel safe."

Flying back to Miami, Luke thought about the friend he'd been speaking to on the phone until just before he was shot. "I mean, I'm on the plane, and the thought of him just goin' out there with the intentions of goin' to the awards, having a good time, and now he has to come back in a box up under the plane? That just stayed in my mind. Yo—he's coming back in a box up under the fucking plane."

Comb's people also wanted him to leave Los Angeles, pleading for his safety. But the mogul was paralyzed by his grief. For the first time in his life he didn't know what he really wanted to do anymore, or where he wanted to go.

"I was stuck," Combs told *Rolling Stone*. "I did not want to leave him. I still didn't really cry yet, 'cause I really didn't want to accept it. So then I'm about to get on a plane. And as I'm seeing the plane pull up, that's when I break down. I'm about to leave L.A. without my man, you know what I'm sayin'? He's at the morgue, just lying there. That shit was just so fucked up to me. I wanted him to be with me, sitting right there with me, going back to New York. I would just sleep a lot. I wanted to wake up. I just knew it was a dream."

That was how Christopher Wallace looked in his casket: as though he was sleeping. Lying in a velvet-lined coffin made of beautifully polished mahogany, Wallace was dressed in a white suit with a matching derby—an outfit worthy of his status as a man of respect. His face looked peaceful, but none of the people there felt peace at his passing. Everyone felt the same thing: this was a light that was snuffed out much too soon.

"They had him dressed up like Big Poppa," said DJ Premier. "They dressed him up nice, but it was hard to look at him like that."

The revered rap producer paused momentarily at the memory.

"I've seen many young brothers in a casket before, but the one with Biggie in it was really, really hard to swallow just because it was like, 'Damn, I just saw you when we finished the album.' "

Many of those in attendance were surprised that the casket was open. On one hand, it gave them a chance to see his face one last time, to touch it, to say good-bye. On the other, it was a poignant reminder of the fragility of life, of the fact that someone they all knew, loved, and shared jokes with was now dead. Both Combs and Lance "Un" Rivera broke down when Christopher Jr., held up to the casket by Rivera, smiled and touched his father's face. There were very few people who weren't overwhelmed with intense waves of grief.

"I'm not good with funerals at all," admitted Easy Mo Bee. "I didn't even go to my cousin's own funeral, man. I went to Biggie's funeral."

Seeing the body also had a sobering effect on Wallace's first producer.

"I went past the casket and I seen him laying there," Mo Bee continued. "They had to tell me to keep moving. I was just standing there, staring at him, man. Shit broke me up. I just wanted to go, since I didn't get to go to the studio and see him do his vocals for the last time, and since I wasn't there to tell him, please don't call that song 'Goin' Back to Cali,' please don't do that. Because I didn't get to be there for none of them last moments, I had to go to his funeral."

Over 350 family members and friends packed in to the elegantly appointed viewing room, consoling one another, many with visible masks of grief. Besides obvious people like the members of Junior M.A.F.I.A., and close friends who toured and worked with him, other guests included Busta Rhymes, Jay-Z, DMC of Run-DMC, Mary J. Blige, Heavy D, Foxy Brown, DJ Kool Herc, Flavor Flav, and Queen Latifah. Former Mayor David Dinkins, although he'd never met Wallace, attended at the behest of Clive Davis.

Ms. Wallace read from the Book of Job. The group 112 sang their song "Cry On." Sean Combs said a few words of remembrance. Faith sang a beautiful rendition of "Walk With Me Lord" that made women and tough guys alike openly weep with grief.

As D-Roc and the other pallbearers carried the casket to the hearse, fans and members of the media watched as other people came out from under the funeral home's red awning onto Madison Avenue. Lil' Kim crumpled like a rag doll into Mary J. Blige's waiting arms. Pepa walked out with tears in her eyes, as did Bad Boy recording artist Mase. The rest of the family quietly filed into the waiting limos and SUVs to make the trip to Fresh Ponds Crematory in Middle Village Queens. The driver led the procession of 20 cars south toward the Brooklyn Bridge.

The whole crew was heading for Fulton Street. One last time.

Roughly 800 people crowded both sides of the block on St. James between Fulton and Washington waiting for Wallace to come home. They had been waiting, in the freezing cold, since 10:00 that morning. And now it was after 1:30.

There were so many people out, it was impossible to walk on the sidewalk.

People sat on top of cars, stood on stoops, hung out of windows. Looking. Waiting. Anticipating. Curious. Nervous. The fifteen-year-old mothers with their baby strollers, snapping gum, looking out at the crowd, the kind of girls that Big rhymed about robbing on the train for their "#1 Mom pendant" on his verse on "Gimme the Loot." Eight- and nine-year-old boys who had hung up posters of him on their walls from *Word Up!* and *Fresh* magazine, just as he had years before for his rap heros. Teenage boys and young men, many of whom knew him, who were caught up in the everyday struggle of the illegal paper chase that Big wrote about in many of his rhymes. His music was dedicated to them, and became the soundtrack of their lives, much the way Marvin Gaye's *What's Going On* or Stevie Wonder's *Songs in the Key of Life* was to their parents.

Old women, held candles, saddened to hear about the death of another young black man, one who had done good with his life and had seemingly put the illegality and negativity behind him. Others cried about his tragic death, crying for his mother Voletta, who was known around the community for more than two decades, but also crying for their own sons and nephews, some who had already died, and some who were well on their way to the funeral parlor.

Some of the same women to whom Wallace had defiantly dedicated his song "Juicy"—the ones who used to call the cops on him when he was on the corner selling drugs "trying to feed my daughter"—were out here crying, defending his legacy. Some stared angrily at the cops lying in wait in riot gear, who seemed so sure that something was going to jump off, and at the numerous members of the television and print media, the kind of people who care about black talent only after it's tragically taken away.

One woman, looking down from a stoop, let the visitors know how she felt about their presence. "Fuck these white muthafuckas! Get off my block! Y'all ain't allowed."

A woman with flowers and a Biggie T-shirt hanging over the front of a baby carriage strolled the streets, a wool cap over her head. Her name was Shirley Wright, and she had traveled to St. James all the way from Los Angeles. "I am here representing peace," she said. Others in the crowd weren't feeling the California love.

"We East Coast ridaz now, fuck them West Coast niggas!" one tall black kid said, his eyes brimming with anger. "That was my man right there," said a shorter kid about Wallace. "He never forgot us."

On the stoop in front of 226 St. James, well-wishers created a shrine of cards, hand-drawn pictures of Big, and candles. Audwin Sookra burned the edges of dollar bills and blew them out, placing them on the ground next to a picture of Wallace. "Biggie always wanted money to burn," he said. He raised his head and nodded at a couple of guys standing nearby. "I don't want anyone to steal this," he said, looking down at the partially burnt dollar. "No one should profit from this."

As he spoke, a few brothers walked the sidelines, carrying a box of T-shirts for sale. The message on the front said "In memory of the Notorious B.I.G" with a likeness of his latest magazine cover silkscreened on the front. Wallace's body was not yet in the ground and

people were already trying to make a buck. Judging from the number of T-shirts visible in the crowd, business was booming.

When Wallace's funeral procession reached Brooklyn, a crowd was waiting on the streets. The scene resembled a memorial for a deceased head of state.

The temperature had dropped despite the presence of the sun. People stomped their feet and blew into their hands to keep warm. Anguish turned into tension. Pathos to humor.

Ten more minutes passed. It was five minutes to two.

"Nigga delinquent," one male voice said.

"He better get his ass on," said a woman, "or he ain't gonna see Tasha today. Too cold out here—shit!"

An old man opened his front door and stepped out onto the stoop. He saw a crowd forming around his car, all trying to get the best vantage point for the coming procession. People were sitting on the hood and the trunk of his old Cadillac.

"Get off my car!" he yelled. "Some people have to go to work."

A few people moved, but most just ignored the old man. Everyone was standing on top of whatever they could find, anything that would give them a better view of the motorcade. Along with the TV camera trucks doing live remotes, there were cars parked up and down both sides of the street. Many drivers didn't anticipate a gathering of this size and didn't make the proper arrangements.

Heads turned as car horns blared in the distance. The sounds of applause and screaming could be heard coming down the block.

Biggie was home.

The shiny black hearse rounded the corner and turned onto St. James, heading toward Fulton, moving very slowly. In front of the motorcade rode a black man on a bicycle, holding up a handmade cardboard sign: CHRISTOPHER WALLACE, THE GREATEST OF ALL TIME. He wasn't a Bad Boy affiliate, just a Brooklynite expressing what everyone was feeling. Eight more stretch limos and 20 other cars followed behind the hearse, and through the windows people saw Ms. Wallace, Faith Evans, and the whole Bad Boy family and waved at them. Some waved their fists in a final triumphant gesture, saluting rather than celebrating. Tears flowed from the eyes of hardrocks and babymommas. No one could feel the cold anymore.

Flowered cars moved by, one with the letters B.I.G. spelled out in red carnations. Another arrangement in yellow said, "For Daddy."

In another limo Lil' Cease, D-Roc, and other members of Junior M.A.F.I.A. raised their hands and funeral programs through the open sunroof. Bigging up Brooklyn, sending the love right back, smiling through their tears. It was almost as if they were saying, "Look at all these people out here—our nigga made it." They took a long look so the memory would last. At least nobody could take that away.

And then, just as suddenly as it arrived, the cavalcade was gone. After hours of waiting, the whole thing had lasted ten minutes.

People stood in hushed, stunned silence. Then a great wave of sadness rushed over the collective. Women's breasts heaved with sobs. Men's shoulders shrugged, some of the men embracing total strangers.

Then it happened. The beat to "Hypnotize" erupted from a speaker outside the Underground nightclub at 977 Fulton.

"Uh! Uh! Uh! *Hot!* / Sicker than your average, Poppa twist cabbage off instinct / Niggas don't think shit stink / Pink gators for my Detroit players / Tims for my hooligans from Brooklyn…"

Biggie was alive. Right there. Right then. Yes, everyone went crazy. Euphoria rippled through the crowd. It was just like the moment in a New Orleans jazz funeral when the dirge becomes a party.

Some kids along Fulton jumped on top of a Dumpster and started waving their hands and shaking their hips to the music. Other people started dancing on top of the cars. The old man looking out for his Cadillac suddenly lost his temper. "Get off my car!" Nobody could hear him. They were too busy dancing.

Everyone was having a good time except for New York's finest. The cops didn't like the sudden shift in energy. Fearing that the situation was getting out of hand, they moved forward trying to disperse the crowd. They pulled some of the kids off the cars and arrested them.

The crowd wasn't trying to hear it—not that the cops cared.

A SWAT team appeared on a rooftop. Cops in full riot gear—helmets, Plexiglas shields, and billy clubs—started moving through the crowd randomly handcuffing anyone who didn't get out of the way. People ran, ducking, and diving. A paddy wagon pulled up. Some young men got into shoving matches with the police. News cameras captured the melee.

"He wouldn't have wanted it like this!" a middle-aged brown-skinned woman named Vanessa Edwards yelled frantically, her eyes wet with frustration. The cops kept pulling people off the cars.

One cop wrestled a young man to the ground and began to pummel his head with a can of pepper spray. Julia Campbell, a thirtyish white woman with a cherubic face and a press pass, stepped forward.

"Why are you doing that? Why are you using pepper spray?"

"Move out of the way, lady," he said.

"I'm with the *New York Times*," she protested. "You can't tell me where to go!"

The cop didn't hesitate. He sprayed pepper in her face, and her glasses offered no protection from the stinging, choking cloud.

As she screamed, another cop stepped in behind her and put on handcuffs. A black teenager who saw the whole thing, walked right up to Campbell.

"Now you see how they treat us! Now you know how it feels. Fucked up, ain't it? You all right?"

Within ten minutes, the whole block was cleared of people. The old man stood in front of his Cadillac with a dismayed look on his face. The windows were broken, the hood and the roof dented by heavy boot prints.

"Hypnotize" kept playing somewhere in the background.

"That Brooklyn bullshit," Biggie said, "We on it."

And the beat never stopped.

Sean Combs rode a motorcycle along an isolated country road, surrounded by a bucolic landscape and a pristine blue sky. After so much pain, so much darkness, so much gloom, it was the first beautiful day he could enjoy. He rode tall, the wind blowing on his face, and for a brief moment, all was right in his world.

He didn't see the bump in the road until he ran right into it. His body hit the pavement at the same time as his bike. And as usual, he couldn't have this painful, private, embarrassing moment to himself—never that. Privacy had no place in the world of Puff Daddy.

Of course, there was a camera around to capture the whole thing. Puff wouldn't have it any other way.

"He wiped out," said Hype Williams, the director of "I'll Be Missing You," a tribute song for Christopher Wallace. "It just so happened that we got it on film, so we used it in the video. Luckily we didn't have to take him to the hospital and we were able to keep filming."

Combs' wipe-out suddenly became visual metaphor, and, in a manner that can only be described as Combsian, he managed to flip a negative situation into something that greatly benefited him. His serene motorcycle ride suddenly represented the good times he and Wallace shared in Los Angeles, the bump in the road the Los Angeles beefs they were oblivious to, and the wipe-out the aftermath to Wallace's being murdered right in front of him. All of it captured, and documented for the world to see, not unlike the numerous photos taken right after the shooting, the public outpouring of grief, and now, like Williams's cameras, the whole event recorded for posterity.

Combs's reaction to the accident, despite his injuries, was similar to the way that he handled misfortune so many times before. He picked himself up, dusted himself off, and got right back to work. The process of getting back on his feet started with the recording of "I'll Be Missing You."

After Wallace was killed, Combs had contemplated getting out of the business altogether. He didn't necessarily contemplate suicide, but he thought about death a lot, almost as if he wished it had happened to him. For days at a time, he would lie in bed, unable to sleep, eat, or even move. "Sometimes I wanna pull it, end it all with a bullet," he rapped on the song "Pain," recorded after Wallace's murder. "Hard to live life to the fullest with all this bullshit."

Why not get out? He already had plenty of money—close to $100 million at this point. He could sell the company, take the cream, and whip up some of the other ideas that he had bubbling—fashion, films, restaurants, whatever he wanted. Few people would consider him a sucker for cashing in his chips.

And during the weeks he spent in inconsolable isolation, the people closest to him wondered—when they were out of earshot—if he might just slowly fade away. Do like Russell Simmons and find him a Lyor Cohen type to take over the day-to-day operations of Bad Boy while Puffy collected checks and sat on a white sand beach somewhere, contemplating his next move.

But Combs wasn't ready for his *Godfather II* Corleone-style moment by the lake, watching the sun set and the leaves blow around, remembering happier days. Nobody was better at kicking himself in the ass. Just looking at how other people were reacting was enough to get him jump-started.

"I saw the strength of Biggie's mother," he told *Rolling Stone*. "If she ain't going to give up, if she ain't jumping off no bridges—she's having to get up and go to work, still take care of the kids—I've got to get myself together."

He also saw a music video.

While he was lying in bed early one morning, MTV played the 1983 Police hit, "Every Breath You Take." Listening to the song, which is actually about a disgruntled lover stalking his ex-girl-friend, Combs felt comfort. The "every step you take," aspect of the lyrics made him feel as if he was being watched and protected from above by his new guardian angel—Wallace.

So like the Lox before him—whose "We'll Always Love Big Poppa" was the first song dedicated to Wallace's memory—and like KRS-One before them (who dedicated several of his Boogie Down Production albums to his dear departed

This mural on Ward Avenue in the Bronx was painted within 24 hours of Wallace's death. It was the first of many tributes to the fallen giant.

DJ Scott La Rock, shot down in the streets of New York), Combs decided to move forward in the name of his man—and write a song about it.

He gathered those closest around him to work on the song, figuring that it would be a beneficial place to work out his grief, but at the same time create a lasting tribute. The Bad Boy family immediately got to work on "I'll Be Missing You." It was decided that the proceeds from the single would go into a trust fund for T'Yanna and Christopher Jr. But of course the song was about was more than that—it was a way for Wallace's friends and fellow artists, to express their feelings in song.

The recording session was tense. There were times when Combs and Evans, overwhelmed with grief, would leave the studio in tears.

There was Faith, crying as she lay down her vocals, her voice emoting the strange mixture of emotions that almost always follows the reaction to someone's death. Combs would sometimes have to leave the room, overwhelmed by all the emotion. But of course none of this pain was private. Not only was it being recorded for public consumption, but a reporter was there witnessing the whole thing.

"You can have all the success and money in the world, but at the end of the day it doesn't really mean a thing," Combs told Chuck Philips, who was in the studio watching Combs and Evans record the song. "I can't be happy right now because my best friend is dead. I know God doesn't give you anything you can't handle, but I'm really struggling with it, man. I'm having a tough time here."

"Me, Stevie J, Faith, and 112 sat in a studio four days in a row," remembered Deric "D Dot" Angelettie. "No sleep. We made two versions before that one, but I came into the studio with that Police sample, and I think that was it."

Another version of the song sampled the Harold Melvin and the Bluenotes' classic "I Miss You," but that choice was considered too maudlin. The goal—for the first time in a Bad Boy single release—wasn't to make a song that would rock a dance floor. It was to make a song that could express the conflicted emotions one always feels at a wake—the sadness of someone's passing, and the joy that comes from people getting together to remember someone they all loved. All set to something that rhymed and had a backbeat. The song was supposed to make you cry and nod your head.

"It wasn't always the Police remake," said Faith, "but we kind of knew once we heard it. I was like, yeah, that's definitely going to be it. It was just a more popular song to cover. And then lyrically, I don't think I really strayed too far away from the original lyrics, it's just that the original song was more about a love interest other than the loss of somebody. So I just had to change a few words, write a few phrases. It's not like I had the big idea. But it just came together well, it worked."

"We're party animals," said Combs. "And we just had to say, 'We miss you, but we miss you in a happy way.' We wanted to rejoice and not be sad, because the Lox song was already sad. We had to find a way to pick it up, because at the end of the day, Big was why we were here, so we had to let him know."

If the song was poignant, the video was a celebration.

The most memorable shot in the video isn't Combs grooving on a people mover, Faith Evans singing movingly into the camera, or even Combs leading a group of children (including three-and-a-half-year-old T'Yanna Wallace) up a hillside dressed in their Sunday best. It's a shot of Combs himself. He's alone, dancing in the rain, spinning in a black designer silk suit as the water pours down from above.

It's shamelessly self-centered, and made more than one person question aloud how much did Combs really care about Wallace if he's dancing like that in his video, some even going as far to liken the act to dancing on Wallace's grave. But the failure to understand the beauty of the moment would also be a failure to understand the beauty and genius of Sean "Puff Daddy" Combs.

Before Wallace's death, "Can't Nobody Hold Me Down," sounded like a study in arrogance, the words of a man taunting G-men, God, and gangsters, bragging about how much money he had and a "Benz that he ain't even drove yet." The beat of one of hip hop's most enduring social commentaries, "The Message" had been co-opted and reworked as a party anthem for a man who seemingly cared more about his cars, caviar, and carats then he did about his people.

After Wallace's death, the same song, and the very same lyrics, became a study in perseverance. Now Combs was a man who refused to be stopped—no matter how high the stakes, no matter what the score. It didn't matter how many people hated him, how many people wished him ill, or even, more seriously, how many people wanted to kill him, in the end it didn't matter. He was going to do his thing his way. As he danced, one realized how now the chorus of a throwaway pop song like Matthew Wilder's 1983 "Break My Stride" could become a mantra of resilience, a mission statement: "Can't nobody break my stride. Can't nobody hold me down. *Oh no.* I got to keep on moving."

Lots of other things had changed too. When Puff first decided to make the transition to artist, Big—who was eager to explore the business side of show-biz—was going to be his manager. But in death, Big did more for Puff than any manager could ever do.

Puff also changed the name of his album. Instead of *Hell Up in Harlem,* Puff's solo debut was now called *No Way Out.* "We changed it because it didn't apply no more," Angelettie said. "And [Combs] felt boxed in."

But he wasn't. Instead, the record that was supposed to be his swan song ended up rising from the flames like a phoenix.

Just as *No Way Out* transformed the life of Combs from well-known executive to pop superstar, *Life After Death* transformed Wallace from pop superstar into a figure of iconic status. Perhaps the most surprising thing was that Biggie's death wasn't what made him an icon—it only prevented Wallace from enjoying it. Had he not been murdered, *Life After Death* would have helped Wallace attain the status of KRS-ONE, or Rakim—artists who are damn near worshipped by the rap community like living gods.

The title *Life After Death,* was, as no reviewer failed to note, prophetic. Some of the same people who, before his death, whispered about how the money had gone to Wallace's head, were now some of the same people praising his genius—a genius on ample display. It was an amazing last statement—all the more sad, because it proved that the rapper was reaching a level of talent with his gift that was truly joyous to behold.

Life After Death was nothing short of a gangsta rap *Songs in the Key of Life,* the stylistically diverse Stevie Wonder double album that made listeners wonder if there was anything Stevie couldn't do. It was the same with Biggie's second album—there was so much variety (beats, flows, styles, subjects) all springing fully formed from a skull shaped like a colossal Olmec head.

Songs like "Somebody's Gotta Die" and "Niggas Bleed" showcased Wallace's eye for detail—with narratives so vivid and indelible that a music video would have actually diminished them. "I'm Fuckin' You Tonight," on the surface, was a raunchy sex rhyme that was almost pornographic in detail—but technically it was a tour de force. Instead of simple rhyming couplets, Big buried rhymes in the beginning and middle and end of his lines—an amazing display of poetic skill that was not meant for the page but the ear. "Some say the Ex makes the sex / Spec-TAC-ular, make me lick you from your neck to your BACK then ya / SHIV-erin', tongue de-LIV-erin' / Chills up that spine, that ass is mine."

"Kick in the Door" showed that even in the most off-kilter environment, Wallace could stutter step and fake out the beat with all the dexterity of Allen Iverson's crossover dribble. With "Notorious Thugs," rapping alongside Bone—his emulation of their style wasn't parody but the deepest form of respect. Songs like "Hypnotize" and "Mo' Money, Mo' Problems" proved Wallace to be the master of the pop rhyme—he could still freak a radio edit, and then turn around and drop a "Ten Crack Commandments," which, like its older brother, proved that *nobody* could rip some Premier gutter beat better than the master. Never has an artist attempted to please so many different audiences simultaneously and done it so brilliantly.

Life After Death was quickly certified quadruple platinum. By January 2000 it had sold 10 million copies—becoming the biggest-selling release of the year, and tying *Please Hammer Don't Hurt 'Em* as the top-selling rap album of all time (though it had the numerical advantage of being a double album, multiplying its Soundscan numbers by two.)

Meanwhile Combs was exploding as a solo artist. Wallace and others had encouraged Combs to make a rap album as a way to enjoy his success. And from his appearances in their videos and the way he told them how to attack their vocals, it was clear that he wanted to be a performer too. This was the very thing Suge had taunted him about at the Source Music Awards. And now it was reality.

But nobody expected it to work this well. "Can't Nobody Hold Me Down," a one-off experiment, had shot up the pop charts. "I'll Be Missing You" became a smash, going triple platinum within weeks of release and occupying the No. 1 spot on the pop charts for most of the year. It remains the biggest-selling single in the whole Bad Boy catalog, raising $TKTK for the Christopher Wallace Foundation.

Combs was right—his authenticity was his marketing. It wasn't as if he was proclaiming himself a gangster—that was more the world of his father and his friends—but he was selling himself as someone who knew enough about the underworld to rise above it, even if he was, by association, a part of it. The more he defended himself, the more he sounded more deeply involved. He sounded like John F. Kennedy denying his father's bootlegging past, or Frank Sinatra urging people that his connections to various crime families was nothing more than him being polite to the guys he grew up with in Hoboken.

"I wish people would judge me by my actions, not by these ridiculous rumors," Combs said. "I'm not some evil underworld mobster from the 'hood. I'm a young, educated, hardworking black man trying to perfect my craft and earn an honest living. I'm building a legacy here. I'm not going to go down in history for some stupid gangsta B.S. No way, man. History is going to remember me as one of the greatest entrepenuers and entertainers the world has ever encountered."

No Way Out was released on July 29, 1997, selling 2 million copies in less than two months. *No Way Out* and *Life After Death* traded places on the pop chart as Bad Boy cornered the market on both record sales and coolness. Wallace and the Lox gave him the street cred, but now Combs was the public face of not only of the company but of New York hip hop. Grit was no longer the shit. Combs was playing gangsta glam on a whole new level.

"I've always been like a walking billboard for my company," Combs said. "The way I dress. The way I move. The way I dance. It all became a part of the Bad Boy lifestyle."

By the time that the Paul Hunter-directed videos for "Been Around the World" and "All About the Benjamins" were in heavy rotation on MTV, Combs not only seemed comfortable in the star role; he seemed born to it. One minute, as in the "World" video, he was a secret agent jumping out of planes—next he was dancing with Jennifer Lopez to War's "Galaxy" in a sensual mambo that got tongues wagging and gossip columnists typing (she was married to waiter turned restaurateur Ojani Noa at the time). Then with the kinetic "Benjamins" video, Combs tap-danced with Savion Glover. The two had a hoofing contest, trading staccato steps like two MCs in a battle. Amazingly, though Combs was dancing against one of the world's most respected tap dancers, he kept up.

It seemed as if there was nothing he couldn't do.

The September 1997 MTV Video Music Awards, the engineer of so many dramatic hip hop moments, set the stage for the most dramatic of all. With a 50-person choir dressed in white, Combs danced and bopped to the beat of "I'll Be Missing You." From a riser emerging near the front of the stage, Sting appeared, singing his original version of his Police hit "Every Breath You Take." From stage left, Faith appeared, singing the chorus about her slain husband. Above everyone, there was a huge monitor, playing footage from Biggie videos "Hypnotize," "One More Chance," and "Juicy," among others.

Four male dancers came out, spinning and dancing with Combs as he stood at the center of the stage, whipping the audience into a frenzy.

"Clap your hands for Big! Clap your hands for Tupac Shakur! Clap your hands for everybody we lost!" he said, his arms stretched out as sparks rained down from the ceiling, icing the finale.

For a few fleeting moments, Combs was the king of the rap game. Even his detractors, a group growing by the minute, had to admit that Combs had the genre on lock; either with hits he produced, hits on his label, or, damn, himself at the center.

"He's passed all these hurdles," said one music executive who preferred to remain nameless. "Those kids dying at CCNY, getting fired from Uptown, Biggie's death, the whole Suge Knight and Tupac shit. It's almost like he's a little superhero. I hate to sound like I'm on his dick, 'cause I'm not, but he's a very smart man."

But even Achilles had his heel, Superman his Kryptonite, and Sampson his shorn locks. The one thing that did hold Combs down, even at the height of his success, was the specter of death.

He couldn't even escape it during the video shoot for the Hype Williams's directed "Mo Money, Mo Problems," another posthumous platinum smash off *Life After Death*. The clip, with its faux golf tournament, its dancers, and its scenes of him and Mase doing the wop in a zero-gravity parachute chamber, were calculated to make up for the fact that Wallace's only appearance in the video was from an old interview filmed in 1994. That's the incovenient thing about being dead. There could be no new pictures of Big Poppa. No more verses committed to tape. Though to be sure, every last scrap got resurrected and put to use.

But what could be obscured in a video was harder to gloss over in real life.

"How do you spell 'kill'?" T'Yanna asked her grandmother, Voletta Wallace. T'Yanna and Voletta were passing time at the golf course on Long Island where Combs and Mase were filming their faux golf tournament.

"K-I-L-L," her grandmother replied. The little girl drew a childlike likeness of Puffy, with big oversized tear drops. She held up her picture, which had a caption scrawled beneath her drawing: "Come Kill Us. Kill us please. Daddy dead, killed by gun."

Spin editor-in-chief Sia Michel, who covered the video shoot for the magazine, witnessed the entire exchange.

"For the rest of our interview, Puffy is visibly deflated," she wrote.

Despite the success of the album, Combs had a bittersweet feeling about the entire affair.

"I don't give a fuck if when this shit drops, I sell four million copies, I will not be happy," he said. "Give me Biggie back and you can take all the records you want. Take every record off the radio. That's just not the bottom line. I'm not happy. I want my muthafuckin' man."

WHO SHOT YA?

CHAPTER 10

❝ I can hear sweat trickling down your cheek
Your heartbeat sound like Sasquatch feet
Thundering, shaking the concrete
Then the shit stop when I foil the plot... **❞**

Voletta Wallace still didn't have her man: the one who killed her son.

While Christopher Wallace's friends grieved, and the Bad Boy staff figured out how to market his album respectfully, his mother's primary concern—after trying to pull herself together emotionally—was to figure out who would want to kill her only child, and to make sure that the Los Angeles Police Department didn't just sweep the investigation under the rug.

She didn't want to believe that police would ignore the death of a young black man who also happened to be a rapper. But she had seen Tupac Shakur's murder go unsolved for months. Even more people witnessed her son's shooting than saw Shakur catch bullets on that street in Las Vegas. Christopher was shot shortly after the party he was attending got shut down, forcing all the guests out onto Wilshire Boulevard at once. Somebody had to have seen something.

Yet besides the statements given by Wallace's closest associates: D-Roc, Lil' Cease, Paul Offord, Gregory "G" Young, and Combs (who answered questions only when accompanied by legal counsel) no one who didn't have to talk stepped forward with any helpful information for the police. The investigation stalled for months. The code of the streets was in effect.

"When it's a situation like that, you can't just spill," said one street dude who was at the party. "You always gotta alter shit. You puttin' niggas' business out there. It's not no little kiddie shit. That shit is real. What you say can have your ass killed the next day. That's what people gotta understand. When it's serious business like that, the best person is the silent person that shuts the fuck up. Let that shit play itself out man. Truth'll get out there one day."

Ms. Wallace wasn't having it.

"I'm sick to my stomach over the way this case has been handled," she told the *Los Angeles Times* in December 1997. "There is a murderer out there laughing at my family and laughing at the cops. I've held my tongue for months now, but I'm fed up with the police just pussyfooting around."

"We are trying to do everything in our power to solve this murder," Detective Russell Poole, the newly installed lead investigator on the case, told the *Los Angeles Times*. "I understand that Mrs. Wallace is upset, but I've tried to explain to her that you can't just throw a case like this together. You need witnesses—and we have none. We've interviewed hundreds of witnesses and the majority of them are not being totally candid with us. It's very frustrating."

Poole had no idea just how frustrating the case would become, nor that uncooperative witnesses would be the least of his problems. Two years after taking over the investigation he resigned from the LAPD because he believed the department did not want the case solved. And now, in the seventh year since Wallace's murder, there have been lots of theories, but no arrests, and no sign of real progress in the police investigation.

The scenarios that Poole uncovered came to resemble a lost chapter from a James Ellroy novel—a mixture of police corruption, gang violence, and a cover-up reaching the highest power circles of the city of angels. As Ice Cube once put it, "L.A. ain't all surf and sun."

On Tuesday, March 18, 1997, the same afternoon Christopher Wallace's remains were being taken on that last ride down St. James—another case involving a green SUV and gunshots slammed into the Wallace investigation.

While waiting at a red light on Ventura Boulevard, a white undercover narcotics cop named Frank Lyga got into a heated argument with a black man driving a Green Montero who was acting very much like a gang member. After threatening to "put a cap in your ass" the mad motorist chased Lyga through busy traffic, and eventually pointed a gun at him—but Lyga shot him first. The motorist's body was identified as Kevin Gaines, a seven-year veteran of the Pacific Division Patrol—one of the LAPD's own.

The press had a field day with the story: a black cop killed by a white cop who claimed that he acted in self-defense. And it happened just seven months after the O.J. Simpson verdict split Los Angeles (and the rest of America) along racial fault lines. An organization of black LAPD officers called for Lyga's dismissal, and the Gaines family hired Johnnie Cochran. The eye of the storm was Detective Poole, a regular Joe Friday type of cop who was assigned to the case.

As far as Poole could tell, Lyga's story checked out. A security camera confirmed that he was being pursued by Gaines's Montero, and he called for backup three times. The pistol found near the body was registered to Gaines, eliminating the possibility that it was planted after the shooting. And this wasn't Gaines's first road-rage incident; he'd threatened motorists by whipping out a gun before.

And then there was the question of the Montero itself, fully tricked out with an onboard TV and VCR. How could a cop with a family of four afford such a fancy car on a $50,000 salary? Actually, he couldn't. Gaines did not own the customized SUV he was killed in. That car was registered to Death Row Records. As it turned out, the patrolman had been having an affair with Sharitha Knight, Suge Knight's ex-wife and Snoop Dogg's ex-manager. Gaines was also one of several cops who moonlighted as security guards for Death Row—which helped explain how he could afford the Benz, the BMW, and the Explorer he did own.

When Poole asked for permission to fully investigate Gaines's background, he was instructed to back off and let Internal Affairs handle it. His superiors decided that Poole's discoveries didn't merit a search warrant. And by keeping the investigation internal, public scrutiny of crooked cops could be avoided. Poole was furious.

"We had dozens of officers who worked for Suge Knight and that's a no-no," Poole said. "The more police officers Suge had in his pocket, the more power he had. He was able to get certain police officers to do certain things for him. Death Row was being investigated for racketeering and dope dealing. He was able to beat felony raps because police were present." Then on April 9, 1997, Poole got an anonymous tip that suggested Gaines might have been involved in the Christopher Wallace murder. He used it as an excuse to take over the murder investigation that no one else really wanted.

There were two main theories as to who could have killed Wallace, and both of them depended on who you held responsible for Shakur's murder. Although there was no solid evidence that the deaths were related, it seem impossible that they weren't.

Many people assumed that friends of Tupac—perhaps Suge Knight himself, although he was incarcerated at the time—had Biggie shot to avenge Shakur's shooting six months earlier. Whether or not Big had anything to do with Pac's death, the rappers' well-publicized beef could have been enough to make Wallace a target.

Then there was the Southside theory, which held that the same gang set implicated in Tupac's murder was also responsible for Wallace's. The variations on this theory usually involved a disagreement over money for security services or a snatched Death Row medallions. The theory persisted despite the fact that Bad Boy staff denied any involvement with gangs whatsoever.

The *Los Angeles Times* reported that Wallace had hung out in Compton signing autographs a week before his shooting. Wallace reportedly spent part of Saturday, March 8, the last day of his life, shooting hoops in a park with

This Death Row chain was worn by a Compton gang member arrested as part of the Shakur murder investigation. But if a chain-snatching did lead to Tupac's murder, why was Wallace killed?

Southside Crips. Members of the gang, like Dwayne Keith "Keefee Dee" Davis and his nephew, Orlando Anderson—both of whom were associated, though not charged, with Tupac Shakur's murder in Las Vegas—were at the Petersen Automotive Museum party on the night Wallace was killed.

Combs nonetheless maintained that he did not even know any Crips, and he certainly did not hire them to provide security. "I would never use people who did not have a security background," Combs said. "Whenever I was in L.A. I hired off-duty police officers and bonded security men. He neglected to mention Paul Offord and Anthony "Wolf" Jones, two longtime associates who pack heat even though they are not licensed to carry firearms. (Jones is a convicted felon.)

Combs's link to the Crips was said to have come from an old school Harlem hustler nicknamed "Zip," who first introduced the young baller to Cristal champagne. Zip may also have helped Puff arrange extra security for the Bad Boy crew while they were touring California in 1995. Puffy has never denied knowing Zip; indeed, he was thanked in the liner notes of both of Biggie's albums. The *L.A. Times* reported that Zip spent a month each year in Compton, where he would visit the Southside Crip "Keefee D." Some people even called him "Zip the Crip." Months before Tupac's shooting, Puffy and Zip held a meeting where Combs met leaders of the gang. "I was in a room full of Crip killers," said a source close to the Bad Boy camp. "Puff said, 'They're going to be doing security for us.' " Just how secure the gangbangers were themselves was debatable from the start. One New Yorker who was present for that initial meeting in the penthouse suite of the Fairfield Inn in Anaheim recalled guns being drawn by Crips who were offended that they'd been offered a less expensive brand of champagne than others in the room were drinking. Combs denied that such a meeting ever took place.

One problem with the gang theory was that Wallace's murder was so well executed. It had all the makings of a professional hit—not the kind of haphazard, gang-related killing where somebody just dumps lead in your car. The element of surprise, the placement of the cars, and the getaway were all too perfect.

And unlike the Shakur killing, many of Wallace's associates had cooperated with the police, helping them come up with a composite sketch of the shooter. According to eyewitnesses, the person who killed Wallace was a black man with a receding hairline and a bow tie. His appearance seemed more consistent with a member of the Nation of Islam than a gangbanger. Also, Poole received word from a confidential informant that a contract killer named "Amir" or "Ashmir" had carried out the hit.

So Poole delved deeper into his "dirty cop" angle. Although Gaines's links to Wallace's killing were tenuous at best, Detective Poole's investigation led him to look into Death Row's practice of employing so many off-duty police officers. All roads led to Wrightway Security.

Reggie Wright Jr. was one of Suge Knight's closest childhood friends. He started his security company shortly after the launch of Death Row Records with a $300,000 loan from Knight. Using his police contacts (Wright's dad ran Compton's Gang Homicide Unit), Wright hired off-duty black cops to work as Death Row's security force. As police officers they were allowed to carry guns all the time, anywhere within the state of California. They were supposed to get permission from their supervisors for moonlighting assignments, especially when working for rappers with criminal records, but these rules were often ignored.

One of Tupac's former bodyguards, Kevin Hackie—himself a former police officer—made Poole aware of the fact that Shakur and Knight had an ongoing financial disagreement. The rapper felt Death Row owed him money. Hackie also supported the Las Vegas Police Department's claim that, despite public declarations that he'd been "shot in the head" during Shakur's shooting, Knight was merely cut by glass.

But how could Knight be responsible for Tupac's death if he had to sit in the line of fire? He could have been killed just as easily as 'Pac. Still, Hackie, Snoop, and others close to Death Row speculated that Knight was ballsy enough to sit next to Shakur during the shooting—presumably to erase himself from the list of suspects. And what about Orlando Anderson, the Southside Crip who had been stomped by Tupac, Suge, and other Death Row riders shortly before 'Pac was shot? Was he just a convenient scapegoat? In a 1997 VIBE interview, he denied any involvement with gangs or Shakur's killing. The following year he was shot at a Compton car wash in what police said was an unrelated incident.

"Puffy hired Southside Crips and the Southside Crips started extorting them for more money," Reggie Wright Jr. told VIBE. "Southside wanted $100,000 for security services," said Wright Jr. "[Puffy] offered them ten thousand. That's why Biggie Smalls is dead today."

Combs steadfastly denied Wright's allegations. "That's not even possible," he said. "I don't have debts, period."

Why would Wright finger the Southside Crips and Bad Boy as the ones to blame for Wallace's murder? Was he trying to divert attention from Death Row, a label with well-known ties to various Blood sets? Kevin Hackie reasoned that Knight would have supported the Wallace murder because not only would he be eliminating his rival's biggest star, but he would also be obscuring the real cause of Shakur's death. In the public eye, Biggie's shooting would look like payback. Since "the streets" had settled it, many would consider the case closed.

Instead, it got deeper. One former Death Row employee claimed that Knight bragged about being behind Wallace's murder. A prison informant, whose cellmate was down with Mob Piru, said that Knight hired another Piru Blood to execute the hit. Others speculated that David Kenner, Knight's lawyer, was behind the killing. It wouldn't have been the only time the attorney's name had been implicated in extralegal activities. Afeni Shakur's $150 million lawsuit, filed in April 1998, accused Knight and Kenner of conspiring to defraud her late son. Kenner had drafted the three-page handwritten contract that brought Shakur to Death Row Records less than a year before his death. The agreement, which Tupac signed from a prison cell, made it clear that getting down with Death Row meant getting down with David Kenner.

With so much attention focused on the big black intimidating figure of Suge Knight, Kenner often gets left out of the Death Row story. But it was Kenner who introduced Knight to incarcerated drug kingpins like Michael "Harry-O" Harris and Ricardo Crockett, who in turn provided the seed money to start Death Row in 1991. After the label was launched, the defense attorney billed Death Row for millions of dollars' worth of criminal defense and contract work. Was he a just lawyer or also a partner in the label? Kenner was smart enough to keep that relationship vague. But he was photographed with Knight at a party, both men rocking glittery Death Row pendants. The clincher was that Tupac was gunned down just a few days after he fired Kenner as his personal lawyer.

Within a year of Wallace's death, Kenner underwent heart surgery, and he has remained incommunicado ever since due to failing health. Whenever he did speak—whether to the press or in a court of law—he flatly denied any wrongdoing.

There were good reasons to doubt whether Suge Knight had anything to do with Tupac's murder. It was clear to anybody who saw them together that Knight had a lot of love for Tupac. According to sources close to Shakur, Suge let him get away with the kind of open disrespect that would earn lesser artists an immediate beat down. Suge sometimes called Tupac "my little brother."

Brotherly love aside, Knight was also a smart businessman who retained a percentage of anyone he ever worked with. To this day, he makes as much money off Snoop Dogg and Dr. Dre as he ever did, and still co-administers their publishing rights—if he doesn't own them outright. Nobody will say for sure. Imagine how much Tupac would have been worth alive, with his prodigious musical talent and his lucrative career as an actor. He'd probably be making $20 million a picture by now—or at the very least $7 to 10 million, which is DMX's asking price. Suge might have beaten Tupac's ass for leaving the label, but if his "little brother" was dead, he couldn't make any money off him. Sure Tupac had already recorded more than 50 songs with Death Row, but why kill the goose that lays the golden eggs? Between Knight's cut of Shakur's movie earnings, as well as earnings from any future recordings he made—for Death Row or his own as-yet-unformed Euthanasia label—it would be a lot more lucrative to keep Tupac alive.

In 1999, Harry Billups, a.k.a. Amir Muhammad, was named as a possible suspect in Wallace's murder. He told the press he was a mortgage broker, not an assassin. He has never been questioned by police.

Detective Poole first heard the name David Mack from Shakur's bodyguard Kevin Hackie. He learned that Mack was a police officer who was closer to Knight than most. And then in November 1997, Officer Mack was implicated in the armed robbery of $700,000 cash from the Bank of America on South Hoover Street in Los Angeles. His girlfriend, assistant branch manager Errolyn Romero, admitted to police that she had ordered a bigger delivery of cash from Brinks that day because she knew Mack was planning to rob her branch.. "Why did I get involved in this?" Romero said as they put the cuffs on her.

Mack was arrested later that night with $1,400 cash in his wallet. A subsequent search of his house unearthed a Tec-9 like the one used in the robbery, plus $18,000 in cash receipts and another $2,600 cash.

"Take your best shot," he told the arresting officer defiantly.

All these details were highly suspicious. But what really made the hair on the back of Poole's neck stand up was the black Impala SS parked in Mack's garage. It was the same color, make, and model that Wallace's assassin had driven. That in itself might have been a coincidence, except that the vehicle was parked directly opposite what could only be described as a shrine of posters and photographs dedicated to Tupac Shakur.

The more Poole looked into Mack, the more prevalent his links to Death Row became. Mack was a Compton native who grew up in the same Mob Piru neighborhood as Suge Knight and Reggie Wright. When he was cornered by some inmates in jail, licking their chops because they had an ex-cop in their midst, he coolly instructed them to back off—he was down with the Bloods.

The first person to visit Mack at Montebello City Jail was his old friend from the University of Oregon track team, Harry Billups a.k.a. Amir Muhammad. Detective Poole remembered receiving an anonymous tip that Wallace had been shot by a contract killer who went by the name Amir or Ashmir. But Poole was even more blown away when he saw a photocopy of the driver's license Muhammad presented when he went to visit Mack.

When Poole showed photos of Mack to people who had worked at the Petersen Automotive Museum the night Wallace was murdered, some of them placed Mack at the party, but Mack clearly didn't match the composite sketch of the shooter that Lil' Cease and G had described. D-Roc picked Mack's mug shot from a photo lineup, recognizing him as the man standing near the entrance when they entered the party—but not as the shooter.

Amir Muhammad's photo, however, was an eerie match to that charcoal drawing of Wallace's killer. Moreover, the address and Social Security number he left when he signed in to visit Mack in jail were fakes, raising further suspicion.

When Poole checked Mack's work records, he discovered that he'd taken "family illness" days off prior to both the Bank of America robbery and the weekend of Wallace's murder.

That's when Poole went to the brass—and got stopped at the door.

He wasn't allowed to run any forensic tests on Mack's Impala, nor to do another search of Mack's house to look for the murder weapon or anything else that might help him crack the Wallace case.

"The LAPD said they didn't want to step on the FBI's toes," Poole said. It was true that the Feds were investigating Bad Boy and Death Row. But they weren't making much progress in solving the killings of Wallace or Shakur. "What they didn't want was to find out that one of our officers was implicated in Biggie

Smalls's murder."

If the department was trying to avoid bad publicity, they got it anyway.

By the fall of 1998, Mack was at the center of the biggest scandal in LAPD history. His former partner, Rafael Perez, an officer with the city's Rampart Division, had been arrested for signing out six pounds of cocaine from a police evidence locker, replacing it with Bisquick, and selling the coke himself. Facing serious jail time, Perez turned state's evidence in exchange for a reduced sentence. It turned out to be a very bad deal for the LAPD: Perez gave testimony about the misdeeds of fellow officers who made Frank Serpico look like Mickey Mouse.

Mack was a mentor to Perez when he first joined the department, until Perez was transferred to Rampart in 1994. Rampart was the home of CRASH—the Community Resources Against Street Hoodlums program, an elite unit of cops who went head to head against the city's black and Latino gangs. The unit had its own subculture. In fact, CRASH was as much a gang as the bangers it went up against. All the CRASH cops had tattoos: a logo fashioned after the poker hand Wild Bill Hickok died holding—aces and eights. Every time an officer shot somebody, a special insignia was tattooed beside their logo.

Because he had worked on the David Mack case, Detective Poole was asked to join a special Robbery-Homicide task force to investigate rogue cops. Perez's name first came up in connection with the missing cocaine, but Poole was interested in Perez for other reasons. For one, Perez said he owed his life to Mack—who saved his ass during a drug buy that turned into a shootout—and Poole wanted to find out if he was still close to his former partner. For another, it turned out that Perez had been messing around with another batch of cocaine that Frank Lyga—the same officer who shot Kevin Gaines—had confiscated in a street bust. Perez had the coke transferred to Rampart and then made sure it ended up missing. It looked like an attempt to discredit Lyga, perhaps out of revenge for Gaines's death.

"Somehow, some way, they were going to make Lyga's life miserable," said one investigator of Perez, Gaines, and Mack. "All of these guys knew each other. They had worked together or they were friends." And they were all a part of Death Row's inner circle. Tupac's bodyguard Kevin Hackie told Detective Poole he had seen the trio at label parties and at the desert video shoot for Tupac and Dr. Dre's "California Love."

After Perez was arrested, he became very talkative. Fifty hours and 2,000 transcript pages later, Perez had accused more than 70 CRASH officers of planting false evidence, ripping off drug dealers, selling drugs, pimping prostitutes, and needlessly beating and shooting suspects. Hundreds of convictions were overturned as a result of what came to be known as the Rampart Scandal. Numerous gangbangers were let go, and the City of Los Angeles was forced to

Three former LAPD officers steeped in controversy: Kevin Gaines, left, lived with Suge Knight's ex-wife and worked as a part-time security guard for Death Row until he was shot by an undercover cop in a road-rage incident. David Mack, center, was convicted of bank robbery and suspected of having ties to Death Row and to Wallace's murder. Mack's friend Officer Rafael Perez, right, was caught stealing pounds of cocaine from a police evidence room. He became the star witness in the LAPD's ignominious Rampart Scandal.

pay tens of millions of dollars in damages.

When inconsistencies in Perez's testimony arose, he was subjected to five polygraph tests, and failed them all. But by this time, the damage was done, and his immunity deal was in place. Yet despite his immunity deal, Perez said nothing damaging about Mack or Gaines.

Poole was frustrated because he wanted information about David Mack and his links to Christopher Wallace's murder. But suddenly Perez was the central focus, damage control was the order of the day, and none of the LAPD brass seemed interested in solving the Wallace killing, especially if it involved one of their own officers.

"The racial politics of this city have become so ridiculous that the police department and the district attorney's office don't want to solve the Biggie Smalls case," said former deputy police chief Steve Downing. "They're afraid Johnnie Cochran will defend whoever is charged and we'll have another O.J. situation."

No matter what he found, Poole said his investigation was undercut by the indifference of then police chief Bernard Parks. "I don't want you to investigate any more," he says the chief told him. "Give me a report in two weeks."

Poole's 40-page report laid out everything from the shootout between Lyga and Gaines to the LAPD's links to Death Row Records to, finally, Wallace's murder. Poole said his superiors forwarded only two pages of the report—those describing an unrelated police brutality case—to the district attorney's office. It looked as if he had been shut down. But he had one more chance.

In May of 1999, Detective Poole was set to testify in the lawsuit brought by the family of Kevin Gaines (represented by Johnnie Cochran) against the LAPD. Poole saw his testimony as a chance to put into the public record all the things he had discovered about the links between Death Row, the LAPD, and L.A.'s gang world. But before that could happen, the city's lawyer (and future mayor) James Hahn, worked out a $250,000 settlement with the Gaines family, thus sealing the case forever.

In September of 2000, Poole resigned from the LAPD, furious that three years of investigative work had been thwarted. Later that month he sued the LAPD and Chief Parks, claiming that the chief violated his First Amendment right to talk about the case when he began to uncover things the department would rather not see made public.

"Why would we ignore information that was relevant?" asked Chief Parks, who remembers his meetings with Poole very differently. "It's completely illogical. And in my judgment, it's kind of interesting that he only brought this information up after he had been personally disciplined and removed from the task force." Parks says he "can't go into" what Poole was disciplined for, but maintains that he was "removed from the task force, disciplined, and then retired before he had vested his pension. Why would he do all of those things? It wasn't because we did anything to him."

"I never claimed to know for certain who killed Biggie Smalls," Poole told Randall Sullivan, who wrote a book called *LAbyrinth* that was based largely on Poole's theories. "All I'm sure of is that the best clues we had were put aside, and that someone has gotten away with murder. I think I have a pretty good idea of who that someone is. I wouldn't mind seeing my theory proved wrong, so long as there was a full investigation of the evidence. But there hasn't been."

On April 9, 2002, Voletta Wallace and Faith Evans filed a civil suit against the LAPD, Chief Bernard Parks, former chief Willie Williams and interim chief Bayan Lewis, claiming "deliberate indifference" to Christopher Wallace's death. The lawsuit cited many of Poole's theories, naming David Mack and Amir Muhammad as suspects, and mentioning a confidential informant who fingered Mack a day after the murder, as well as a witness who identified Muhammad as having been at the Petersen Automotive Museum on the night of the murder. "Defendant Parks intentionally, willfully, and recklessly delayed and stopped the investigation," the complaint charged, "as soon as it became apparent officers employed by the Los Angeles Police Department were involved in the murder."

Capt. Jim Tatreau, head of the LAPD's Robbery-Homicide division, dismissed the lawsuit's allegations as ridiculous. "I'd be so happy to be able to develop any information to solve that case," Tatreau said. "If they were LAPD cops, so be it. Like we haven't taken hits before."

The following year, Poole eroded his position somewhat by striking a movie deal in which Sylvester Stallone would play him. The catch was that Stallone asked Suge Knight, one of Poole's chief suspects, to portray himself in the film.

Steven Katz, the new lead detective on the Wallace murder case, appears to have disregarded Poole's Mack/Muhammad theory. According to a report in the *Washington Post*, police said they had not interviewed Muhammad because he'd missed every meeting they set up with his attorney.

"We've attempted to locate him," Katz said. "At the time we went to look for him, we could not find him."

It was a dubious claim, since *Los Angeles Times* reporter Chuck Philips was able to find Muhammad in three days. In the process, he set off an internal war at the paper (between the Metro and the Business sections) that lingers to this day.

The Death Row Records story was part of Chuck Philips's turf as a music business reporter for the *Times*. Philips had covered the company from the very beginning, when no one else was paying attention. Suge Knight respected him because of what he wasn't—not some white boy who wanted to be black, nor an angry white man with a vendetta against a black company with street roots. Philips was very much what Knight termed "12 o'clock"—straight up and down. If you were in the right, you were right; if you were in the wrong, he was going to nail you.

Despite his professional respect for Knight, Philips did not shy away from writing pieces that did great damage to Death Row. It was Philips who reported on Knight's dealings with Barry Longo, the Los Angeles D.A. responsible for overseeing Knight's probation. Longo's daughter Gina had signed a recording contract with Death Row, and he rented his beach house in the exclusive Malibu Colony compound to the label. It was Philips who reported both sides of the Steve Cantrock story, the accountant who accused Knight of making him sign a confession of cooking the books at gunpoint. Those pieces created the atmosphere that helped get Knight sent to prison on a parole violation. They also laid the foundation for Connie Bruck's famous Tupac profile in the *New Yorker* as well as Ronin Ro's seminal *Have Gun Will Travel*.

Even while in prison, Knight did not refuse Philips's interview requests. He was the only person at the *Times* who could get to Suge Knight—or to Puffy Combs. It was Chuck who broke the story about Zip and Combs's links to the Southside Crips. But the biggest and most contentious story of his career was still a few years away.

When Chuck Philips's front-page piece "Who Killed Tupac Shakur?" appeared on the sixth anniversary of the rapper's shooting—September 7, 2002—it set off a firestorm that hadn't been seen since Shakur and Wallace were murdered.

Philips claims that the Southside Crips or Orlando "Baby Lane" Anderson were involved in Tupac's murder weren't groundbreaking to anyone who had been reading Rob Marriott's work in VIBE magazine. Knight himself had told a VIBE correspondent who visited him in prison that "Baby Lane" was the one who shot Tupac.

What set off the firestorm was Philips's theory about where the murder weapon came from. Philips asserted that Christopher Wallace was in Las Vegas on the night of the shooting and that he agreed to pay the Southside Crips $1 million to kill Shakur. He wrote that the Crips "sent an emissary to a penthouse suite at the MGM Grand, where Wallace was booked under a false name. In Vegas to party, he didn't attend the Tyson-Seldon fight but had quickly learned about Shakur's scuffle with Anderson. Wallace gathered a handful of thugs and East Coast rap associates to hear what the Crips had to say." Philips said he based his dramatic account on anonymous sources who were present at the meeting. "The Crips envoy explained that the gang was prepared to kill Shakur but expected to collect $1 million for its efforts," he wrote. "Wallace agreed, with one condition, a witness said. He pulled out a loaded .40-caliber Glock pistol and placed it on the table in front of him. He didn't just want Shakur dead. He wanted the satisfaction of knowing the fatal bullet came from his gun."

Philips wrote that after Orlando Anderson's beat down, he departed the MGM Grand to go back to his room at the Excalibur, where he had checked in with a girlfriend, and that, as soon as fellow Crips heard about the beat down, he was summoned to Treasure Island, a hotel farther down the Strip that Philips characterized as a Crip hangout during big fight weekends. He wrote that a call was made to a "safe house," where a cache of weapons was waiting, and someone was sent over to pick them up. Then, according to Philips, someone in the room got the bright idea to hit up Wallace for some money. That's when someone was supposedly sent to Wallace's secret hotel suite to get the go-ahead. Instead, Philips said, they came back with Wallace's Glock .40. The rest was history.

After the shooting, Wallace supposedly returned to New York to begin work on *Life After Death*—paying only $50,000 of the $1 million he promised. This part of Philips's story aligned with previous theories about Wallace being murdered because of an unpaid debt to the gang. According to Philips's theory, Wallace paid the ultimate price because he welched on a million dollar debt.

It wasn't just the explosive and shocking nature of what Philips was writing that was so mind-blowing. It was also how ambiguously the story was sourced.

An admisson is in order here. I know Chuck Philips. I've worked with him before and consider him a friend. In fact, with Eric Lictbau, we cowrote the front-page story of Christopher Wallace's murder on March 9 when I worked at the *L.A. Times*. He is one of the most thorough, evenhanded, responsible, and dedicated journalists I know.

There are those who claim that Philips was Suge Knight's stoolie, that he was paid off to write the story, or that he had a vendetta against hip hop and black people. I don't believe any of that. I had to take the article seriously because Chuck Philips wrote it. Coming from anybody else, it would have been much easier to dismiss the whole thing.

That being said, the piece was not as exhaustively documented as most of Philips's articles.

With the exception of E.D.I. Mean, a member of Shakur's Outlaws crew, nobody in the piece was quoted by name. Philips said he based the report on "police affidavits and court documents as well as interviews with investigators, witnesses to the crime, and members of the Southside Crips who had never before discussed the killing outside the gang." Nevertheless everything in the piece was stated as an unequivocal fact. The whole piece read like a screenplay treatment rather than a solid investigative piece in which a theory is presented and scrutinized from all sides before a conclusion is drawn. Some questioned his motive, but at least his story might embarrass the Las Vegas authorities into tracking these Crips down for questioning.

Still, nobody in six years had ever suggested that the Notorious B.I.G. was

anywhere near Las Vegas on the night in question. Philips wrote that Wallace was checked in at the MGM Grand under a pseudonym without offering any evidence whatsoever. His unnamed sources offered no explanation of how someone so large (in every sense of the word) could slip into Vegas unnoticed on a hectic fight night.

Even the timeline seemed off: Orlando Anderson got beat down around 9 P.M., then met with his homies, and paged the Notorious B.I.G. Then somebody went to meet with him, got the gun, and went to kill Tupac—all within the space of two hours? Anyone who understands how slowly things move in the hip hop world would realize how preposterous this is. And remember, this was in the days before two-way pagers. Factoring in the traffic on a Saturday night in Las Vegas, it might take half an hour to get from one end of the Strip to the other. On a fight night it would be twice as bad. Yet, according to Philips's theory, there was enough time for someone to go from Treasure Island, all the way at one end of the Strip, to the MGM Grand, at the other end, then meet with Wallace, and come back to Treasure Island, get a car out of valet parking (which can take 20 minutes even for a high-roller), and then run into Suge and Tupac on the street.

If you can get past all of that, there's still a major problem with that cinematic scene in which Christopher Wallace handed a loaded gun to someone he didn't know to commit a murder for him. Christopher Wallace was much too cautious to take that kind of risk with a stranger. If he would do anything like that, it would be with D'Roc, or Lil' Cease, or one of his boys who, if caught, would go to the grave protecting his name. He knew one of the first rules of the street was never to have someone you didn't really know put in serious work for you. They could always flip on you if things went wrong.

Why then would he hand this cat a loaded Glock, knowing that the gun could be traced back to him? Wallace wouldn't even write a rap song with a character stupid enough to do that—unless he was trying to show baby ballers what *not* to do in this kind of situation.

And what about the one million dollars? Wallace loved money. And he knew anybody could get someone killed for $10,000—maybe less depending on the situation. These guys were in a gang, and if they were truly down for their set, they were gonna do 'Pac anyway. Why pay someone for something they're going to do with or without your money?

Wallace had made half-million-dollar videos, gone on promotional tours, and run up huge studio tabs—all of which were counted against his royalties. No matter what he portrayed on the records—he was no millionaire yet. Wallace didn't start making money on his music until after he died. At the time Shakur was shot, Wallace would have been hard-pressed to find $50,000 in a hurry, let alone a million. Yet Philips's piece names only Wallace among the group of East Coast thugs and associates who supposedly plotted Shakur's murder with the Crips.

It just wasn't believable.

The morning before the piece was published, I reached Lil' Cease on the phone. He already knew about the story, because Puffy had told him the night before.

"Where is this shit coming from?" Cease said, outraged, but steady of voice. "I don't know where they're coming from with this bullshit."

Cease insisted that he and Wallace were at home in Teaneck, New Jersey, when they heard about Tupac's shooting on television. He didn't mention anything about going to the studio, as Bad Boy would later contend in its official statement on the matter. In a little-known 1997 interview with veteran music journalist Charlie Braxton, Wallace himself said, "I think me and Lil' Cease was at a restaurant in New York" when he heard the news. "Somebody paged me and told me about it," he said. In any case everyone was emphatic that Biggie was on the East Coast.

"He wouldn't do that shit," Cease said about Wallace. "That's not in Duke's character."

Wallace had learned to be distrustful and paranoid when it came to criminal activity. He was also convinced that he was under surveillance—and as it turned out, he was right. Federal agents showed members of Junior M.A.F.I.A. photos taken of Biggie just minutes before he was shot.

"I had to think to myself, like, 'Them motherfuckas was there?'" Cease said. "And nobody saw who did this? I just don't understand it. Y? I can't put it together."

When Philips's article hit, adamant denials flew coast to coast. Radio phone lines were flooded, and the story was all anyone could talk about. Power 106 in Los Angeles played Tupac tracks for four straight hours, as if he had just gotten shot that morning. Morning jock Big Boy read from the paper as if it were fact. And even though callers like Tupac's brother, Mopreme Shakur, urged restraint, plenty of people were happy to rush to judgment. The murder had gone unsolved for too long. People wanted someone to blame.

On the East Coast it was the opposite. Many people felt that there were forces at work trying to smear Wallace's name. Others claimed that Chuck Philips was a racist. No one was countering Philips's allegations with the hard facts that could kill his theory. And some of the lyrics on *Life After Death* were, upon closer inspection, a bit troublesome. In "The Long Kiss Goodnight," Biggie says "I'm flamin' gats aimin' at / These maniacs put my name in raps." Later he mentions his "team in the marine-blue coupe" (the Crip color) and describes a shooting that's eerily similar to Tupac's: "Slugs hit your chest / Tap your spine / Flatline / Heard through the grapevine you got fucked fo' times." Then Puffy closes the tune like an angry, demented preacher: "I told y'all to stop . . ." he roars. "All we have to do now is say a prayer for you." Of course, it's impossible to draw any real conclusions from a record. But it is worth noting that Big performed this song live on the radio in San Francisco just three days before he was shot. Perhaps somebody took his song the wrong way.

A few days after Philips's story broke, Bad Boy released documents purporting to show that Wallace was at Daddy's House recording studio from around noon on the day of Shakur's shooting. The notes say he "wrote half the session," was "in and out/sat around" and "laid down a ref," or a reference vocal for the song "Nasty Boy." This behavior was customary, and fell into precisely the pattern D-Dot Angelettie described. But Wallace's sessions were almost always at night, never during the afternoon.

When talking with John Leland of the *New York Times,* Louis Alfred, the engineer listed on the song, remembered a night session, not a day session

Sass Ong, the studio director at Daddy's House, claimed that the notes were stored in an unalterable database. But the fact remains that none of the studio documents shown to the public were dated. Nor has Wallace's family yet cited telephone, credit card, or other documents that could prove once and for all that Wallace wasn't in Vegas. The family did announce that they were bringing a lawsuit against the *Los Angeles Times,* although six months after the story appeared, the suit was not yet filed. "My immediate reaction when I saw the article was shock and anger," said Faith Evans. "It's this type of irresponsible journalism that leads to people losing their lives."

Voletta Wallace called the piece "patently false," adding that her son "wept openly at the news of Tupac's death."

Throughout the controversy, Sean Combs declined comment through his publicist. Chuck Philips has offered no further information except that he stands by his story. While Philips's allegations about Wallace grabbed the most attention, they remain unproven. Yet the central, outrageous truth of his story stands unrefuted: that a newspaper journalist was able to find key murder witnesses who have never been interviewed by police. No wonder that the case has remained unsolved for six years.

SKY'S THE LIMIT

66 While we out here, say the hustlas prayer
If the game shakes me or breaks me
I hope it makes me a better man... 99

Dripping wet, the chubby little boy dressed in red, white, and blue swim trunks stares at the stranger standing in his grandmother's driveway with wide, curious eyes.

I stare back at him, just as curious. I'm smiling because he's gotten so big so quickly. He doesn't look anything like his baby pictures anymore. He's practically grown, with long thick limbs and a belly inherited from his dad. He's going to be a big kid—6'3", 225 at least. Even with his mother's fair skin, Christopher Wallace Jr. looks just like his father.

"Hi, C.J.," I say. I'm a little shaken, because, as I look at his face, I can't stop thinking about my last conversation with his father. The thought that strikes me is how much he would have loved to see his son get this big.

"Is your grandmother here?"

"Yes," he replies, pointing toward the door, "she's inside." And without another word he scurries off toward the backyard to join his big sister T'Yanna and his little brother, Todd Jr., who are already splashing around in the pool.

Ms. Wallace appears in the door and invites me into the house with a warm smile and a hug. We've only met a couple of times, but she welcomes me like family. "You just missed Faith," she says. Evans has dropped off her sons to stay with "Mee-maw" (as they call their grandmother) while she performs a few concerts in the New York area. Ms. Wallace is all smiles today; the former elementary school teacher loves taking care of children—especially her grandchildren.

The house in the Poconos is bright and comfortable. Christopher Wallace bought the land and started the construction; Sean Combs paid to finish the job after Christopher was murdered. There's enough land in the back for Ms. Wallace to do a bit of gardening, as she used to do when she was growing up in Jamaica. "I love flowers," she says. "If you call me in the summertime, I'm not in here, I'm out there in the garden. I'm all over the place. I love my house." The

Christopher Jordan Wallace, age five. He bears a striking resemblance to his father, whose love of music he shares.

air is filled with the smell of food cooking and the sound of kids laughing and playing. Right now Mrs. Wallace is the happiest she's been since her only child was killed.

The house's sitting room is like a small museum dedicated to Christopher Wallace. There's a huge oil painting of him over the fireplace, and framed photographs from various stages of his life stand on every flat surface. There are trophies from *The Source* and *Billboard* and MTV and platinum sales plaques from Bad Boy. Over on the mantel is an artifact from the days before Christopher became Biggie—the first award he ever won, a tiny fireman with a hose in his hand, commemorating an outstanding elementary school report on fire prevention.

For the first few years, it was hard for her to talk about Christopher without crying. She still cries sometimes—but happier thoughts surface, too.

We're sitting down now, looking at pictures that bring memories flooding back. She can still reenact entire conversations with her son. Like the day she walked into his first apartment, the Brooklyn duplex that he rented after *Ready to Die* started selling. She wasn't surprised to find it as much of a pigsty as his old room at 226 St. James.

"I looked around and said, 'My God! Is any human being supposed to be living like this?' " She plays up the disgust for comic effect. "And he would look at me with his most loving smile and say, 'Tell me something, Ma'am. Whose house is this? Is this 2645 Eliot? Yo, this is *my* house. I can do whatever I want to do.' " Ms. Wallace is cracking herself up as she continues both parts of the dialog. "Did the cleaning lady even come into this room?' I asked. And he said, 'Yeah, but I told her don't touch my drawers. Ma, you want to wash my drawers for me?' "

When Ms. Wallace does her Biggie impression, her shoulders hunch back, and her voice drops a few registers. Her Jamaican accent and regal bearing disappear, and, for a few seconds, she speaks with a Fulton Street lilt. The tilt of her head, the way her eyes sparkle—it's clear where her son got his charisma.

She talks about cooking him his favorite food: He loved her sea bass seasoned with scallions. She remembers how after he broke his leg the second time he adopted a healthier diet. She recalls his excitement over losing 30 pounds.

" 'Can you imagine me, boy,' " she says in his voice, sounding just as excited. " 'getting out of this hospital and losing a hundred pounds? I'm gonna be sporting those Calvin Klein drawers, Ma!' "

She laughs when I ask about the other women in Christopher's life.

"Everybody was his mistress," she says, "and they keep saying, Biggie loves me. And, he is gonna marry me." She rolls her eyes. "*Please*. Biggie loved that almighty dollar. That's what Biggie loved. That and his children."

What about Lil' Kim?

"Kim was my son's business partner. Do you hear me? Yes, they had an affair, but trust me, I did not hear him say, 'She's my wife, love of my life.' And the same thing with Ms. Baltimore, Ms. Chicago, Ms. Maryland, and Ms. California. Everybody wants to say, 'Oh, I was his heart. I was his eyes. I was his nose.' How are you breathing then?" she says, laughing. "Why couldn't you say you were a good friend or a groupie? Say 'I slept with him two or three times,' but don't walk around saying he was gonna marry you. *Hello*—he wasn't divorced. Get a life!"

As a solo artist, Lil' Kim has wrapped herself in the legend of Biggie Smalls. On one record, she refers to herself as "Miss White, the Queen of New York."

The lives that Kim and Charli Baltimore have made for themselves are both showbiz lives. But they are very different. Charli left her deal with Untertainment, the label founded by Biggie's old partner Un Rivera, to sign with Irv Gotti at Murder Inc. It was important for her to define herself outside of Biggie Smalls' enormous shadow. "Yeah I knew Big, but come on," she says. "We don't have to ride with that forever, like *Biggie, Biggie, Biggie*. I don't think he would appreciate that. It's been seven years. Let the man rest." She does hang on to certain lessons he taught her. "He was just like, Always keep going," she recalls. "And study your own flaws. He would always listen to *Ready To Die*, like. 'I could've did this different. I could've said this better.' I'm like, You're bugging. This is a classic album. But that's what inspired him to do better.'"

If Charli has tried to distance herself from the legend of Biggie Smalls, Lil' Kim has wrapped herself up in it like a blanket. "I love him with all my heart, like I've never loved anyone in my life," she told VIBE. "I still feel his spirit with me, like right now he's sitting right here. I could be on the toilet and I feel his spirit. I talk to him every night. I just feel blessed because Biggie has been with me every step of the way." For a time she lived with other members of Junior M.A.F.I.A. but they have drifted apart. "You came up with us," says Lil Cease of Kim. "Of course there's love there. But she just exploited that shit too much, and it wasn't really that. Big had love for her 'cause she was part of the team. She was from around the way." During an interview with VH-1, Kim said that she became pregnant with Wallace's child and that he pressured her to terminate the pregnancy shortly before her debut album, *Hard Core*, was released. DJ Enuff, who traveled many miles on the road with Big and Kim, says their relationship was based on music first. "Kim was Bonnie to his Clyde. Kim was his protégée. I think he fell in love with his work. You know what I mean? He turned young Kimberly Jones in The Queen Bitch, you feel what I'm saying? I'm proud of her. She's taken it to another level." Kim still credits Wallace as executive producer of her solo albums, and laces her songs with echoes of his rhymes. She's even taken to calling herself "Miss White, the Queen of New York."

When Voletta Wallace talks about Jan Jackson—who lives with her daughter T'Yanna in the house next door on this secluded country road—Voletta Wallace's tone is totally warm. Time and grandkids have helped to heal any lingering misgivings. She has nothing but love for the only woman who knew her son before the stardom.

And as for her son's widow, she thinks Faith has been better off since Wallace's death. "If Christopher was alive today, Faith wouldn't be as happy," she says. Not that she thinks her son didn't love Faith or vice versa. It's just that she knows how possessive her son could be, and how selfish. "I think Christopher would be calling her as if he still owned her," she says. Ms. Wallace is happy that Evans has found stability with her husband and manager Todd Russaw. She's glad Evans doesn't have to deal with Christopher's infidelity, and other problems associated with getting married too quickly. She's happy that Faith has finally found peace.

Ms. Wallace's life is peaceful for the most part. She divides her time between the Catskills and Brooklyn, where she oversees the Christopher Wallace Foundation, which provides resources for various schools under a program called B.I.G., which now stands for "Books Instead of Guns." The foundation is also making plans for a permanent community center in Biggie's old neighborhood.

"My goal is to have something strong in his name," she says. "If we have a community center, I can take a lot more kids off the street," she says. There is so much work to be done. The phone always seems to be ringing with one initiative or another. She is working on a book of her own, the story of a single mother's journey, raising a son, then losing him to the forces of

Faith sings "Walk With Me Jesus" at the 2003 B.I.G. Night Out benefit in New York. On her album Faithfully, she used the beats to "Juicy" and "Who Shot Ya" as a way of "paying homage to him without singing about him."

darkness, and somehow carrying on.

The only time she gets really angry is when she talks about Los Angeles and the LAPD. That's her other main goal—bringing her son's killers to justice.

What irks her the most isn't just that her son was under surveillance on the night he died, but if they were on his case like that, why can't anyone solve his murder? She receives anonymous tips from time to time, and passes them on to her own private investigator. She's convinced that lots of people out there know more than they are telling.

"Where was this surveillance?," she asks. "Who were you surveilling? Everybody is just hush hush! Why this great conspiracy? When my son died, they had twenty-one police officers working on the case. Then one day I called and it was ten. Then there were five. Then there were two. Then Russell Poole quit. Now everyone's resigning. Are you handing over information to those new people?"

It frustrates her that, with the exception of Faith and a few of Wallace's closest friends, no one else seems terribly bothered by the fact that the case hasn't been solved. "If they loved him so much," she asks bitterly, "how come they never ask about the investigation?"

"Yes, I'm angry! I'm mad," she says, exhaling loudly. Hell hath no fury like a mom who's been disrespected. And for all the people paying tribute to the Notorious B.I.G., she detects a lack of respect for Christopher Wallace. The *Los Angeles Times* accused him of Tupac Shakur's murder without providing any hard evidence. Before that it was Randall Sullivan's book *LAbyrinth*. While she appreciated the attention the book brought to the LAPD cover-up, she was horrified to open the book and find her son's autopsy photo inside. (She complained to the publisher, and the photograph was removed from the paperback edition.)

"I cried for three days," she says, still visibly upset. "I had to hide the book, to make sure that T'Yanna and C.J. didn't see it."

At that moment, C.J. and his half sister walk in from the pool wrapped in towels, and ask "Mee-maw" for some food. Just like that, her mood brightens.

She has never claimed that her son was an angel, but she wants the world to remember the person she knew and loved. Not just the rap star who died in the so-called East Coast–West Coast war. She still doesn't care much for rap, though she does collect half of her son's royalties thanks to Faith, who looked out for her like a good daughter-in-law. Voletta Wallace wants people to remember the smiles and the humor, the prodigious talent that he displayed as a graphic artist as well as on records. She still has the drawing he did on the night before he was killed. It's a picture of his heart breaking with his kids' names written inside.

And so she keeps on going. Working. Watching her granddaughter T'Yanna grow up a little more every day. And sometimes, during quiet moments, thinking about the little boy who she loved so much—and who the rest of the world barely even knows.

"Things are smiling with me," she says as I prepare to take my leave. "I'm doing good. My son took care of me. Social Security will chip in." She pauses, looking out toward her backyard in the afternoon sun.

"Time will take care of them," she says. "Everyone that tried to get over on my son, time will take care of them."

DJ Premier leans back in his chair behind the mixing board in Studio B at D&D studios. Behind him sits a well-worn MPC60 drum machine, the same one he's had for the last 14 years. I feel as if I'm looking at Charlie Parker's saxophone. He's made magic with that thing, bent over in the corner of a loud, smoky room. Like an old man who mistrusts newfangled technology, Premier wants nothing to do with the latest Pro-Tools software. "When you record to tape, you get more of a raw, full sound because the tape can withstand a certain amount of pressure, decibel-wise," he says. "With digital, everything is compressed. It sounds good, and it's clear, but it cuts out all the beef that comes with it when you lay it down." He leans toward the dilapidated 24-track board and caresses it for a second, like an old lover. "Analog is straight raw," he says. "You get a better thickness."

Studio B is the smallest room in the building with the oldest board, but that doesn't matter to Premier. This is the room where all the history was made. Ever since he laced the Gangstarr sureshot "Dwyck" in this room, this is the only place he works. Nas's "New York State of Mind" was recorded in this room. So was "Unbelievable." Within months of our conversation, the studio will be closed.

From the time he finished chopping up "Impeach the President" to make the beat to the time Biggie walked through the door, smoked a blunt, had his wick dipped by two groupies, and laced the track with his vocals, a classic song was made. The whole thing took maybe three or four hours.

One of Primo's boys, a big cat from Brooklyn, sweatshirt, Timberlands, and all, nods his head as Primo talks, smiling when he thinks about Biggie. "Damn," he says, shaking his head. "That nigga took three or four hours to make some shit that'll last three or four hundred years."

"I've learned that you just gotta put out more weapons," Premier says. "You gotta cut through the bullshit, and just constantly flood the industry with that stuff," he says. "Otherwise, the people get used to hearing the same old shit. So if you give them something new, they start to adjust to that, and they want something new."

Premier doesn't even listen to rap anymore. The world's finest hip hop producer says that since the death of Biggie and Tupac something happened to the music he loves. The thrill is gone. Everyone is so concerned with selling records than making dope beats and rhymes. "Now it's about watering it down to where it's not even pure anymore," he says. "It's definitely rap—not hip hop."

He insists that if Run-D.M.C. were an unknown group trying to shop a song like "Rock Box" right now, they couldn't get a record deal. And he's probably right. "People be like 'Oh, it's too hardcore,'" he says with disgust. "Back then you have to be hardcore to even think about selling a record."

So which way is hip hop going?

"You know what's going to happen with hip hop? Whatever's happening with us." So writes the Brooklyn MC Mos Def in his song "Fear Not of Man," from the album *Black on Both Sides*. "If we smoked out, hip hop is gonna be smoked out, if we doing all right, hip hop is gonna be doing all right. People talk about hip hop like its some giant living in the hillside coming down to visit the townspeople. We are hip hop. So the next time you ask yourself where hip hop is going, ask yourself, "Where am I going? How am I doing?"

In the words of Don Pooh, "Hip hop now is like this really fly girl with a big-ass scar across her face," Pooh said. "She still fly, but you can always see that scar. She didn't die. She's not dead. She's just not as pretty."

"If you strike me down," Obi-Wan Kenobi warned Darth Vader in Star Wars, "I shall become more powerful than you can possibly imagine."

The old man parried, blocking each of Vader's blows, waiting for his audience. And as soon as the kid, Luke Skywalker, stepped into view, Kenobi put up his saber, allowing himself to be cut down—strangely enough, it seemed to be just what he wanted. He vanished into thin air as soon as he was cut. He had become one with the Force, the essence of all living things. And dying only made him that much more influential.

The essence of hip hop is a lot like the Force. It permeates all aspects of popular media, from the songs you hear in beer commercials to the cars you drive, to the clothes that you wear. Only a select few possess the ability to manipulate this Force. Instead of being called Jedi knights, they're called MCs.

Christopher "Obi-Wan" Wallace and Tupac "Anakin" Shakur (also known as Darth "Makaveli" Vader) loom even larger over hip hop in death than they did in life. Both men died by their twenty-fifth birthdays and have sold more records posthumously than while they were alive. Their images have become fixtures in the popular imagination. They've also proven to a tough act to follow for other hip hop artists.

D.M.C. and Run look on as DJ Jam Master Jay shows younng Biggie some love. Just a few years later, both were gone.

From Nas to Jay-Z to Ja Rule to Ol' Dirty Bastard, damn near every MC in the game has compared themselves to the twin titans. When introducing his bullet-scarred protégé 50 Cent to the world, Eminem rapped: "Take some Big and some Pac and you mix 'em up in a pot . . . What the fuck do you got? / You got the realest and illest killers tied up in a knot." "Those two mutha-fuckas were bigger than life," says Nas, who was dissed on record by both of artists—and has outlived them both. "There's gonna be all kinds of shit said about them. Forever. They were bigger than life. Bigger than Elvis."

Yes, Biggie Smalls was the illest—no doubt. Was he the best pure MC hip hop has ever seen? That's a question best left to those heads who were fortunate enough to compare his flow with that of, say, Grandmaster Caz rocking live with the Cold Crush Brothers. After Biggie's passing, Caz himself called up a radio station to give Wallace maximum respect. "He was a genius who actually inspired me to stay on point," said Caz. That would have pleased Biggie, who once told Chairman Mao that he simply wanted to be considered "The best that ever did it."

In Quincy Jones III's insightful documentary *Thug Angel,* Shock G of Digital Underground compares the artistic legacies of Wallace and Shakur. "Biggie's gonna win hands down when you're talking flow," he said. "Strictly from a rhythm standpoint, Biggie is a swinger. He swings like a horn player over jazz . . ."

Tupac by contrast, rhymed "from the pit of his stomach," Shock G said. "When people say Pac is the best rapper of all time, they don't just mean he's the best rapper. They mean what he had to say was most potent, most relevant. Tupac pulled from Martin Luther King, Malcolm X, all the great speakers."

Tupac's image itself has become a symbol of cult revolution—sandwiched on the T-shirt racks between Bob Marley and Che Guevara. Biggie's legacy is different. "I may be a big black ugly dude, but I got style," Wallace observed. "I kinda uplifted big black ugly dudes for real." Wallace didn't have movie star looks. He looked like what he rapped about: a former drug dealer from the 'hood who made good. The fact that he was large and out of shape only endeared him to an audience that thought hip hop was getting too pretty anyway. More than his image it was his craftsmanship. The brother wasn't joking when he said he had "techniques dripping out my butt cheeks."

And of course, Big and 'Pac are inextricably linked in the public imagination as warriors to the death. All this, even though they never really had a battle per se.

"That wasn't a battle," says Nas, "it was beef. Tupac was on some straight war shit. Big was on some straight mafia shit with class without saying names. Like, 'If we got beef I ain't gonna say your name. You know, I'm a just see you in the street.' But take these subliminal words muthafucka 'cause I ain't like you either. And 'Pac's shit was like, 'Fuck that. Let's blow down the buildings down. Let's blow the city up.' They're two different kinds of geniuses, like Malcolm and Martin."

Like Nas, Jay-Z admired both Big and 'Pac. "I had known Big since high school," he told VIBE. "When we reconnected in 1996 to do 'Brooklyn's Finest' for my album, we became real close. He was hilarious, with a big heart and I never doubted he was keeping it real with me. I thought he was smart to stay silent when Tupac started his war of words. And on the real, I could tell the whole situation made him depressed. We had worked hard to leave a certain kind of life behind, and from the beginning that thing felt like more than a rap battle."

Others, like Wiz of Nas's Braveheart crew, feel that Big could have cleared the air by answering in rhyme. "Everybody wanted to see the skill battle," he said. "Believe me, that would have calmed the tension down if they woulda gone at it. Just like Nas and Jay-Z. The fact that Nas responded back to Jay makes the people around him feel like, at least he said something. We're not gonna be walking around with the grudge forever, like we got to get him back. No, Son got him back lyrically."

It is perhaps a testament to how much things had changed that Nas and Jay-Z kept the battle on wax. Jay-Z himself felt as if he had gone too far with "Superugly"—his own mother even called him about the record—and contacted the community's mix-tape DJs to pull it out of circulation.

Despite their differences, the two men thought about their own legacy, and that of the man who led to their falling out in the first place: Biggie. They didn't want something as simple as a perceived dis to lead to the repeat that led to the deaths of Tupac Shakur and Christopher Wallace.

In his video for "Got Urself a Gun," directed by Benny Boom, Nas did a re-creation of both Shakur and Wallace's assassinations Oliver Stone–style. But morphed himself into both rappers. The implication was that he was carrying on their spirits, but also making comments about his own struggle with Jay-Z.

The video ends in a graveyard with Nas pouring out liquor to give respect to the deceased. But at the same time it could be read as a squashing of lyrical beefs before they turn into physical confrontations. In the end the battle gave both men a deeper respect for each other. "I can't sit here and boo-hoo about it," said Nas. "I'm not the first guy whose family's been dragged into the public—whether you're talking about actors and their Hollywood lives or Biggie with Faith and 'Pac."

"The Jay and Nas battle was respectfully the greatest battle in hip hop. You can't ruin that by going out and shooting somebody. That was two armies, two empires that went at it for lyrical supremacy. A Battle of the minds or whatever you want to call it."

Who would have thought that rappers even in their ugliest moments could finally reach this level of maturity? That more than anything is a testament to Biggie's legacy. Maybe people have learned from his and Tupac's mistakes. Maybe we really are starting to realize what we have all lost.

AUTHOR'S NOTE

"What were the old days like?"

I walked into the offices of VIBE magazine on a humid August afternoon in 1998 and associate editor Hyun Kim asked me the question that made time stand still. I was only 29, and his question made me feel like an old man. But I knew exactly what he was talking about.

Back in 1989, when I was a high school senior and serious hip hop fanatic, I used to dream about following my favorite rap artists around, talking to them, gaining insights to their music and their personalities, living through them.

Hip hop coverage at the time was scarce. You might see the occasional article posing the question "Will This Rap Fad Ever Fade?" or perhaps a nightly news segment about break dancing. If you were lucky enough to find a magazine, it was probably, *Word Up, Fresh,* or *Yo!* There was usually a cut-out poster inside and a story about Big Daddy Kane's favorite food.

Certain articles, like James Bernard's *Village Voice* review of Brand Nubian's *All for One* and Frank Owens's pieces for *Spin* on N.W.A adorned the walls of my Stanford University dorm instead of posters.

The old days. The golden age of rap journalism: between 1988 and 1995, when we thought we could change the world. Before the big money, backstabbing, and bullshit came into play. We referred to ourselves as the "Hip Hop Nation," which now sounds like the most absurd and corny phrase imaginable. Back then it meant something that we took very seriously. We were united by a righteous cause: to turn the urban youth culture of hip hop into a movement for positive social and political change. The movement had songs, like "Self-Destruction" and "We're All in the Same Gang" that sparked debate about issues like drug abuse and black-on-black violence. We had magazines, like *The Source* and VIBE, that could properly document the music that inspired the movement instead of treating it like a fad. Hell, we even had directors like John Singleton and the Hughes Brothers who were disciples of the music, and whose cinematic vision splashed hip hop on Hollywood's big screen.

Those were the heady days when we felt that, by the very act of following rap artists around and telling their stories, we could not only change the mainstream's opinion of the art form, but perhaps even elevate the art form itself. Keep it pure. Police it by reminding the rappers what they promised us as listeners. Tell the truth.

And the rappers made it pretty easy for us. There were few messy cover negotiations in those early days. You just showed up at the studio, came to the neighborhood, or, in some cases, went right to somebody's mama's house to conduct the interview. Most of the time, the artists were happy to see their names in print with their quotes, naked and raw, right on the page—as unadulterated as anything they were doing on the microphone.

Artists weren't judged by how much money they made or how brightly their Bentley coupe shined. Many didn't even know what a Bentley was, nor could they fathom paying $250,000 for a house, let alone a car. Fuck a video. Did you write your own rhymes? If I started beat-boxing right now, could you blow my mind with the deadly lyrics about to explode off your tongue?

It seemed as if there were lyricists everywhere. You went to a New York hip hop club like the Muse, and half the time nobody would be dancing. It was just circles of kids, bobbing their heads, listening intently as freestyler after freestyler stepped up to kick a spontaneous rhyme off the top of his head, on and on till the break of dawn.

What were the old days like?

I snapped back to attention.

"Man, I don't even know how to begin," I said. "They were beautiful."

"Imagine being a sportswriter when Willie Mays and Mickey Mantle were playing," Hyun said. "That's what it must have been like."

The longer we talked, the more I thought about the person who epitomized what those days were all about. Out of the hundreds of rappers, singers, producers, directors, actors, and ex-politicians I'd interviewed since 1991, one man stood out as the most powerful and candid speaker I've ever encountered: the Notorious B.I.G.

Interviewing Biggie was always a joy because he never said, "No comment." He was easy to find, not pretentious in the least, and funny as a muthafucka. He told the stories of his life in stark visual terms, much like his raps. His tales were often darkly comedic, in the same way that, despite its brutal violence, Quentin

Tarantino's *Pulp Fiction* is essentially a comedy. Whether talking about his sheltered childhood, his experiences as a drug dealer, or his newfound fame in the rap game, Biggie always said something interesting and usually provocative.

The first conversation I had with him was on September 27, 1994, two weeks after *Ready to Die* came out. He was standing out there on the block in baggy jeans and Tims, waiting for his boys to show up and take him to a record-release party for Parish from EPMD. He was the only cat on the block who could afford a new car, but he never learned how to drive. His wife, Faith, his friend Klept, or another member of Junior M.A.F.I.A. would chauffeur him everywhere while he sat by the window, taking it all in, playing with words in his brain.

Our paths wouldn't cross again for three more years, until that afternoon by the pool in L.A. We spoke again a few days later on the set of the video for his song "Hypnotize," and finally in his suite at the Westwood Marquis Hotel.

Those six hours of conversation with Christopher Wallace led to the creation of this book. I've done lots of additional reporting since then. And where noted, I've drawn on other interviews he gave to fellow hip hop journalists and other media outlets—as well as reporting done by people who helped me with the enormous task of compiling research for this book.

In a way, writing about his life was something that Christopher Wallace didn't want. He preferred to keep people he didn't know at a distance. It was a hard lesson he'd learned on the street, where any stranger could be a rival, a snitch, or an undercover cop.

"You never want anybody to know everything about you," he once told me. Yet that's exactly what this book will attempt to do, to tell you just as much about Christopher Wallace as it does about the Notorious B.I.G.

The challenge of writing a book about Christopher Wallace is daunting in itself. How do you represent someone who had so many different personalities—and a name to go with each one? There was Big Chris, the shy guy who loved kung fu movies and chilling at home with his kids, and then there was Biggie Smalls, the freestyle legend, cee-lo dice champion, and unofficial mayor of St. James Place. And he did it all for the same reason he spent so much time in Cali—all in the pursuit of fun.

Which is precisely what's been missing from other books that have been written about the Notorious B.I.G., books that focused on his still-unsolved murder, his disagreements with Tupac, his more violent songs. But they offer very little of Christopher Wallace—what made him laugh, what made him cry, what he was like as a person. That's because these writers had only videos, CDs, and press clippings to tell them who he was. If you listen to a song like "Suicidal Thoughts" without the benefit of spending time with Wallace, you might conclude that he really was, as he put it, "on some killing himself shit." You might hear him say, on the remix to "One More Chance," that he's "black and ugly as ever," and figure that he had self-esteem problems. In fact, Wallace had such a strong sense of self that he could poke fun at himself, make light of what people whispered about him behind his back, and laugh with them.

Who knows what kind of records Wallace—or Shakur—would have made had they lived longer lives. We do know is that they always took risks with their work, trying things that no one else had tried before. Make your money. Get your paper. Cause that's what Big would want you to do. But at the same time, never stop making records that make people think. Sometimes it feels as though what died with Wallace and Shakur was the potential for greatness in hip hop. The desire to write record songs that could change the way people think about life, instead of dumbing-down and pandering to the lowest common denominator.

Get it together.

ABOUT THE AUTHOR

Cheo Hodari Coker, 30, has published cover stories, major features, and reviews in VIBE, *The Bomb Hip-Hop Magazine, The Source, XXL, Rap Pages* SPIN, the *Los Angeles Times, Premiere, Essence, Details, The Face, Rolling Stone,* the *San Francisco Bay Guardian,* and the *Village Voice.* He began his writing career while still enrolled at Stanford University, where he completed his bachelor of arts degree in English in 1995. He became a pop music staff writer for the Calendar section of the *Los Angeles Times* by the fall of that year and stayed there for two years, contributing more than 200 articles for the section.

Coker wrote the May 1997 VIBE cover story "Chronicle of a Death Foretold," which was published shortly after the murder of Christopher Wallace, a.k.a. the Notorious B.I.G. The article contained excerpts from Wallace's last full-length interview. Coker left the *Times* in September 1997 to pursue a screenwriting career. He co-wrote the hip-hop thriller *Flow* with Richard (*Uptown Saturday Night*) Wesley, which was purchased by New Line Cinema for John (*Boyz 'N The Hood*) Singleton to produce and direct, and has worked on subsequent feature film scripts about Bob Marley, Tupac Shakur, and Marion Barry for Warner Bros., MTV Networks, and H.B.O. Coker also wrote, executive-produced and created the animated series "The Devil's Music" for www.urbanentertainment.com.

Unbelievable is Coker's first book. He also wrote the N.W.A chapter in the *VIBE History of Hip Hop,* published by Three Rivers Press, and the liner notes for *N.W.A's Greatest Hits* on Ruthless/Priority Records.

Coker lives across the street from the land of Oz with his wife, Dr. Tumaini Rucker Coker, along with an extensive collection of vinyl, CDs, DVDs, video games, paperbacks, and comic books that he refuses to put in storage, and a 1966 Ford Mustang that he refuses to sell. He also refuses to grow up.

ACKNOWLEDGMENTS

First things first: Our deepest gratitude goes to Voletta Wallace, whose strength of spirit is an inspiration to all who are fortunate enough to know her. Thank you for raising such an unbelievable young man, and thank you for making this book possible. We could not have done it without you.

Unbelievable was more than two years in the making, but the book actually flows out of VIBE magazine's entire ten-year history. Biggie was a guest performer at VIBE's launch party in September 1993, jumping onstage to thrill the crowd with a rendition of "Party and Bullshit." He was first featured in the magazine's NEXT section in August 1994, in a piece written by Mimi Valdés. He appeared on the cover three times: in October 1995 with Faith, in September 1996 with Puffy, and then in May 1997 after he was killed while leaving a party co-sponsored by VIBE. I know I speak for everyone who worked on this book when I say that it was more than a labor of love. We viewed it as our solemn responsibility to get this one right.

Big respect to the VIBE Books splinter cell: Art Director Mark Shaw, Photo Editor Adrienne Williams, Research Editor Sun Singleton, and Reporter at Large Raqiyah Mays. Your steadfast devotion to this effort has made all the difference.

To our wise and wonderful editor, Kristin Kiser at Three Rivers Press, who patiently allowed this book to become all that it needed to be: thank you for your vision.

To the rest of the Three Rivers team, copy editor extraordinaire Jim Walsh, production and design guru Lauren Dong, publisher Philip Patrick, and the indefatigable assistants Claudia Gabel and Ellen Rubenstein: thanks for remembering that it's darkest before the dawn.

To all of Biggie's family, friends, and colleagues who spoke with the author or the research team: thanks for entrusting us with your memories and insights.

Peace to all the journalists whose works are listed in the end notes. Write on.

To VIBE veterans Emil Wilbekin and Mimi Valdés, thanks for your guidance.

Thanks to Kenard Gibbs for supporting VIBE Books from day one.

Thanks to our agent Sarah Lazin for finally believing the unbelievable.

Thanks to Jeff Miller, David Korzenik, and Katherine Trager for sound legal advice.

Special thanks to Carter Harris, Beverly Smith, Karla Radford, Hyun Kim, Serena Kim, Kim Ford, Ali Muhammad, Damien Lemon, and Jacquie Juceam.

Big up to B-zo, Mao, and Uncle Ralph for dropping gems as usual.

And, of course, to Cheo: thank you for rising to this major challenge.

And to Sue and Tumaini, thank you for believing in both of us. We did it.

And to A, I, and M... everlasting love.

ROB KENNER
Editorial Director, VIBE Books

Our titles interlace action, crime, and the urban lifestyle depicting the harsh realities of life on the streets. Call it street literature, urban drama, we call it hip-hop literature. This exciting genre features fast-paced action, gritty ghetto realism, and social messages about the high price of the street life style.

DEAD AND STINKIN'
STEPHEN HEWETT

A GOOD DAY TO DIE
JAMES HENDRICKS

WHEN LOVE TURNS TO HATE
SHARRON DOYLE

IF IT AIN'T ONE THING IT'S ANOTHER
SHARRON DOYLE

WOMAN'S CRY
VANESSA MARTIR

BLACKOUT
JERRY LaMOTHE
ANTHONY WHYTE

HUSTLE HARD
BLAINE MARTIN

A BOOGIE DOWN STORY
KEISHA SEIGNIOUS

CRAVE ALL LOSE ALL
ERICK S GRAY

LOVE AND A GANGSTA
ERICK S GRAY

AMERICA'S SOUL
ERICK S GRAY

LIES OF A REAL HOUSEWIFE
ANGELA STANTON

Mail us a List of the titles you would like include $14.95 per Title + shipping charges $3.95 for one book & $1.00 for each additional book. Make all checks payable to: Augustus Publishing 33 Indian Rd. NY, NY 10034

HARD WHITE
SHANNON HOLMES
ANTHONY WHYTE

STREET CHIC
ANTHONY WHYTE

BOOTY CALL *69
ERICK S GRAY

POWER OF THE P
JAMES HENDRICKS

STREETS OF NEW YORK VOL. 1
ERICK S GRAY, ANTHONY WHYTE
MARK ANTHONY, SHANNON HOLMES

STREETS OF NEW YORK VOL. 2
ERICK S GRAY, ANTHONY WHYTE
MARK ANTHONY, K'WAN

STREETS OF NEW YORK VOL. 3
ERICK S GRAY, ANTHONY WHYTE
MARK ANTHONY, TREASURE BLUE

SMUT CENTRAL
BRANDON McCALLA

GHETTO GIRLS
ANTHONY WHYTE

GHETTO GIRLS TOO
ANTHONY WHYTE

GHETTO GIRLS 3:
SOO HOOD
ANTHONY WHYTE

GHETTO GIRLS IV:
YOUNG LUV
ANTHONY WHYTE

SPOT RUSHERS
BRANDON McCALLA

IT CAN HAPPEN
IN A MINUTE
S.M. JOHNSON

LIPSTICK DIARIES
CRYSTAL LACEY WINSLOW
VARIOUS FEMALE AUTHORS

LIPSTICK DIARIES 2
WAHIDA CLARK
VARIOUS FEMALE AUTHORS